FOREWORD

The collection of "Everything Will Be Okay" travel phrasebooks published by T&P Books is designed for people traveling abroad for tourism and business. The phrasebooks contain what matters most - the essentials for basic communication. This is an indispensable set of phrases to "survive" while abroad.

This phrasebook will help you in most cases where you need to ask something, get directions, find out how much something costs, etc. It can also resolve difficult communication situations where gestures just won't help.

This book contains a lot of phrases that have been grouped according to the most relevant topics. The edition also includes a small vocabulary that contains roughly 3,000 of the most frequently used words. Another section of the phrasebook provides a gastronomical dictionary that may help you order food at a restaurant or buy groceries at the store.

Take "Everything Will Be Okay" phrasebook with you on the road and you'll have an irreplaceable traveling companion who will help you find your way out of any situation and teach you to not fear speaking with foreigners.

TABLE OF CONTENTS

T&P Books Publishing

PRONUNCIATION

Letter	Danish example	T&P phonetic alphabet	English example
Aa	Afrika, kompas	[æ], [ɑ], [ɑː]	man, father
Bb	barberblad	[b]	baby, book
Cc	cafe, creme	[k]	clock, kiss
Cc [1]	koncert	[s]	city, boss
Dd	direktør	[d]	day, doctor
Dd [2]	facade	[ð]	weather, together
Ee	belgier	[e], [ə]	medal, elm
Ee [3]	elevator	[ɛ]	man, bad
Ff	familie	[f]	face, food
Gg	mango	[g]	game, gold
Hh	høne, knurhår	[h]	home, have
Ii	kolibri	[i], [iː]	feet, Peter
Jj	legetøj	[j]	yes, New York
Kk	leksikon	[k]	clock, kiss
Ll	leopard	[l]	lace, people
Mm	marmor	[m]	magic, milk
Nn	natur, navn	[n]	name, normal
ng	omfang	[ŋ]	English, ring
nk	punktum	[ŋ]	English, ring
Oo	fortov	[o], [ɔ]	drop, baught
Pp	planteolie	[p]	pencil, private
Qq	sequoia	[k]	clock, kiss
Rr	seriøs	[ʁ]	French (guttural) R
Ss	selskab	[s]	city, boss
Tt	strøm, trappe	[t]	tourist, trip
Uu	blæksprutte	[uː]	pool, room
Vv	børnehave	[ʊ]	vase, winter
Ww	whisky	[w]	vase, winter
Xx	Luxembourg	[ks]	box, taxi
Yy	lykke	[y], [ø]	fuel, eternal
Zz	Venezuela	[s]	city, boss

Letter	Danish example	T&P phonetic alphabet	English example
Ææ	ærter	[ɛ], [ɛː]	habit, bad
Øø	grønsager	[ø], [œ]	church, eternal
Åå	åbent, afgå	[ɔ], [oː]	sun, lucky

Comments

[1] before **e, i**
[2] after a stressed vowel
[3] at the beginning of words

LIST OF ABBREVIATIONS

English abbreviations

ab.	-	about
adj	-	adjective
adv	-	adverb
anim.	-	animate
as adj	-	attributive noun used as adjective
e.g.	-	for example
etc.	-	et cetera
fam.	-	familiar
fem.	-	feminine
form.	-	formal
inanim.	-	inanimate
masc.	-	masculine
math	-	mathematics
mil.	-	military
n	-	noun
pl	-	plural
pron.	-	pronoun
sb	-	somebody
sing.	-	singular
sth	-	something
v aux	-	auxiliary verb
vi	-	intransitive verb
vi, vt	-	intransitive, transitive verb
vt	-	transitive verb

Danish abbreviations

f	-	common gender
f pl	-	common gender plural
i	-	neuter
i pl	-	neuter plural
i, f	-	neuter, common gender
ngn.	-	somebody
pl	-	plural

DANISH PHRASEBOOK

This section contains
important phrases that may
come in handy in various
real-life situations.
The phrasebook will help
you ask for directions, clarify
a price, buy tickets, and
order food at a restaurant

T&P Books Publishing

PHRASEBOOK
CONTENTS

T&P Books Publishing

The bare minimum

Excuse me, ...	**Undskyld, ...** [ˈɔnˌskylʔ, ...]
Hello.	**Hej.** [ˈhɑj]
Thank you.	**Tak.** [tɑk]
Good bye.	**Farvel.** [fɑˈvɛl]
Yes.	**Ja.** [ˈjæ]
No.	**Nej.** [nɑjʔ]
I don't know.	**Jeg ved det ikke.** [jɑj ve de ˈekə]
Where? | Where to? | When?	**Hvor? | Hvorhen? | Hvornår?** [ˈvɒʔ? | ˈvɒʔˌhɛn? | vɒˈnɒʔ?]

I need ...	**Jeg har brug for ...** [jɑ hɑʔ ˈbʁuʔ fə ...]
I want ...	**Jeg vil ...** [jɑj ve ...]
Do you have ...?	**Har du ...?** [ˈhɑʔ du ...?]
Is there a ... here?	**Er der en ... her?** [æɐ̯ ˈdɛʔɐ̯ en ... hɛʔɐ̯?]
May I ...?	**Må jeg ...?** [mɔʔ jɑ ...?]
..., please (polite request)	**... venligst** [... ˈvɛnlist]

I'm looking for ...	**Jeg leder efter ...** [jɑ ˈleːðə ˈɛftʌ ...]
restroom	**toilet** [toaˈlɛt]
ATM	**udbetalingsautomat** [uðˈbeˈtæʔleŋs ɑwtoˈmæʔt]
pharmacy (drugstore)	**apotek** [ɑpoˈteʔk]
hospital	**hospital** [hɔspiˈtæʔl]
police station	**politistation** [poliˈti staˈɕoʔn]
subway	**metro** [ˈmeːtʁo]

taxi	**taxi** ['tɑksi]
train station	**togstation** ['tɔw staˈɕoʔn]

My name is ...	**Mit navn er ...** [mit 'nɑwˀn 'æɐ̯ ...]
What's your name?	**Hvad er dit navn?** ['vað 'æɐ̯ dit nɑwˀn?]
Could you please help me?	**Kan du hjælpe mig?** ['kan du 'jɛlpə mɑj?]
I've got a problem.	**Jeg har fået et problem.** [jɑ hɑˀ foˀ et pʁoˈbleˀm]
I don't feel well.	**Jeg føler mig dårlig.** [jɑ 'føːlɐ mɑj 'dɔːli]
Call an ambulance!	**Ring efter en ambulance!** ['ʁɐ̯ŋə 'ɛftʌ en ɑmbu'lɑŋsə]
May I make a call?	**Må jeg foretage et opkald?** [mɔˀ jɑ 'foːɒˌtæˀ et 'ʌpkalˀ?]

I'm sorry.	**Det er jeg ked af.** [de 'æɐ̯ jɑ 'keðˀ æˀ]
You're welcome.	**Selv tak.** [sɛlˀ tak]

I, me	**Jeg, mig** [jɑj, mɑj]
you (inform.)	**du** [du]
he	**han** [han]
she	**hun** [hun]
they (masc.)	**de** [di]
they (fem.)	**de** [di]
we	**vi** [vi]
you (pl)	**I, De** [I, di]
you (sg, form.)	**De** [di]

ENTRANCE	**INDGANG** ['enˌgɑŋˀ]
EXIT	**UDGANG** ['uðˌgɑŋˀ]
OUT OF ORDER	**UDE AF DRIFT** ['uːðə æˀ 'dʁɛft]
CLOSED	**LUKKET** ['lɔkəð]

OPEN   **ÅBEN**
['ɔːbən]

FOR WOMEN   **TIL KVINDER**
[te 'kvenʌ]

FOR MEN   **TIL MÆND**
[te 'mɛnˀ]

Questions

Where?	**Hvor?** ['vɒˀ?]
Where to?	**Hvorhen?** ['vɒˀˌhɛn?]
Where from?	**Hvorfra?** ['vɒˀˌfʁɑˀ?]
Why?	**Hvorfor?** ['vɔfʌ?]
For what reason?	**Af hvilken grund?** [æˀ 'velkən 'gʁɔnˀ?]
When?	**Hvornår?** [vɒ'nɒˀ?]
How long?	**Hvor længe?** [vɒˀ 'lɛŋə?]
At what time?	**På hvilket tidspunkt?** [pɔ 'velkəð 'tiðspɔŋˀt?]
How much?	**Hvor meget?** [vɒˀ 'mɑɑð?]
Do you have ...?	**Har du ...?** ['hɑˀ du ...?]
Where is ...?	**Hvor er ...?** [vɒˀ 'æɐ̯ ...?]
What time is it?	**Hvad er klokken?** ['vað 'æɐ̯ 'klʌkən?]
May I make a call?	**Må jeg foretage et opkald?** [mɔˀ ja 'fɒːɒˌtæˀ et 'ʌpkalˀ?]
Who's there?	**Hvem der?** [vɛm 'dɛˀɐ̯?]
Can I smoke here?	**Må jeg ryge her?** [mɔˀ ja 'ʁyːə 'hɛˀɐ̯?]
May I ...?	**Må jeg ...?** [mɔˀ ja ...?]

Needs

I'd like ...	**Jeg vil gerne ...** [jɑj ve 'gæɐ̯nə ...]
I don't want ...	**Jeg ønsker ikke ...** [jɑ 'ønskɐ̯ 'ekə ...]
I'm thirsty.	**Jeg er tørstig.** ['jɑj 'æɐ̯ 'tœɐ̯sti]
I want to sleep.	**Jeg ønsker at sove.** [jɑ 'ønskɐ̯ ʌ 'sɒwə]

I want ...	**Jeg vil ...** [jɑj ve ...]
to wash up	**at vaske** [ʌ 'vaskə]
to brush my teeth	**at børste mine tænder** [ʌ 'bœɐ̯stə 'mi:nə 'tɛnʌ]
to rest a while	**at hvile en stund** [ʌ 'vi:lə en 'stɔnˀ]
to change my clothes	**at klæde mig om** [ʌ 'klɛˀ 'mɑj ʌm]

to go back to the hotel	**at gå tilbage til hotellet** [ʌ 'gɔˀ te'bæːjə te ho'tɛlˀəð]
to buy ...	**at købe ...** [ʌ 'kø:bə ...]
to go to ...	**at gå til ...** [ʌ 'gɔ te ...]
to visit ...	**at besøge ...** [ʌ be'søˀjə ...]
to meet with ...	**at mødes med ...** [ʌ 'mø:ðəs mɛ ...]
to make a call	**at foretage et opkald** [ʌ 'fɒːɒˌtæˀ et 'ʌpkalˀ]

I'm tired.	**Jeg er træt.** ['jɑj 'æɐ̯ 'tʁat]
We are tired.	**Vi er trætte.** ['vi 'æɐ̯ 'tʁatə]
I'm cold.	**Jeg fryser.** [jɑ 'fʁy:sʌ]
I'm hot.	**Jeg har det varmt.** [jɑ hɑˀ de 'vɑˀmt]
I'm OK.	**Jeg er OK.** ['jɑj 'æɐ̯ ɔw'kɛj]

I need to make a call.

Jeg har brug for at foretage et opkald.
[ja hɑˀ ˈbʁuˀ fə ʌ ˈfɔːɒˌtæˀ et ˈʌpkalˀ]

I need to go to the restroom.

Jeg har brug for at gå på toilettet.
[ja hɑˀ ˈbʁuˀ fə ʌ gɔˀ pɔ toaˈlɛət]

I have to go.

Jeg er nødt til at gå.
[ˈjaj ˈæɐ̯ nøˀt te ʌ gɔˀ]

I have to go now.

Jeg er nødt til at gå nu.
[ˈjaj ˈæɐ̯ nøˀt te ʌ gɔˀ nu]

Asking for directions

Excuse me, ...
Undskyld, ...
['ɔnˌskylˀ, ...]

Where is ...?
Hvor er ...?
[vɒˀ 'æɐ̯ ...?]

Which way is ...?
Hvilken vej er ...?
['velkən 'vajˀ 'æɐ̯ ...?]

Could you help me, please?
Er du sød at hjælpe mig?
[æɐ̯ du 'søðˀ ʌ 'jɛlpə majˀ?]

I'm looking for ...
Jeg leder efter ...
[ja 'leːðə 'ɛftʌ ...]

I'm looking for the exit.
Jeg leder efter udgangen.
[ja 'leːðə 'ɛftʌ 'uðˌgaŋən]

I'm going to ...
Jeg har tænkt mig at ...
[ja haˀ 'tɛŋkt majˀ ʌ ...]

Am I going the right way to ...?
Går jeg den rigtige vej til ...?
[gɒˀ ja dən 'ʁɛgtiə vajˀ te ...?]

Is it far?
Er det langt væk?
[æɐ̯ de 'laŋˀt vɛk?]

Can I get there on foot?
Kan jeg komme derhen til fods?
['kanˀ ja 'kʌmə 'dɛˀɐ̯'hɛn te 'foˀðs?]

Can you show me on the map?
Kan du vise mig på kortet?
['kan du 'viːsə majˀ pɔ 'kɒːtəð?]

Show me where we are right now.
Vis mig, hvor vi er lige nu.
['viˀs majˀ, vɒˀ vi 'æɐ̯ 'liːə nu]

Here
Her
['hɛˀɐ̯]

There
Der
[dɛˀɐ̯]

This way
Denne vej
['dɛnə vajˀ]

Turn right.
Drej til højre.
[dʁajˀ te 'hʌjʁʌ]

Turn left.
Drej til venstre.
[dʁajˀ te 'vɛnstʁʌ]

first (second, third) turn
første (anden, tredje) vej
['fœɐ̯stə ('anən, 'tʁɛðjə) vajˀ]

to the right
til højre
[te 'hʌjʁʌ]

to the left

til venstre
[te ˈvɛnstʁʌ]

Go straight ahead.

Gå ligeud.
[ˈgɔˀ ˈliːəˈuðˀ]

Signs

WELCOME!	**VELKOMMEN!** ['vɛl̩kʌm'ən]
ENTRANCE	**INDGANG** ['enˌgɑŋ']
EXIT	**UDGANG** ['uðˌgɑŋ']
PUSH	**SKUB** [skɔb]
PULL	**TRÆK** ['tʁak]
OPEN	**ÅBEN** ['ɔːbən]
CLOSED	**LUKKET** ['lɔkəð]
FOR WOMEN	**TIL KVINDER** [te 'kvenʌ]
FOR MEN	**TIL MÆND** [te 'mɛn']
GENTLEMEN, GENTS (m)	**MÆND** [mɛn']
WOMEN (f)	**KVINDER** ['kvenʌ]
DISCOUNTS	**UDSALG** ['uðˌsal']
SALE	**RESTSALG** ['ʁast ˌsal']
FREE	**GRATIS** ['gʁɑːtis]
NEW!	**NYT!** [nyt]
ATTENTION!	**OBS!** [ʌbs]
NO VACANCIES	**ALT OPTAGET** ['al't 'ʌpˌtæˀəð]
RESERVED	**RESERVERET** [ʁɛsæɐ̯'veˀʌð]
ADMINISTRATION	**ADMINISTRATION** [aðministʁɑ'ɕoˀn]
STAFF ONLY	**KUN PERSONALE** [kɔn pæɐ̯so'næːlə]

BEWARE OF THE DOG!	**PAS PÅ HUNDEN!** [pas pɔ 'hunən]
NO SMOKING!	**RYGNING FORBUDT!** ['ʁy:neŋ fʌ'byˀd]
DO NOT TOUCH!	**RØR IKKE!** ['ʁœˀɐ̯ 'ekə]
DANGEROUS	**FARLIGT** ['fɑ:lit]
DANGER	**FARE** ['fɑ:ɑ]
HIGH VOLTAGE	**STÆRKSTRØM** ['stæɐ̯k 'stʁœmˀ]
NO SWIMMING!	**SVØMNING FORBUDT!** ['svœmneŋ fʌ'byˀt]

OUT OF ORDER	**UDE AF DRIFT** ['u:ðə æˀ 'dʁɛft]
FLAMMABLE	**BRANDFARLIG** ['bʁɑn‚fɑ:li]
FORBIDDEN	**FORBUDT** [fʌ'byˀt]
NO TRESPASSING!	**ADGANG FORBUDT!** ['að‚gɑŋˀ fʌ'byˀð]
WET PAINT	**VÅD MALING** ['vɔˀð 'mæ:leŋ]

CLOSED FOR RENOVATIONS	**LUKKET PGA. RENOVERING** ['lɔkəð pɔˀ 'gʁɔnˀ a ʁɛno've'ɐ̯eŋ]
WORKS AHEAD	**ARBEJDE FORUDE** ['ɑ:‚bɑjˀdə 'fɔ:‚u:ðə]
DETOUR	**OMKØRSEL** [ɒm'køɐ̯səl]

Transportation. General phrases

plane	**fly** [fly']
train	**tog** ['tɔ'w]
bus	**bus** [bus]
ferry	**færge** ['fæɐ̯wə]
taxi	**taxi** ['tɑksi]
car	**bil** [bi'l]

schedule	**køreplan** ['kø:ʌˌplæ'n]
Where can I see the schedule?	**Hvor kan jeg se køreplanen?** [vɒ' kan jɑ se' 'kø:ʌˌplæ'nən?]
workdays (weekdays)	**hverdage** ['væɐ̯ˌdæ'ə]
weekends	**weekender** ['wi:ˌkɛndʌ]
holidays	**helligdage** ['hɛliˌdæ'ə]

DEPARTURE	**AFGANG** ['awˌgɑŋ']
ARRIVAL	**ANKOMST** ['anˌkʌm'st]
DELAYED	**FORSINKET** [fə'sen'kəð]
CANCELLED	**AFLYST** ['awˌly'st]

next (train, etc.)	**næste** ['nɛstə]
first	**første** ['fœɐ̯stə]
last	**sidste** ['sistə]

When is the next ...?	**Hvornår er den næste ...?** [vɒ'nɒ' 'æɐ̯ dən 'nɛstə ...?]
When is the first ...?	**Hvornår er den første ...?** [vɒ'nɒ' 'æɐ̯ dən 'fœɐ̯stə ...?]

When is the last ...?

Hvornår er den sidste ...?
[vɒˈnɒˀ ˈæɐ̯ dən ˈsistə ...?]

transfer (change of trains, etc.)

skift
[ˈskift]

to make a transfer

at skifte
[ʌ ˈskiftə]

Do I need to make a transfer?

Behøver jeg at skifte?
[beˈhøˀvə ˈjɑj ʌ ˈskiftə?]

Buying tickets

Where can I buy tickets?	**Hvor kan jeg købe billetter?** [vɒˀ kan jɑ ˈkøːbə biˈlɛtʌ?]
ticket	**billet** [biˈlɛt]
to buy a ticket	**at købe en billet** [ʌ ˈkøːbə en biˈlɛt]
ticket price	**billetpris** [biˈlɛtˌpʁiˀs]

Where to?	**Hvorhen?** [ˈvɒˀˌhɛn?]
To what station?	**Til hvilken station?** [te ˈvelkən staˈɕoˀn?]
I need ...	**Jeg har brug for ...** [jɑ hɑˀ ˈbʁuˀ fə ...]
one ticket	**én billet** [en biˈlɛt]
two tickets	**to billetter** [toˀ biˈlɛtʌ]
three tickets	**tre billetter** [ˈtʁɛˀ biˈlɛtʌ]

one-way	**enkelt** [ˈɛŋˀkəlt]
round-trip	**retur** [ʁɛˈtuɐˀ]
first class	**første klasse** [ˈfœɐ̯stə ˈklasə]
second class	**anden klasse** [ˈanən ˈklasə]

today	**i dag** [i ˈdæˀ]
tomorrow	**i morgen** [i ˈmɒːɒn]
the day after tomorrow	**i overmorgen** [i ˈɒwʌˌmɒːɒn]
in the morning	**om morgenen** [ʌm ˈmɒːɒnən]
in the afternoon	**om eftermiddagen** [ʌm ˈɛftʌmeˌdæˀən]
in the evening	**om aftenen** [ʌm ˈaftənən]

aisle seat

gangplads
['gɑŋplas]

window seat

vinduesplads
['vendus 'plas]

How much?

Hvor meget?
[vɒˀ 'mɑɑð?]

Can I pay by credit card?

Kan jeg betale med kreditkort?
['kanˀ ja be'tæˀlə mɛ kʁɛ'dit kɒːt?]

Bus

bus	**bus** [bus]
intercity bus	**rutebil** ['ʁuːtəˌbiʔl]
bus stop	**busstoppested** ['busˌstɒpəstɛð]
Where's the nearest bus stop?	**Hvor er det nærmeste busstoppested?** [vɒʔ 'æɐ̯ de 'næɐ̯məstə 'busˌstɒpəstɛð?]
number (bus ~, etc.)	**nummer** ['nɔmʔʌ]
Which bus do I take to get to ...?	**Hvilken bus skal jeg tage for at komme til ...?** ['velkən bus skalʔ jɑ 'tæʔə fə ʌ 'kʌmə te ...?]
Does this bus go to ...?	**Kører denne bus til ...?** ['køːɐ̯ 'dɛnə bus te ...?]
How frequent are the buses?	**Hvor hyppigt kører busserne?** [vɒʔ 'hypit 'køːɐ̯ 'busɐnə?]
every 15 minutes	**hvert kvarter** ['vɛʔɐ̯t kvɑ'teʔɐ̯]
every half hour	**hver halve time** ['vɛɐ̯ halʔvə 'tiːmə]
every hour	**hver time** ['vɛɐ̯ 'tiːmə]
several times a day	**flere gange om dagen** ['fleːʌ 'ɡɑŋə ʌm 'dæʔən]
... times a day	**... gange om dagen** [... 'ɡɑŋə ʌm 'dæʔən]
schedule	**køreplan** ['køːʌˌplæʔn]
Where can I see the schedule?	**Hvor kan jeg se køreplanen?** [vɒʔ kan jɑ seʔ 'køːʌˌplæʔnən?]
When is the next bus?	**Hvornår kører den næste bus?** [vɒ'nɒʔ 'køːɐ̯ dən 'nɛstə bus?]
When is the first bus?	**Hvornår kører den første bus?** [vɒ'nɒʔ 'køːɐ̯ dən 'fœɐ̯stə bus?]
When is the last bus?	**Hvornår kører den sidste bus?** [vɒ'nɒʔ 'køːɐ̯ dən 'sistə bus?]

stop

stop
['stʌp]

next stop

næste stop
['nɛstə 'stʌp]

last stop (terminus)

sidste stop
['sistə 'stʌp]

Stop here, please.

Stop her, tak.
['stʌp 'hɛˀɐ̯, tɑk]

Excuse me, this is my stop.

Undskyld, det er mit stop.
['ɔnˌskylˀ, de 'æɐ̯ mit 'stʌp]

Train

train	**tog** ['tɔˀw]
suburban train	**regionaltog** [ʁɛgjoˈnæˀl tɔˀw]
long-distance train	**intercitytog** [entʌˈsiti tɔˀw]
train station	**togstation** ['tɔw staˈɕoˀn]
Excuse me, where is the exit to the platform?	**Undskyld, hvor er udgangen til perronen?** ['ɔnˌskylˀ, vɒˀ 'æɐ̯ 'uðˌgɑŋən te paˈʁʌŋən?]

Does this train go to ...?	**Kører dette tog til ...?** ['køːɐ̯ 'dɛtə tɔˀw te ...?]
next train	**næste tog** ['nɛstə 'tɔˀw]
When is the next train?	**Hvornår afgår det næste tog?** [vɒˈnɒˀ 'awˌgɒˀ de 'nɛstə tɔˀw?]
Where can I see the schedule?	**Hvor kan jeg se køreplanen?** [vɒˀ kɑ jɑ seˀ 'køːʌˌplæˀnən?]
From which platform?	**Fra hvilken perron?** [fʁɑˀ 'velkən paˈʁʌŋ?]
When does the train arrive in ...?	**Hvornår ankommer toget til ...?** [vɒˈnɒˀ 'anˌkʌmʌ 'tɔˀwəð te ...?]

Please help me.	**Vær sød at hjælpe mig.** ['vɛɐ̯ˀ 'søðˀ ʌ 'jɛlpə mɑj]
I'm looking for my seat.	**Jeg leder efter min plads.** [jɑ 'leːðə 'ɛftʌ min plas]
We're looking for our seats.	**Vi leder efter vores pladser.** ['vi 'leːðə 'ɛftʌ 'vɒɒs 'plasʌ]
My seat is taken.	**Min plads er taget.** [min 'plas 'æɐ̯ 'tæəð]
Our seats are taken.	**Vore pladser er taget.** ['vɒːɒ 'plasʌ 'æɐ̯ 'tæəð]

I'm sorry but this is my seat.	**Jeg beklager, men dette er min plads.** [jɑ beˈklæˀjə, mɛn 'dɛtə 'æɐ̯ min 'plas]
Is this seat taken?	**Er denne plads taget?** [æɐ̯ 'dɛnə plas 'tæəð?]
May I sit here?	**Må jeg sidde her?** [mɔˀ jɑ 'seðə 'hɛˀɐ̯?]

On the train. Dialogue (No ticket)

Ticket, please.

Billet, tak.
[bi'lɛt, tɑk]

I don't have a ticket.

Jeg har ikke nogen billet.
[jɑ hɑˀ 'ekə 'noən bi'lɛt]

I lost my ticket.

Jeg har mistet min billet.
[jɑ hɑˀ 'mestəð min bi'lɛt]

I forgot my ticket at home.

Jeg har glemt min billet derhjemme.
[jɑ hɑˀ 'glɛmt min bi'lɛt dɑ'jɛmə]

You can buy a ticket from me.

Du kan købe en billet af mig.
[du kan 'kø:bə en bi'lɛt æˀ mɑj]

You will also have to pay a fine.

**Du bliver også nødt
til at betale en bøde.**
[du 'bliɐ̯ˀ ˈʌsə nøˀt
te ʌ be'tæˀlə en 'bø:ðə]

Okay.

OK.
[ɔw'kɛj]

Where are you going?

Hvor skal du hen?
[vɒˀ skalˀ du hɛn?]

I'm going to …

Jeg har tænkt mig at …
[jɑ hɑˀ 'tɛŋkt mɑj ʌ …]

How much? I don't understand.

Hvor meget? Jeg forstår det ikke.
[vɒˀ 'maɑð? jɑ fə'stɒ̞ de 'ekə]

Write it down, please.

Skriv det ned, tak.
['skʁiwˀ de neðˀ, tɑk]

Okay. Can I pay with a credit card?

OK. Kan jeg betale med kreditkort?
[ɔw'kɛj. kan jɑ be'tæˀlə mɛ kʁɛ'dit kɒːt?]

Yes, you can.

Ja, det kan du godt.
['jæ, de kan du 'gʌt]

Here's your receipt.

Her er din kvittering.
['hɛˀɐ̯ 'æɐ̯ din kvi'teˀɐ̯eŋ]

Sorry about the fine.

Undskyld bøden.
['ɔnˌskylˀ 'bø:ðən]

That's okay. It was my fault.

Det er OK. Det var min skyld.
[de 'æɐ̯ ɔw'kɛj. de vɑ min skylˀ]

Enjoy your trip.

Nyd turen.
[nyð 'tuɐ̯ˀn]

Taxi

taxi	**taxi** ['taksi]
taxi driver	**taxichauffør** ['taksi ɕo'fø'ɐ̯]
to catch a taxi	**at få fat i en taxi** [ʌ fɔ' fat i en 'taksi]
taxi stand	**taxiholdeplads** ['taksi 'hʌlə‿plas]
Where can I get a taxi?	**Hvor kan jeg finde en taxi?** [vɒ' kan jaj 'fenə en 'taksi?]
to call a taxi	**at ringe efter en taxi** [ʌ 'ʁɛŋə 'ɛftʌ en 'taksi]
I need a taxi.	**Jeg har brug for en taxi.** [ja ha' 'bʁu' fə en 'taksi]
Right now.	**Lige nu.** ['li:ə 'nu]
What is your address (location)?	**Hvad er din adresse?** ['vað 'æɐ̯ din a'dʁasə?]
My address is ...	**Min adresse er ...** [min a'dʁasə 'æɐ̯ ...]
Your destination?	**Hvor skal du hen?** [vɒ' skal' du hɛn?]
Excuse me, ...	**Undskyld, ...** ['ɔn‿skyl', ...]
Are you available?	**Er du ledig?** [æɐ̯ du 'le:ði?]
How much is it to get to ...?	**Hvor meget koster det at komme til ...?** [vɒ' 'maɑð 'kʌstɐ̯ de ʌ 'kʌmə te ...?]
Do you know where it is?	**Ved du, hvor det er?** [ve du, vɒ' de 'æɐ̯?]
Airport, please.	**Lufthavnen, tak.** ['lɔft‿haw'nən, tak]
Stop here, please.	**Stop her, tak.** ['stʌp 'hɛ'ɐ̯, tak]
It's not here.	**Det er ikke her.** [de 'æɐ̯ 'ekə 'hɛ'ɐ̯]
This is the wrong address.	**Det er den forkerte adresse.** [de 'æɐ̯ dən fə'keɐ̯'tə a'dʁasə]

Turn left.

Drej til venstre.
[dʁɑjˀ te 'vɛnstʁʌ]

Turn right.

Drej til højre.
[dʁɑjˀ te 'hʌjʁʌ]

How much do I owe you?

Hvor meget skylder jeg dig?
[vɒˀ 'mɑɑð 'skylə jɑ dɑjˀ]

I'd like a receipt, please.

Jeg vil gerne have en kvittering, tak.
[jɑj ve 'gææɡnə hæˀ en kvi'teˀɡeŋ, tɑk]

Keep the change.

Behold resten.
[be'hʌlˀ 'ʁɑstən]

Would you please wait for me?

Vil du venligst vente på mig?
['ve du 'vɛnlist 'vɛntə pɔ mɑjˀ]

five minutes

fem minutter
[fɛmˀ me'nutʌ]

ten minutes

ti minutter
['tiˀ me'nutʌ]

fifteen minutes

femten minutter
['fɛmtən me'nutʌ]

twenty minutes

tyve minutter
['tyːvə me'nutʌ]

half an hour

en halv time
[en 'halˀ 'tiːmə]

Hotel

Hello.	**Hej.** ['hɑj]
My name is …	**Mit navn er …** [mit 'nɑw'n 'æɐ̯ …]
I have a reservation.	**Jeg har en reservation.** [ja ha' en ʁɛsæɐ̯va'ɕo'n]
I need …	**Jeg har brug for …** [ja ha' 'bʁu' fə …]
a single room	**et enkeltværelse** [et 'ɛŋ'kəlt‚væɐ̯ʌlsə]
a double room	**et dobbeltværelse** [et 'dʌbəlt 'væɐ̯ʌlsə]
How much is that?	**Hvor meget bliver det?** [vɒ' 'mɑɑð 'bliɐ̯' de?]
That's a bit expensive.	**Det er lidt dyrt.** [de 'æɐ̯ lit 'dyɐ̯'t]
Do you have anything else?	**Har du nogen andre muligheder?** ['hɑ' du 'noən 'ɑndʁʌ 'mu:li‚heð'ʌ?]
I'll take it.	**Det tager jeg.** [de 'tæ'ɐ̯ jɑj]
I'll pay in cash.	**Jeg betaler kontant.** [ja be'tæ'lʌ kɔn'tan't]
I've got a problem.	**Jeg har fået et problem.** [ja ha' fɒ' et pʁo'ble'm]
My … is broken.	**Mit … er gået i stykker.** [mit … 'æɐ̯ 'gɔ:əð 'støkʌ]
My … is out of order.	**Mit … virker ikke.** [mit … 'viɐ̯kʌ 'ekə]
TV	**TV** ['te'‚ve']
air conditioner	**klimaanlæg** ['kli:ma'an‚lɛ'g]
tap	**hane** ['hæ:nə]
shower	**bruser** ['bʁu:sʌ]
sink	**vask** ['vask]
safe	**pengeskab** ['pɛŋə‚skæ'b]

door lock	**dørlås** ['dœɐ̯loˀs]
electrical outlet	**stikkontakt** ['stek kɔn'tɑkt]
hairdryer	**hårtørrer** ['hɒːˌtœɐ̯ʌ]

I don't have ...	**Jeg har ikke nogen ...** [jɑ hɑˀ 'ekə 'noən ...]
water	**vand** ['vanˀ]
light	**lys** ['lyˀs]
electricity	**elektricitet** [elɛktʁisi'teˀt]

Can you give me ...?	**Kan du give mig ...?** ['kan du giˀ mɑj ...?]
a towel	**et håndklæde** [ed 'hʌnˌklɛːðə]
a blanket	**et tæppe** [ed 'tɛpə]
slippers	**hjemmesko** ['jɛməˌskoˀ]
a robe	**en kåbe** [en 'kɔːbə]
shampoo	**shampoo** ['ɕæːmˌpuː]
soap	**sæbe** ['sɛːbə]

I'd like to change rooms.	**Jeg vil gerne skifte værelse.** [jɑj ve 'gæɐ̯nə 'skiftə 'væɐ̯ʌlsə]
I can't find my key.	**Jeg kan ikke finde min nøgle.** [jɑ kan 'ekə 'fenə min 'nʌjlə]
Could you open my room, please?	**Kunne du låse op til mit værelse?** ['kunə du 'lɔːsə ʌp te mit 'væɐ̯ʌlsə?]
Who's there?	**Hvem der?** [vɛm 'dɛˀɐ̯?]
Come in!	**Kom ind!** [kʌmˀ enˀ]
Just a minute!	**Et øjeblik!** [ed 'ʌjə'blek]
Not right now, please.	**Ikke lige nu, tak.** ['ekə 'liːə nu, tɑk]

Come to my room, please.	**Kom til mit værelse, tak.** [kʌmˀ te mit 'væɐ̯ʌlsə, tɑk]
I'd like to order food service.	**Jeg vil gerne bestille roomservice.** [jɑj ve 'gæɐ̯nə be'stelˀə 'ʁuːmˌsœːvis]
My room number is ...	**Mit værelsesnummer er ...** [mit 'væɐ̯ʌlsə'nɔmˀʌ 'æɐ̯ ...]

I'm leaving ...   **Jeg forlader ...**
                                       [jɑ fəˈlæˀðə ...]

We're leaving ...   **Vi forlader ...**
                                       [ˈvi fəˈlæˀðə ...]

right now   **lige nu**
                                       [ˈliːə ˈnu]

this afternoon   **i eftermiddag**
                                       [I ˈɛftʌmeˌdæˀ]

tonight   **i aften**
                                       [i ˈɑftən]

tomorrow   **i morgen**
                                       [i ˈmɒːɒn]

tomorrow morning   **i morgen tidlig**
                                       [i ˈmɒːɒn ˈtiðli]

tomorrow evening   **i morgen aften**
                                       [i ˈmɒːɒn ˈɑftən]

the day after tomorrow   **i overmorgen**
                                       [i ˈɒwʌˌmɒːɒn]

I'd like to pay.   **Jeg vil gerne betale.**
                                       [jɑj ve ˈgæɡnə beˈtæˀlə]

Everything was wonderful.   **Alt var vidunderligt.**
                                       [ˈalˀt vɑ viðˈɔnˀʌlit]

Where can I get a taxi?   **Hvor kan jeg finde en taxi?**
                                       [vɒˀ kan jɑj ˈfenə en ˈtɑksi?]

Would you call a taxi for me, please? **Vil du ringe efter en taxi for mig, tak?**
                                       [ˈve du ˈʁɛŋə ˈɛftʌ en ˈtɑksi fə mɑj, tɑk?]

Restaurant

Can I look at the menu, please?	**Kan jeg se menuen?** ['kan' ja se' me'nyən?]
Table for one.	**Bord til én.** ['bo'ɐ̯ te 'en]
There are two (three, four) of us.	**Vi er to (tre, fire).** [vi 'æɐ̯ to' ('tʁɛ', 'fi'ʌ)]

Smoking	**Rygning** ['ʁy:neŋ]
No smoking	**Rygning forbudt** ['ʁy:nen fʌ'by'd]
Excuse me! (addressing a waiter)	**Undskyld!** ['ɔnˌskyl']
menu	**menu** [me'ny]
wine list	**vinkort** ['vi:nˌkɒːt]
The menu, please.	**Menuen, tak.** [me'nyən, tak]

Are you ready to order?	**Er du klar til at bestille?** [æɐ̯ du klɑ' te ʌ be'stel'ə?]
What will you have?	**Hvad vil du have?** ['vað ve du hæ'?]
I'll have ...	**Jeg vil gerne have ...** [jɑj ve 'gæɐ̯nə hæ' ...]

I'm a vegetarian.	**Jeg er vegetar.** ['jɑj 'æɐ̯ vegə'tɑ']
meat	**kød** ['køð]
fish	**fisk** ['fesk]
vegetables	**grøntsager** ['gʁœntˌsæ'jʌ]
Do you have vegetarian dishes?	**Har du vegetarretter?** ['hɑ' du vegə'tɑ''ʁatə?]
I don't eat pork.	**Jeg spiser ikke svinekød.** [jɑ 'spi:sɐ 'ekə 'svi:nə'køð]
He /she/ doesn't eat meat.	**Han /hun/ spiser ikke kød.** [han /hun/ 'spi:sɐ 'ekə 'køð]
I am allergic to ...	**Jeg er allergisk over for ...** ['jɑj 'æɐ̯ a'læɐ̯'gisk 'ɒw'ʌ fə ...]

Would you please bring me ...	**Er du sød at give mig ...** [æɐ̯ du 'søð' ʌ 'gi' maj ...]
salt | pepper | sugar	**salt | peber | sukker** ['sal'̩t | 'pewʌ | 'sɔkʌ]
coffee | tea | dessert	**kaffe | te | dessert** ['kafə | te' | de'sɛɐ̯'t]
water | sparkling | plain	**vand | med brus | uden brus** ['van' | mɛ 'bʁu's | 'uðən 'bʁu's]
a spoon | fork | knife	**en ske | gaffel | kniv** [en ske' | 'gafəl | 'kniw']
a plate | napkin	**en tallerken | serviet** [en ta'læɐ̯kən | sæɐ̯vi'ɛt]

Enjoy your meal!	**Nyd dit måltid!** [nyð dit 'mʌlˌtið']
One more, please.	**En til, tak.** [en te, tak]
It was very delicious.	**Det var meget lækkert.** [de va 'maɑð 'lɛkʌt]

check | change | tip	**regningen | byttepenge | drikkepenge** ['ʁajneŋən | 'bytəˌpɛŋə | 'dʁɛkəˌpɛŋə]
Check, please. (Could I have the check, please?)	**Regningen, tak.** ['ʁajneŋən, tak]
Can I pay by credit card?	**Kan jeg betale med kreditkort?** ['kan' ja be'tæ'lə mɛ kʁɛ'dit kɔ:t?]
I'm sorry, there's a mistake here.	**Undskyld, men der er en fejl her.** ['ɔnˌskyl', mɛn 'dɛ'ɐ̯ 'æɐ̯ en 'faj'l 'hɛ'ɐ̯]

Shopping

Can I help you?	**Kan jeg hjælpe?**
	['kan' ja 'jɛlpə?]
Do you have ...?	**Har du ...?**
	['hɑ' du ...?]
I'm looking for ...	**Jeg leder efter ...**
	[ja 'le:ðə 'ɛftʌ ...]
I need ...	**Jeg har brug for ...**
	[ja hɑ' 'bʁu' fə ...]

I'm just looking.	**Jeg kigger bare.**
	[ja 'kigʌ 'bɑ:ɑ]
We're just looking.	**Vi kiggede bare.**
	['vi 'kigəðə 'bɑ:ɑ]
I'll come back later.	**Jeg kommer tilbage senere.**
	[ja 'kʌmʌ te'bæ:jə 'se'nʌʌ]
We'll come back later.	**Vi kommer tilbage senere.**
	['vi 'kʌmʌ te'bæ:jə 'se'nʌʌ]
discounts | sale	**rabatter | udsalg**
	[ʁɑ'batʌ | 'uð‚sal']

Would you please show me ...	**Vil du være sød at vise mig ...**
	['ve du 'vɛɐ̯' søð' ʌ 'vi:sə maj ...]
Would you please give me ...	**Vil du give mig ...**
	['ve du gi' maj ...]
Can I try it on?	**Kan jeg prøve det på?**
	['kan' ja 'pʁœ:wə de pɔ'?]
Excuse me, where's the fitting room?	**Undskyld, hvor er prøverummet?**
	['ɔn‚skyl', vɒ' 'æɐ̯ 'pʁœ:wə 'ʁɔməð?]
Which color would you like?	**Hvilken farve vil du have?**
	['velkən 'fɑ:və ve du hæ'?]
size | length	**størrelse | længde**
	['stœɐ̯ʌlsə | 'lɛŋ'də]
How does it fit?	**Hvordan passer det?**
	[vɒ'dan 'pasʌ de?]

How much is it?	**Hvor meget bliver det?**
	[vɒ' 'maɑð 'bliɐ̯' de?]
That's too expensive.	**Det er for dyrt.**
	[de 'æɐ̯ fə 'dyɐ̯'t]
I'll take it.	**Det tager jeg.**
	[de 'tæ'ɐ̯ jaj]
Excuse me, where do I pay?	**Undskyld, hvor kan jeg betale?**
	['ɔn‚skyl', vɒ' kan' ja be'tæ'lə?]

Will you pay in cash or credit card?

Vil du betale kontant eller med kreditkort?
['ve du be'tæˀlə kɔn'tanˀt mɛ kʁɛ'dit kɒːt?]

In cash | with credit card

Kontant | med kreditkort
[kɔn'tanˀt | mɛ kʁɛ'dit kɒːt]

Do you want the receipt?

Vil du have kvitteringen?
['ve du hæˀ kvi'teˀɡeŋən?]

Yes, please.

Ja, tak.
['jæ, tɑk]

No, it's OK.

Nej, det er OK.
[nɑjˀ, de 'æɡ ɔw'kɛj]

Thank you. Have a nice day!

Tak. Hav en dejlig dag!
[tɑk. 'hɑˀ en 'dɑjli 'dæˀ]

In town

Excuse me, please.	**Undskyld mig.** ['ɔn,skyl' maj]
I'm looking for …	**Jeg leder efter …** [ja 'le:ðə 'ɛftʌ …]
the subway	**metroen** ['me:tʁoən]
my hotel	**mit hotel** [mit ho'tɛl']
the movie theater	**biografen** [bio'gʁa'fən]
a taxi stand	**en taxiholdeplads** [en 'taksi 'hʌlə,plas]
an ATM	**en udbetalingsautomat** [en uð'be'tæ'leŋs awto'mæ't]
a foreign exchange office	**et vekselkontor** [et 'vɛksəl kɔn'to'ɐ̯]
an internet café	**en internetcafé** [en 'entʌ,nɛt ka'fe']
… street	**… gade** [… 'gæ:ðə]
this place	**dette sted** ['dɛtə 'stɛð]
Do you know where … is?	**Ved du, hvor … er?** [ve du, vɒ' … 'æɐ̯?]
Which street is this?	**Hvilken gade er dette?** ['velkən 'gæ:ðə 'æɐ̯ 'dɛtə?]
Show me where we are right now.	**Vis mig, hvor vi er lige nu.** ['vi's maj, vɒ' vi 'æɐ̯ 'li:ə nu]
Can I get there on foot?	**Kan jeg komme derhen til fods?** ['kan' ja 'kʌmə 'dɛ'ɐ̯'hɛn te 'fo'ðs?]
Do you have a map of the city?	**Har du et kort over byen?** ['ha' du et 'kɒːt 'ɒw'ʌ 'byən?]
How much is a ticket to get in?	**Hvor meget koster en billet for at komme ind?** [vɒ' 'maað 'kʌstɐ en bi'lɛt fə ʌ 'kʌmə 'en'?]
Can I take pictures here?	**Må jeg tage billeder her?** [mɔ' ja tæ' 'beləðʌ 'hɛ'ɐ̯?]
Are you open?	**Har du åbent?** ['ha' du 'ɔ:bənt?]

When do you open?

Hvornår åbner du?
[vɒ'nɒ' 'ɔːbnʌ du?]

When do you close?

Hvornår lukker du?
[vɒ'nɒ' 'lɔkɐ du?]

Money

money	**penge** ['pɛŋə]
cash	**kontanter** [kɔn'tanˀtʌ]
paper money	**sedler** ['sɛðˀlʌ]
loose change	**småmønter** [ˌsmʌ'mønˀtʌ]
check | change | tip	**regningen | byttepenge | drikkepenge** ['ʁajnenən | 'bytəˌpɛŋə | 'dʁɛkəˌpɛŋə]

credit card	**kreditkort** [kʁɛ'dit kɒːt]
wallet	**tegnebog** ['tajnəbɔˀw]
to buy	**at købe** [ʌ 'køːbə]
to pay	**at betale** [ʌ be'tæˀlə]
fine	**bøde** ['bøːðə]
free	**gratis** ['gʁɑːtis]

Where can I buy ...?	**Hvor kan jeg købe ...?** [vɒˀ kan ja 'køːbə ...?]
Is the bank open now?	**Har banken åbent nu?** ['haˀ 'baŋkən 'ɔːbənt nu?]
When does it open?	**Hvornår åbner den?** [vɒ'nɒˀ 'ɔːbnʌ dɛnˀ?]
When does it close?	**Hvornår lukker den?** [vɒ'nɒˀ 'lɔkɐ dɛnˀ?]

How much?	**Hvor meget?** [vɒˀ 'maɑð?]
How much is this?	**Hvor meget bliver det?** [vɒˀ 'maɑð 'bliɐˀ de?]
That's too expensive.	**Det er for dyrt.** [de 'æɐ fɐ 'dyɐ̯ˀt]

Excuse me, where do I pay?	**Undskyld, hvor kan jeg betale?** ['ɔnˌskylˀ, vɒˀ kanˀ ja be'tæˀlə?]
Check, please.	**Regningen, tak.** ['ʁajnenən, tak]

Can I pay by credit card?

Kan jeg betale med kreditkort?
['kan' ja be'tæ'lə mɛ kʁɛ'dit kɒ:t?]

Is there an ATM here?

**Er der en
udbetalingsautomat her?**
[æɐ̯ 'dɛ'ɐ̯ en
uð'be'tæ'leŋs ɑwto'mæ't 'hɛ'ɐ̯?]

I'm looking for an ATM.

**Jeg leder efter
en udbetalingsautomat.**
[ja 'le:ðə 'ɛftʌ
en uð'be'tæ'leŋs ɑwto'mæ't]

I'm looking for a foreign exchange office.

Jeg leder efter et vekselkontor.
[ja 'le:ðə 'ɛftʌ et 'vɛksəl kɔn'to'ɐ̯]

I'd like to change ...

Jeg vil gerne veksle ...
[jaj ve 'gæɐ̯nə 'vɛkslə ...]

What is the exchange rate?

Hvad er vekselkursen?
['vað 'æɐ̯ 'vɛksəl 'kuɐ̯'sən]

Do you need my passport?

Har du brug for mit pas?
['hɑ' du 'bʁu' fə mit 'pas?]

Time

What time is it?	**Hvad er klokken?** ['vað 'æɐ̯ 'klʌkən?]
When?	**Hvornår?** [vɒ'nɒˀ?]
At what time?	**På hvilket tidspunkt?** [pɔ 'velkəð 'tiðspɔŋˀt?]
now | later | after ...	**nu | senere | efter ...** ['nu | 'seˀnʌʌ | 'ɛftʌ ...]
one o'clock	**klokken et** ['klʌkən et]
one fifteen	**kvart over et** ['kvɑːt 'ɒwˀʌ et]
one thirty	**halv to** ['halˀ 'toˀ]
one forty-five	**kvart i to** ['kvɑːt i 'toˀ]

one | two | three	**et | to | tre** [ed | toˀ | tʁɛˀ]
four | five | six	**fire | fem | seks** ['fiˀʌ | fɛmˀ | 'sɛks]
seven | eight | nine	**syv | otte | ni** ['sywˀ | 'ɔːtə | niˀ]
ten | eleven | twelve	**ti | elleve | tolv** ['tiˀ | 'ɛlvə | tʌlˀ]

in ...	**om ...** [ʌm ...]
five minutes	**fem minutter** [fɛmˀ me'nutʌ]
ten minutes	**ti minutter** ['tiˀ me'nutʌ]
fifteen minutes	**femten minutter** ['fɛmtən me'nutʌ]
twenty minutes	**tyve minutter** ['tyːvə me'nutʌ]
half an hour	**en halv time** [en 'halˀ 'tiːmə]
an hour	**en time** [en 'tiːmə]
in the morning	**om morgenen** [ʌm 'mɒːɒnən]
early in the morning	**tidligt om morgenen** ['tiðlit ʌm 'mɒːɒnən]

this morning	**her til morgen** ['hɛʔɐ te 'mɒːɒn]
tomorrow morning	**i morgen tidlig** [i 'mɒːɒn 'tiðli]

in the middle of the day	**midt på dagen** ['met pɔ 'dæʔən]
in the afternoon	**om eftermiddagen** [ʌm 'ɛftʌme̩dæʔən]
in the evening	**om aftenen** [ʌm 'ɑftənən]
tonight	**i aften** [i 'ɑftən]

at night	**om natten** [ʌm 'nɛtn]
yesterday	**i går** [i 'gɒʔ]
today	**i dag** [i 'dæʔ]
tomorrow	**i morgen** [i 'mɒːɒn]
the day after tomorrow	**i overmorgen** [i 'ɒwʌˌmɒːɒn]

What day is it today?	**Hvilken dag er det i dag?** ['velkən 'dæʔ 'æɐ de i 'dæʔ?]
It's …	**Det er …** [de 'æɐ …]
Monday	**Mandag** ['manʔda]
Tuesday	**tirsdag** ['tiɐʔsda]
Wednesday	**onsdag** ['ɔnʔsda]

Thursday	**torsdag** ['tɒʔsda]
Friday	**Fredag** ['fʁɛʔda]
Saturday	**Lørdag** ['lœɐda]
Sunday	**søndag** ['sœnʔda]

Greetings. Introductions

Hello.
Hej.
['haj]

Pleased to meet you.
Glad for at møde dig.
['glað fə ʌ 'mø:ðə 'daj]

Me too.
Det samme her.
[de 'samə 'hɛ'ɐ̞]

I'd like you to meet ...
Jeg vil gerne have at du møder ...
[jaj ve 'gæɐ̞nə hæ' ʌ du 'mø:ðə ...]

Nice to meet you.
Rart at møde dig.
['ʁa'ʔt ʌ 'mø:ðə daj]

How are you?
Hvordan har du det?
[vɒ'dan ha' du de?]

My name is ...
Mit navn er ...
[mit 'nɑw'n 'æɐ̞ ...]

His name is ...
Hans navn er ...
[hans 'nɑw'n 'æɐ̞ ...]

Her name is ...
Hendes navn er ...
['henəs 'nɑw'n 'æɐ̞ ...]

What's your name?
Hvad hedder du?
['vað 'heðʌ du?]

What's his name?
Hvad hedder han?
['vað 'heðʌ han?]

What's her name?
Hvad hedder hun?
['vað 'heðʌ hun?]

What's your last name?
Hvad er dit efternavn?
['vað 'æɐ̞ did 'ɛftʌˌnɑw'n?]

You can call me ...
Du kan ringe til mig ...
[du kan 'ʁɛŋə te maj ...]

Where are you from?
Hvor er du fra?
[vɒ' 'æɐ̞ du fʁa']

I'm from ...
Jeg er fra ...
['jaj 'æɐ̞ fʁa' ...]

What do you do for a living?
Hvad arbejder du med?
['vað 'ɑːˌbajʔdʌ du mɛ?]

Who is this?
Hvem er det?
[vɛm 'æɐ̞ de?]

Who is he?
Hvem er han?
[vɛm 'æɐ̞ han?]

Who is she?
Hvem er hun?
[vɛm 'æɐ̞ hun?]

Who are they? | **Hvem er de?**
[vɛm 'æɐ̯ di?]

This is ... | **Dette er ...**
['dɛtə 'æɐ̯ ...]

my friend (masc.) | **min ven**
[min 'vɛn]

my friend (fem.) | **min veninde**
[min vɛn'enə]

my husband | **min mand**
[min 'manˀ]

my wife | **min kone**
[min 'koːnə]

my father | **min far**
[min 'fɑː]

my mother | **min mor**
[min 'moɐ̯]

my brother | **min bror**
[min 'bʁoɐ̯]

my sister | **min søster**
[min 'søstʌ]

my son | **min søn**
[min 'sœn]

my daughter | **min datter**
[min 'datʌ]

This is our son. | **Dette er vores søn.**
['dɛtə 'æɐ̯ 'vɒɒs 'sœn]

This is our daughter. | **Dette er vores datter.**
['dɛtə 'æɐ̯ 'vɒɒs 'datʌ]

These are my children. | **Dette er mine børn.**
['dɛtə 'æɐ̯ 'miːnə 'bœɐ̯ˀn]

These are our children. | **Dette er vores børn.**
['dɛtə 'æɐ̯ 'vɒɒs 'bœɐ̯ˀn]

Farewells

Good bye!	**Farvel!** [fɑ'vɛl]
Bye! (inform.)	**Hej hej!** ['hɑj 'hɑj]
See you tomorrow.	**Ses i morgen.** ['seˀs i 'mɒːɒn]
See you soon.	**Vi ses snart.** ['vi 'seˀs 'snɑˀt]
See you at seven.	**Vi ses klokken syv.** ['vi 'seˀs 'klʌkən 'sywˀ]
Have fun!	**Have det sjovt!** ['hɑˀ de 'ɕɒwd]
Talk to you later.	**Vi snakkes ved senere.** ['vi 'snɑkəs ve 'seˀnʌʌ]
Have a nice weekend.	**Ha' en dejlig weekend.** [ha en 'dɑjli 'wiːˌkɛnd]
Good night.	**Godnat.** [go'nad]
It's time for me to go.	**Det er på tide at jeg smutter.** [de 'æɐ̯ pɒ 'tiːðə ʌ ja 'smutə]
I have to go.	**Jeg bliver nødt til at gå.** [ja 'bliɐ̯ˀ nøˀt te ʌ 'gɔˀ]
I will be right back.	**Jeg kommer straks tilbage.** [ja 'kʌmʌ 'stʁɑks te'bæːjə]
It's late.	**Det er sent.** [de 'æɐ̯ 'seˀnt]
I have to get up early.	**Jeg er nødt til at stå tidligt op.** ['jɑj 'æɐ̯ nøˀt te ʌ 'stɔˀ 'tiðlit 'ʌp]
I'm leaving tomorrow.	**Jeg rejser i morgen.** [ja 'ʁɑjsə i 'mɒːɒn]
We're leaving tomorrow.	**Vi rejser i morgen.** ['vi 'ʁɑjsə i 'mɒːɒn]
Have a nice trip!	**Hav en dejlig tur!** ['hɑˀ en 'dɑjli 'tuɐ̯ˀ]
It was nice meeting you.	**Det var rart at møde dig.** [de vɑ 'ʁɑˀt ʌ 'møːðə 'dɑj]
It was nice talking to you.	**Det var rart at tale med dig.** [de vɑ 'ʁɑˀt ʌ 'tæːlə mɛ 'dɑj]
Thanks for everything.	**Tak for alt.** [tɑk fə 'alˀt]

I had a very good time.

Jeg nød tiden sammen.
[ja nøːð 'tiðən 'samˀən]

We had a very good time.

Vi nød virkeligt tiden sammen.
['vi nøːð 'viɛ̯kəlit 'tiðən 'samˀən]

It was really great.

Det var virkeligt godt.
[de va 'viɛ̯kəlit 'gʌt]

I'm going to miss you.

Jeg kommer til at savne dig.
[ja 'kʌmʌ te ʌ 'sawnə 'daj]

We're going to miss you.

Vi kommer til at savne dig.
['vi 'kʌmʌ te ʌ 'sawnə 'daj]

Good luck!

Held og lykke!
['hɛlˀ ʌ 'løkə]

Say hi to ...

Sig hej til ...
['saj 'haj te ...]

Foreign language

I don't understand.	**Jeg forstår det ikke.** [ja fə'stɐ̯ de 'ekə]
Write it down, please.	**Skriv det ned, tak.** ['skʁiw' de neð', tɑk]
Do you speak …?	**Taler du …?** ['tæːlʌ du …?]
I speak a little bit of …	**Jeg taler en lille smule …** [ja 'tæːlʌ en 'lilə 'smuːlə …]
English	**engelsk** ['ɛŋ'əlsk]
Turkish	**tyrkisk** ['tyɐ̯kisk]
Arabic	**arabisk** [ɑ'ʁɑ'bisk]
French	**fransk** ['fʁɑn'sk]
German	**tysk** ['tysk]
Italian	**italiensk** [ital'jɛ'nsk]
Spanish	**spansk** ['spɑn'sk]
Portuguese	**portugisisk** [pɒtu'gi'sisk]
Chinese	**kinesisk** [ki'ne'sisk]
Japanese	**japansk** [ja'pæ'nsk]
Can you repeat that, please.	**Kan du gentage det, tak.** ['kan du 'gɛn,tæ' de, tɑk]
I understand.	**Jeg forstår.** [ja fə'stɐ̯]
I don't understand.	**Jeg forstår det ikke.** [ja fə'stɐ̯ de 'ekə]
Please speak more slowly.	**Tal langsommere.** ['tal 'laŋ,sʌm'əʌ]
Is that correct? (Am I saying it right?)	**Er det rigtigt?** [æɐ̯ de 'ʁɛgtit?]
What is this? (What does this mean?)	**Hvad er dette?** ['vað 'æɐ̯ 'dɛtə?]

Apologies

Excuse me, please.	**Undskyld mig.** ['ɔnˌskyl' maj]
I'm sorry.	**Det er jeg ked af.** [de 'æɡ ja 'keð' æ']
I'm really sorry.	**Jeg er virkelig ked af det.** ['jaj 'æɡ 'viɡkəli 'keð' æ' de]
Sorry, it's my fault.	**Beklager, det er min skyld.** [be'klæ'jə, de 'æɡ min 'skyl']
My mistake.	**Min fejl.** [min 'faj'l]
May I ...?	**Må jeg ...?** [mɔ' ja ...?]
Do you mind if I ...?	**Har du noget imod, hvis jeg ...?** ['ha' du 'noːəð i'moð', 'ves jaj ...?]
It's OK.	**Det er OK.** [de 'æɡ ɔw'kɛj]
It's all right.	**Det er OK.** [de 'æɡ ɔw'kɛj]
Don't worry about it.	**Tag dig ikke af det.** ['tæ' 'daj 'ekə æ' de]

Agreement

Yes.	**Ja.** ['jæ]
Yes, sure.	**Ja, helt sikkert.** ['jæ, 'heˀlt 'sekʌt]
OK (Good!)	**Godt!** ['gʌt]
Very well.	**Meget godt.** ['maað 'gʌt]
Certainly!	**Bestemt!** [be'stɛmˀt]
I agree.	**Jeg er enig.** ['jɑj 'æɐ̯ 'eːni]
That's correct.	**Det er korrekt.** [de 'æɐ̯ ko'ʁakt]
That's right.	**Det er rigtigt.** [de 'æɐ̯ 'ʁɛgtit]
You're right.	**Du har ret.** [du hɑˀ 'ʁat]
I don't mind.	**Jeg har ikke noget imod det.** [jɑ hɑˀ 'ekə 'noːəð i'moðˀ de]
Absolutely right.	**Helt korrekt.** ['heˀlt ko'ʁakt]
It's possible.	**Det er muligt.** [de 'æɐ̯ 'muːlit]
That's a good idea.	**Det er en god idé.** [de 'æɐ̯ en 'goðˀ i'deˀ]
I can't say no.	**Jeg kan ikke sige nej.** [jɑ kan 'ekə 'si: 'nɑjˀ]
I'd be happy to.	**Jeg ville være glad for.** [jɑj 'vilə 'vɛɐ̯ˀ 'glað fə]
With pleasure.	**Med glæde.** [mɛ 'glɛːðə]

Refusal. Expressing doubt

No.	**Nej.** [nɑjˀ]
Certainly not.	**Bestemt ikke.** [beˈstɛmˀt ˈekə]
I don't agree.	**Jeg er ikke enig.** [ˈjɑj ˈæɐ̯ ˈekə ˈeːni]
I don't think so.	**Jeg tror det ikke.** [ja ˈtʁoˀɐ̯ de ˈekə]
It's not true.	**Det er ikke sandt.** [de ˈæɐ̯ ˈekə ˈsant]
You are wrong.	**Du tager fejl.** [du ˈtæˀɐ̯ ˈfɑjˀl]
I think you are wrong.	**Jeg tror, du tager fejl.** [ja ˈtʁoˀɐ̯, du ˈtæˀɐ̯ ˈfɑjˀl]
I'm not sure.	**Jeg er ikke sikker.** [ˈjɑj ˈæɐ̯ ˈekə ˈsekʌ]
It's impossible.	**Det er umuligt.** [de ˈæɐ̯ uˈmuˀlit]
Nothing of the kind (sort)!	**Overhovedet ikke!** [ɒwʌˈhoːədəð ˈekə]
The exact opposite.	**Det stik modsatte.** [de ˈstek ˈmoðˌsatə]
I'm against it.	**Jeg er imod det.** [ˈjɑj ˈæɐ̯ iˈmoðˀ de]
I don't care.	**Jeg er ligeglad.** [ˈjɑj ˈæɐ̯ ˈliːəˌglað]
I have no idea.	**Jeg aner det ikke.** [ˈjɑj ˈæːnə de ˈekə]
I doubt it.	**Jeg tvivler på det.** [ja ˈtviwlə pɔˀ de]
Sorry, I can't.	**Undskyld, jeg kan ikke.** [ˈɔnˌskylˀ, ja kanˀ ˈekə]
Sorry, I don't want to.	**Undskyld, jeg ønsker ikke at.** [ˈɔnˌskylˀ, ja ˈønskɐ ˈekə ʌ]
Thank you, but I don't need this.	**Tak, men jeg har ikke brug for dette.** [tɑk, mɛn ja ˈhaˀ ˈekə ˈbʁuˀ fə ˈdɛtə]
It's getting late.	**Det bliver sent.** [de ˈbliɐ̯ˀ ˈseˀnt]

I have to get up early.

Jeg er nødt til at stå tidligt op.
['jaj 'æɛ nø'̩t te ʌ 'stɔˀ 'tiðlit ʌp]

I don't feel well.

Jeg føler mig dårlig.
[ja 'føːlɛ̩ maj 'dɒːli]

Expressing gratitude

Thank you.	**Tak.** [tak]
Thank you very much.	**Mange tak.** ['maŋə 'tak]
I really appreciate it.	**Jeg sætter virkeligt pris på det.** [ja sɛtʌ 'viɐ̯kəlit 'pʁiˀs pɔˀ de]
I'm really grateful to you.	**Jeg er dig virkeligt taknemmelig.** ['jaj 'æɐ̯ da 'viɐ̯kəlit tak'nɛmˀəli]
We are really grateful to you.	**Vi er dig virkeligt taknemmelige.** ['vi 'æɐ̯ da 'viɐ̯kəlit tak'nɛmˀəliə]

Thank you for your time.	**Tak for din tid.** [tak fə din 'tiðˀ]
Thanks for everything.	**Tak for alt.** [tak fə 'alˀt]
Thank you for ...	**Tak for ...** [tak fə ...]
your help	**din hjælp** [din 'jɛlˀp]
a nice time	**en dejlig tid** [en 'dajli 'tiðˀ]

a wonderful meal	**et vidunderligt måltid** [ed við'ɔnˀʌlit 'mʌlˌtiðˀ]
a pleasant evening	**en hyggelig aften** [en 'hygəli 'aftən]
a wonderful day	**en vidunderlig dag** [en við'ɔnˀʌli 'dæˀ]
an amazing journey	**en fantastisk rejse** [en fan'tastisk 'ʁajsə]

Don't mention it.	**Glem det.** ['glɛm de]
You are welcome.	**Du er velkommen.** [du 'æɐ̯ 'vɛlˌkʌmˀən]
Any time.	**Når som helst.** ['nɒˀ sʌm 'hɛlˀst]
My pleasure.	**Intet problem.** ['entəð pʁo'bleˀm]
Forget it.	**Glem det.** ['glɛm de]
Don't worry about it.	**Tag dig ikke af det.** ['tæˀ 'daj 'ekə æˀ de]

Congratulations. Best wishes

Congratulations!	**Til lykke!** [te 'løkə]
Happy birthday!	**Tillykke med fødselsdagen!** [tə'løkə mɛ 'føsəls͵dæˀən]
Merry Christmas!	**Glædelig jul!** ['glɛːðəli 'juˀl]
Happy New Year!	**Godt Nytår!** ['gʌt 'nyt͵ɒˀ]
Happy Easter!	**God påske!** ['goðˀ 'pɔːskə]
Happy Hanukkah!	**Glædelig Hanukkah!** ['glɛːðəli 'hanuka]
I'd like to propose a toast.	**Jeg vil gerne udbringe en skål.** [jɑj ve 'gæɐ̯nə 'uð͵bʁɛŋˀə en 'skɔˀl]
Cheers!	**Skål!** ['skɔˀl]
Let's drink to …!	**Lad os skåle for …!** [laðˀ ʌs 'skɔːlə fə …!]
To our success!	**Til vores succes!** [te 'vɒɒs syk'se]
To your success!	**Til din succes!** [te din syk'se]
Good luck!	**Held og lykke!** ['hɛlˀ ʌ 'løkə]
Have a nice day!	**Hav en dejlig dag!** ['haˀ en 'dɑjli 'dæˀ]
Have a good holiday!	**Hav en god ferie!** ['haˀ en 'goðˀ 'feɐ̯ˀiə]
Have a safe journey!	**Har en sikker rejse!** ['hɑˀ en 'sekʌ 'ʁɑjsə!]
I hope you get better soon!	**Jeg håber du får det bedre snart!** [jɑ 'hɔːbʌ du fɒˀ de 'bɛðʁʌ 'snɑˀt]

Socializing

Why are you sad?
Hvorfor er du ked af det?
['vɔfʌ 'æɐ du 'keð' æ' de?]

Smile! Cheer up!
Smil! Op med humøret!
['smi'l! ʌb mɛ hu'mø'ɐ̯əð]

Are you free tonight?
Er du fri i aften?
[æɐ du 'fʁi' i 'aftən?]

May I offer you a drink?
Må jeg tilbyde dig en drink?
[mɔ' ja 'tel,by'ðə 'daj en 'driŋk?]

Would you like to dance?
Kunne du tænke dig at danse?
['kunə du 'tɛŋkə daj ʌ 'dansə?]

Let's go to the movies.
Lad os gå i biografen.
[laðʌs 'gɔ' i bio'gʁɑ'fən]

May I invite you to …?
Må jeg invitere dig til …?
[mɔ' ja envi'te'ʌ da te …?]

a restaurant
en restaurant
[en ʁɛsto'ʁɑn]

the movies
biografen
[bio'gʁɑ'fən]

the theater
teatret
[te'æ'tɐ̯əð]

go for a walk
at gå en tur
[ʌ 'gɔ' en 'tuɐ̯']

At what time?
På hvilket tidspunkt?
[pɔ 'velkəð 'tiðspɔŋ't?]

tonight
i aften
[i 'aftən]

at six
klokken seks
['klʌkən 'sɛks]

at seven
klokken syv
['klʌkən 'syw']

at eight
klokken otte
['klʌkən 'ɔ:tə]

at nine
klokken ni
['klʌkən 'ni']

Do you like it here?
Kan du lide det her?
['kan du 'li:ðə de 'hɛ'ɐ̯?]

Are you here with someone?
Er du her med nogen?
[æɐ du 'hɛ'ɐ̯ mɛ 'noən?]

I'm with my friend.
Jeg er sammen med min ven.
['jaj 'æɐ 'sam'ən mɛ min 'vɛn]

I'm with my friends.	**Jeg er sammen med mine venner.** ['jɑj 'æɡ̊ 'sɑm'ən mɛ'miːnə 'vɛnʌ]
No, I'm alone.	**Nej, jeg er alene.** [nɑj', jɑ 'æɡ̊ a'leːnə]
Do you have a boyfriend?	**Har du en kæreste?** ['hɑ' du en 'kæɡ̊ʌstə?]
I have a boyfriend.	**Jeg har en kæreste.** [jɑ hɑ' en 'kæɡ̊ʌstə]
Do you have a girlfriend?	**Har du en kæreste?** ['hɑ' du en 'kæɡ̊ʌstə?]
I have a girlfriend.	**Jeg har en kæreste.** [jɑ hɑ' en 'kæɡ̊ʌstə]
Can I see you again?	**Kan jeg se dig igen?** ['kan' jɑ se' dɑj i'ɡɛn?]
Can I call you?	**Kan jeg ringe til dig?** ['kan' jɑ 'ʁɛŋə te dɑj?]
Call me. (Give me a call.)	**Ring til mig.** ['ʁɛŋə te mɑj]
What's your number?	**Hvad er dit nummer?** ['vað 'æɡ̊ dit 'nɔm'ʌ?]
I miss you.	**Jeg savner dig.** [jɑ 'sɑwnɡ̊ dɑj]
You have a beautiful name.	**Du har et smukt navn.** [du hɑ' et 'smɔkt 'nɑw'n]
I love you.	**Jeg elsker dig.** ['jɑj 'ɛlskʌ dɑj]
Will you marry me?	**Vil du gifte dig med mig?** ['ve du 'ɡiftə 'dɑj mɛ mɑj?]
You're kidding!	**Du spøger!** [du 'spøːjə]
I'm just kidding.	**Jeg spøger.** [jɑ 'spøːjə]
Are you serious?	**Mener du det alvorligt?** ['meːnʌ du de al'vɒ'lit?]
I'm serious.	**Jeg mener det alvorligt.** [jɑ 'meːnʌ de al'vɒ'lit]
Really?!	**Virkeligt?!** ['viɡ̊kəlit?!]
It's unbelievable!	**Det er utroligt!** [de 'æɡ̊ u'tʁo'lit]
I don't believe you.	**Jeg tror dig ikke.** [jɑ 'tʁo'ɡ̊ 'dɑj 'ekə]
I can't.	**Jeg kan ikke.** [jɑ kan 'ekə]
I don't know.	**Jeg ved det ikke.** [jɑj ve de 'ekə]

I don't understand you.

Jeg forstår dig ikke.
[ja fə'stɐ̯ daj 'ekə]

Please go away.

Gå din vej.
['gɔˀ din 'vajˀ]

Leave me alone!

Lad mig være!
[lað maj 'vɛɐ̯ˀ]

I can't stand him.

Jeg kan ikke fordrage ham.
[ja kan 'ekə fə'dʁaˀwə ham]

You are disgusting!

Du er modbydelig!
[du 'æɐ̯ moð'byð'əli]

I'll call the police!

Jeg ringer til politiet!
[ja 'ʁɛŋʌ te poli'tiˀəð]

Sharing impressions. Emotions

I like it.	**Jeg kan lide det.** [ja kan 'liːðə de]
Very nice.	**Meget fint.** ['maɑð 'fiˀnt]
That's great!	**Det er godt!** [de 'æɐ̯ 'gʌt]
It's not bad.	**Det er ikke dårligt.** [de 'æɐ̯ 'ekə 'dɒːlit]

I don't like it.	**Jeg kan ikke lide det.** [ja kan 'ekə 'liːðə de]
It's not good.	**Det er ikke godt.** [de 'æɐ̯ 'ekə 'gʌt]
It's bad.	**Det er dårligt.** [de 'æɐ̯ 'dɒːlit]
It's very bad.	**Det er meget dårligt.** [de 'æɐ̯ 'maɑð 'dɒːlit]
It's disgusting.	**Det er ulækkert.** [de 'æɐ̯ 'uˌlɛkʌt]

I'm happy.	**Jeg er glad.** ['jɑj 'æɐ̯ 'glað]
I'm content.	**Jeg er tilfreds.** ['jɑj 'æɐ̯ te'fʁɛs]
I'm in love.	**Jeg er forelsket.** ['jɑj 'æɐ̯ fə'ɛlˀskəð]
I'm calm.	**Jeg er rolig.** ['jɑj 'æɐ̯ 'ʁoːli]
I'm bored.	**Jeg keder mig.** [ja 'keːðʌ mɑj]

I'm tired.	**Jeg er træt.** ['jɑj 'æɐ̯ 'tʁat]
I'm sad.	**Jeg er ked af det.** ['jɑj 'æɐ̯ 'keðˀ æˀ de]
I'm frightened.	**Jeg er bange.** ['jɑj 'æɐ̯ 'baŋə]

I'm angry.	**Jeg er vred.** ['jɑj 'æɐ̯ 'vʁɛðˀ]
I'm worried.	**Jeg er bekymret.** ['jɑj 'æɐ̯ be'kømˀʁʌð]
I'm nervous.	**Jeg er nervøs.** ['jɑj 'æɐ̯ næɐ̯'vøˀs]

I'm jealous. (envious)

Jeg er misundelig.
['jɑj 'æɐ̯ mis'ɔnˀəli]

I'm surprised.

Jeg er overrasket.
['jɑj 'æɐ̯ 'ɒwʌˌʁɑskəð]

I'm perplexed.

Jeg er forvirret.
['jɑj 'æɐ̯ fʌ'viɐ̯ˀʌð]

Problems. Accidents

I've got a problem.	**Jeg har fået et problem.** [ja ha' fɒ' et pʁoˈbleˀm]
We've got a problem.	**Vi har fået et problem.** ['vi ha' 'fɒ' et pʁoˈbleˀm]
I'm lost.	**Jeg forstår ikke.** [ja fəˈstɒ̯ 'ekə]
I missed the last bus (train).	**Jeg kom for sent til den sidste bus (tog).** [ja 'kʌm' fə 'seˀnt te dən 'sistə bus ('tɔˀw)]
I don't have any money left.	**Jeg har ikke nogen penge tilbage.** [ja ha' 'ekə 'noən 'pɛŋə teˈbæːjə]
I've lost my ...	**Jeg har mistet min ...** [ja ha' 'mestəð min ...]
Someone stole my ...	**Nogen stjal mit ...** ['noən 'stjæˀl mit ...]
passport	**pas** ['pas]
wallet	**tegnebog** ['tajnəbɔˀw]
papers	**papirer** [paˈpiːɐ̯']
ticket	**billet** [biˈlɛt]
money	**penge** ['pɛŋə]
handbag	**håndtaske** ['hʌnˈtaskə]
camera	**kamera** ['kæˀmɐ̯ʁa]
laptop	**laptop** ['lap,tʌp]
tablet computer	**tablet computer** ['tablɛt kʌmˈpjuːtʌ]
mobile phone	**mobiltelefon** [moˈbil teləˈfoˀn]
Help me!	**Hjælp mig!** ['jɛlˀp maj]
What's happened?	**Hvad er der sket?** ['vað 'æ̯ 'dɛˀ̯ 'skeˀð?]
fire	**brand** ['bʁanˀ]

shooting	**skyderi** [skyðʌ'ʁiˀ]
murder	**mord** ['moˀɐ̯]
explosion	**eksplosion** [ɛksplo'ɕoˀn]
fight	**kamp** ['kamˀp]

Call the police!	**Ring til politiet!** ['ʁɛŋə te poli'tiˀəð]
Please hurry up!	**Vær sød at skynde dig!** ['vɛɐ̯ˀ 'søðˀ ʌ 'skønə 'dɑj]
I'm looking for the police station.	**Jeg leder efter politistationen.** [jɑ 'leːðə 'ɛftʌ poli'ti staˀɕoˀnən]
I need to make a call.	**Jeg har brug for at foretage et opkald.** [jɑ hɑˀ 'bʁuˀ fə ʌ 'foːɒ̯ˌtæˀ et 'ʌpkalˀ]
May I use your phone?	**Må jeg bruge din telefon?** [moˀ jɑ 'bʁuːə din teleˈfoˀn?]

I've been ...	**Jeg er blevet ...** ['jɑj 'æɐ̯ 'blewəð ...]
mugged	**overfaldet** ['ɒwʌˌfalˀəð]
robbed	**røvet** ['ʁœwəð]
raped	**voldtaget** ['vʌlˌtæˀəð]
attacked (beaten up)	**angrebet** ['anˌgʁɛˀbəð]

Are you all right?	**Er du okay?** [æɐ̯ du ɔw'kɛj?]
Did you see who it was?	**Så du, hvem det var?** ['soˀ du, vɛm de 'vɑ?]
Would you be able to recognize the person?	**Ville du være i stand til at genkende personen?** ['vilə du 'vɛɐ̯ˀ i 'stan te ʌ 'gɛnˌkɛnˀə pæɐ̯'soˀnən?]
Are you sure?	**Er du sikker?** ['æɐ̯ du 'sekʌ?]

Please calm down.	**Fald til ro.** ['falˀ te 'ʁoˀ]
Take it easy!	**Tag det roligt!** ['tæˀ de 'ʁoːliˀt]
Don't worry!	**Det går nok!** [de gɒˀ 'nʌk]
Everything will be fine.	**Alt vil være OK.** ['alˀt ve 'vɛɐ̯ˀ ɔw'kɛj]
Everything's all right.	**Alt er okay.** ['alˀt 'æɐ̯ ɔw'kɛj]

Come here, please.

Kom her.
[kʌmˀ ˈhɛˀɐ̯]

I have some questions for you.

Jeg har nogle spørgsmål til dig.
[ja haˀ ˈnoːlə ˈsbœɐ̯s‚mɔˀl te ˈdaj]

Wait a moment, please.

Vent et øjeblik.
[ˈvɛnt et ˈʌjə‚blek]

Do you have any I.D.?

Har du nogen ID?
[ˈhaˀ du ˈnoən ˈiˀdeˀ?]

Thanks. You can leave now.

Tak. Du kan gå nu.
[tɑk. du kan ˈgɔˀ nu]

Hands behind your head!

Hænderne bag hovedet!
[ˈhɛnˀʌnə ˈbæˀ ˈhoːðəð]

You're under arrest!

Du er anholdt!
[du ˈæɐ̯ ˈan‚hʌlt]

Health problems

Please help me.	**Vær sød at hjælpe mig.** ['vɛɐ̯ˀ 'søðˀ ʌ 'jɛlpə maj]
I don't feel well.	**Jeg føler mig dårlig.** [ja ˈføːlḛ maj 'dɒːli]
My husband doesn't feel well.	**Min mand føler sig dårlig.** [min 'manˀ ˈføːlḛ saj 'dɒːli]
My son ...	**Min søn ...** [min 'sœn ...]
My father ...	**Min far ...** [min 'faː ...]
My wife doesn't feel well.	**Min kone føler sig dårlig.** [min 'koːnə ˈføːlḛ saj 'dɒːli]
My daughter ...	**Min datter ...** [min 'datʌ ...]
My mother ...	**Min mor ...** [min 'moḛ ...]
I've got a ...	**Jeg har fået ...** [ja haˀ fɒˀ ...]
headache	**hovedpine** ['hoːəðˌpiːnə]
sore throat	**ondt i halsen** ['ɔnt i 'halˀsən]
stomach ache	**mavepine** ['mæːvə 'piːnə]
toothache	**tandpine** ['tanˌpiːnə]
I feel dizzy.	**Jeg føler mig svimmel.** [ja ˈføːlḛ maj 'svemˀəl]
He has a fever.	**Han har feber.** [han haˀ 'feˀbʌ]
She has a fever.	**Hun har feber.** [hun haˀ 'feˀbʌ]
I can't breathe.	**Jeg kan ikke få vejret.** [ja kan 'ekə fɔˀ 'vajˌʁat]
I'm short of breath.	**Jeg er forpustet.** ['jaj 'æḛ fəˈpuˀstəð]
I am asthmatic.	**Jeg er astmatiker.** ['jaj 'æḛ astˈmæˀtikʌ]
I am diabetic.	**Jeg er diabetiker.** ['jaj 'æḛ diaˈbeˀtikʌ]

I can't sleep.
Jeg kan ikke sove.
[jɑ kan 'ekə 'sɒwə]

food poisoning
madforgiftning
['maðfʌˌgiftneŋ]

It hurts here.
Det gør ondt her.
[de 'gœɐ̯ ɔnt 'hɛˀɐ̯]

Help me!
Hjælp mig!
['jɛlˀp mɑj]

I am here!
Jeg er her!
['jɑj 'æɐ̯ 'hɛˀɐ̯]

We are here!
Vi er her!
['vi 'æɐ̯ 'hɛˀɐ̯]

Get me out of here!
Få mig ud herfra!
['fɔˀ mɑj 'uðˀ 'hɛˀɐ̯ˌfʁɑˀ]

I need a doctor.
Jeg har brug for en læge.
[jɑ hɑˀ 'bʁuˀ fə en 'lɛːjə]

I can't move.
Jeg kan ikke bevæge sig.
[jɑ kan 'ekə be'vɛˀjə 'sɑj]

I can't move my legs.
Jeg kan ikke bevæge mine ben.
[jɑ kan 'ekə be'vɛˀjə 'miːnə 'beˀn]

I have a wound.
Jeg har et sår.
[jɑ hɑˀ et 'sɒˀ]

Is it serious?
Er det alvorligt?
[æɐ̯ de al'vɒˀlit?]

My documents are in my pocket.
Mine papirer ligger i min lomme.
['miːnə pa'piːɐ̯ 'legʌ i min 'lʌmə]

Calm down!
Tag det roligt!
['tæˀ de 'ʁoːlit]

May I use your phone?
Må jeg bruge din telefon?
[mɔˀ jɑ 'bʁuːə din teleˈfoˀn?]

Call an ambulance!
Ring efter en ambulance!
['ʁɛŋə 'ɛftʌ en ambu'laŋsə]

It's urgent!
Det haster!
[de 'hastə]

It's an emergency!
Det er en nødsituation!
[de 'æɐ̯ en 'nød sitwa'ɕoˀn]

Please hurry up!
Vær sød at skynde dig!
['vɛɐ̯ˀ 'søðˀ ʌ 'skønə 'dɑj]

Would you please call a doctor?
Vil du venligst ringe til en læge?
['ve du 'vɛnlist 'ʁɛŋə te en 'lɛːjə?]

Where is the hospital?
Hvor er hospitalet?
[vɒˀ 'æɐ̯ hɔspi'tæˀləð?]

How are you feeling?
Hvordan har du det?
[vɒ'dan hɑˀ du de?]

Are you all right?
Er du okay?
[æɐ̯ du ɔw'kɛj?]

What's happened?
Hvad er der sket?
['vað 'æɐ̯ 'dɛˀɐ̯ 'skeˀð?]

I feel better now.

Jeg har det bedre nu.
[ja haʔ de ˈbɛðʁʌ ˈnu]

It's OK.

Det er OK.
[de ˈæɐ̯ ɔwˈkɛj]

It's all right.

Det er OK.
[de ˈæɐ̯ ɔwˈkɛj]

At the pharmacy

pharmacy (drugstore)	**apotek** [ɑpoˈteˀk]
24-hour pharmacy	**døgnåbent apotek** [ˈdʌjˀn ˈɔːbənt ɑpoˈteˀk]
Where is the closest pharmacy?	**Hvor er det nærmeste apotek?** [vɒˀ ˈæɐ̯ de ˈnæɐ̯məstə ɑpoˈteˀk?]
Is it open now?	**Holder det åbent nu?** [ˈhʌlʌ de ˈɔːbənt ˈnu?]
At what time does it open?	**Hvornår åbner det?** [vɒˈnɒˀ ˈɔːbnʌ de?]
At what time does it close?	**Hvornår lukker det?** [vɒˈnɒˀ ˈlɔkɐ̯ de?]
Is it far?	**Er det langt væk?** [æɐ̯ de ˈlɑŋˀt vɛk?]
Can I get there on foot?	**Kan jeg komme derhen til fods?** [ˈkanˀ jɑ ˈkʌmə ˈdɛˀɐ̯ˈhɛn te ˈfoˀðs?]
Can you show me on the map?	**Kan du vise mig på kortet?** [ˈkan du ˈviːsə mɑj pɔ ˈkɒːtəð?]
Please give me something for ...	**Kan du give mig noget for ...** [ˈkan du giˀ mɑj ˈnoːəð fə ...]
a headache	**hovedpine** [ˈhoːəðˌpiːnə]
a cough	**hoste** [ˈhoːstə]
a cold	**forkølelse** [fʌˈkøˀləlsə]
the flu	**influenza** [enfluˈɛnsa]
a fever	**feber** [ˈfeˀbʌ]
a stomach ache	**ondt i maven** [ˈɔnt i ˈmæːvən]
nausea	**kvalme** [ˈkvalmə]
diarrhea	**diarré** [diaˈʁɛˀ]
constipation	**forstoppelse** [fʌˈstʌpəlsə]
pain in the back	**rygsmerter** [ˈʁœg ˈsmæɐ̯tə]

chest pain	**brystsmerter** ['bʁœst 'smæɐ̯tə]
side stitch	**sidesting** ['siːðə 'steŋˀ]
abdominal pain	**mavesmerter** ['mæːvə 'smæɐ̯tə]

pill	**pille** ['pelə]
ointment, cream	**salve, creme** ['salvə, 'kʁɛˀm]
syrup	**sirup** ['siˀʁɔp]
spray	**spray** ['spʁɛj]
drops	**dråber** ['dʁɔːbʌ]

You need to go to the hospital.	**Du er nødt til at tage på hospitalet.** [du 'æɐ̯ 'nøˀt te ʌ tæˀ pɔ hɔspiˈtæˀləð]
health insurance	**sygesikring** ['syːə̩sekʁɛŋ]
prescription	**recept** [ʁɛˈsɛpt]
insect repellant	**mygge-afskrækker** ['mygə-ˈɑwˌskʁakʌ]
Band Aid	**hæfteplaster** ['hɛftə 'plastʌ]

The bare minimum

Excuse me, ...	**Undskyld, ...** ['ɔnˌskylʔ, ...]
Hello.	**Hej.** ['hɑj]
Thank you.	**Tak.** [tɑk]
Good bye.	**Farvel.** [fɑ'vɛl]
Yes.	**Ja.** ['jæ]
No.	**Nej.** [nɑjʔ]
I don't know.	**Jeg ved det ikke.** [jɑj ve de 'ekə]
Where? | Where to? | When?	**Hvor? | Hvorhen? | Hvornår?** ['vɒʔ? | 'vɒʔˌhɛn? | vɒ'nɒʔ?]

I need ...	**Jeg har brug for ...** [jɑ hɑʔ 'bʁuʔ fə ...]
I want ...	**Jeg vil ...** [jɑj ve ...]
Do you have ...?	**Har du ...?** ['hɑʔ du ...?]
Is there a ... here?	**Er der en ... her?** [æɐ̯ 'dɛʔɐ en ... hɛʔɐ̯?]
May I ...?	**Må jeg ...?** [mɔʔ jɑ ...?]
..., please (polite request)	**... venligst** [... 'vɛnlist]

I'm looking for ...	**Jeg leder efter ...** [jɑ 'leːðə 'ɛftʌ ...]
restroom	**toilet** [toa'lɛt]
ATM	**udbetalingsautomat** [uð'be'tæʔleŋs ɑwto'mæʔt]
pharmacy (drugstore)	**apotek** [ɑpo'teʔk]
hospital	**hospital** [hɔspi'tæʔl]
police station	**politistation** [poli'ti sta'ɕoʔn]
subway	**metro** ['meːtʁo]

taxi	**taxi** ['tɑksi]
train station	**togstation** ['tɔw stɑ'ɕoˀn]

My name is ...	**Mit navn er ...** [mit 'nɑwˀn 'æɐ̯ ...]
What's your name?	**Hvad er dit navn?** ['vað 'æɐ̯ dit nɑwˀn?]
Could you please help me?	**Kan du hjælpe mig?** ['kan du 'jɛlpə mɑj?]
I've got a problem.	**Jeg har fået et problem.** [jɑ hɑˀ foˀ et pʁo'bleˀm]
I don't feel well.	**Jeg føler mig dårlig.** [jɑ 'føːlɐ mɑj 'dɒːli]
Call an ambulance!	**Ring efter en ambulance!** ['ʁɛŋə 'ɛftʌ en ɑmbu'lɑŋsə]
May I make a call?	**Må jeg foretage et opkald?** [mɔˀ jɑ 'foːɒ̯ˌtæˀ et 'ʌpkalˀ?]

I'm sorry.	**Det er jeg ked af.** [de 'æɐ̯ jɑ 'keðˀ æˀ]
You're welcome.	**Selv tak.** [sɛlˀ tak]

I, me	**Jeg, mig** [jɑj, mɑj]
you (inform.)	**du** [du]
he	**han** [han]
she	**hun** [hun]
they (masc.)	**de** [di]
they (fem.)	**de** [di]
we	**vi** [vi]
you (pl)	**I, De** [I, di]
you (sg, form.)	**De** [di]

ENTRANCE	**INDGANG** ['enˌgɑŋˀ]
EXIT	**UDGANG** ['uðˌgɑŋˀ]
OUT OF ORDER	**UDE AF DRIFT** ['uːðə æˀ 'dʁɛft]
CLOSED	**LUKKET** ['lɔkəð]

OPEN	**ÅBEN** [ˈɔːbən]
FOR WOMEN	**TIL KVINDER** [te ˈkvenʌ]
FOR MEN	**TIL MÆND** [te ˈmɛnˀ]

T&P BOOKS

TOPICAL
VOCABULARY

This section contains more
than 3,000 of the most
important words.
The dictionary will provide
invaluable assistance while
traveling abroad, because
frequently individual words
are enough for you to be
understood.
The dictionary includes a
convenient transcription of
each foreign word

T&P Books Publishing

VOCABULARY
CONTENTS

T&P Books Publishing

BASIC CONCEPTS

T&P Books Publishing

1. Pronouns

I, me	**jeg**	[ˈjɑj]
you	**du**	[du]
he	**han**	[ˈhan]
she	**hun**	[ˈhun]
it	**den, det**	[ˈdən], [de]
we	**vi**	[ˈvi]
you (to a group)	**I**	[i]
they	**de**	[ˈdi]

2. Greetings. Salutations

Hello! (fam.)	**Hej!**	[ˈhɑj]
Hello! (form.)	**Hallo! Goddag!**	[haˈlo], [goˈdæˀ]
Good morning!	**Godmorgen!**	[goˈmɒːɒn]
Good afternoon!	**Goddag!**	[goˈdæˀ]
Good evening!	**Godaften!**	[goˈɑftən]
to say hello	**at hilse**	[ʌ ˈhilsə]
Hi! (hello)	**Hej!**	[ˈhɑj]
greeting (n)	**hilsen** (f)	[ˈhilsən]
to greet (vt)	**at hilse**	[ʌ ˈhilsə]
How are you? (form.)	**Hvordan har De det?**	[vɒˈdan ha di de]
How are you? (fam.)	**Hvordan går det?**	[vɒˈdan gɒː de]
What's new?	**Hvad nyt?**	[ˈvað ˈnyt]
Goodbye! (form.)	**Farvel!**	[faˈvɛl]
Bye! (fam.)	**Hej hej!**	[ˈhɑj ˈhɑj]
See you soon!	**Hej så længe!**	[ˈhɑj sʌ ˈlɛŋə]
Farewell!	**Farvel!**	[faˈvɛl]
to say goodbye	**at sige farvel**	[ʌ ˈsiː faˈvɛl]
So long!	**Hej hej!**	[ˈhɑj ˈhɑj]
Thank you!	**Tak!**	[ˈtak]
Thank you very much!	**Mange tak!**	[ˈmaŋə ˈtak]
You're welcome	**Velbekomme**	[ˈvɛlbəˈkʌmˀə]
Don't mention it!	**Det var så lidt!**	[de vaˀ sʌ let]
It was nothing	**Det var så lidt!**	[de vaˀ sʌ let]
Excuse me! (fam.)	**Undskyld, ...**	[ˈɔnˌskylˀ, ...]
Excuse me! (form.)	**Undskyld mig, ...**	[ˈɔnˌskylˀ mɑj, ...]

to excuse (forgive)	at undskylde	[ʌ 'ɔn،skylˀə]
to apologize (vi)	at undskylde sig	[ʌ 'ɔn،skylˀə saj]
My apologies	Om forladelse	[ʌm fʌ'læˀðəlsə]
I'm sorry!	Undskyld mig!	['ɔn،skylˀ maj]
to forgive (vt)	at tilgive	[ʌ 'tel،giˀ]
It's okay! (that's all right)	Det gør ikke noget	[de 'gæɡ 'ekə 'nɔːəð]
please (adv)	værsgo	['væɡ'sgoˀ]

Don't forget!	Husk!	['husk]
Certainly!	Selvfølgelig!	[sɛl'føljəli]
Of course not!	Naturligvis ikke!	[na'tuɡˀliˀviˀs 'ekə]
Okay! (I agree)	OK! Jeg er enig!	[ɔw'kɛj], ['jaj 'æɡ 'eːni]
That's enough!	Så er det nok!	['sʌ æɡ de 'nʌk]

3. Questions

Who?	Hvem?	['vɛmˀ]
What?	Hvad?	['vað]
Where? (at, in)	Hvor?	['vɒˀ]
Where (to)?	Hvorhen?	['vɒˀ،hɛn]
From where?	Hvorfra?	['vɒˀ،fʁɑˀ]
When?	Hvornår?	[vɒ'nɒˀ]
Why? (What for?)	Hvorfor?	['vɔfʌ]
Why? (~ are you crying?)	Hvorfor?	['vɔfʌ]

What for?	For hvad?	[fʌ 'vað]
How? (in what way)	Hvordan?	[vɒ'dan]
What? (What kind of ...?)	Hvilken?	['velkən]
Which?	Hvilken?	['velkən]

To whom?	Til hvem?	[tel 'vɛmˀ]
About whom?	Om hvem?	[ʌm 'vɛmˀ]
About what?	Om hvad?	[ʌm 'vað]
With whom?	Med hvem?	[mɛ 'vɛmˀ]

How many?	Hvor mange?	[vɒˀ 'maŋə]
How much?	Hvor meget?	[vɒˀ 'maa ð]
Whose?	Hvis?	['ves]

4. Prepositions

with (accompanied by)	med	[mɛ]
without	uden	['uðən]
to (indicating direction)	til	['tel]
about (talking ~ ...)	om	[ʌm]
before (in time)	før	['føˀɡ]
in front of ...	foran ...	['fɔː'anˀ ...]
under (beneath, below)	under	['ɔnʌ]

above (over)	over	['ɒwʌ]
on (atop)	på	[pɔ]
from (off, out of)	fra	['fʁɑˀ]
of (made from)	af	[a]

| in (e.g., ~ ten minutes) | om | [ʌm] |
| over (across the top of) | over | ['ɒwʌ] |

5. Function words. Adverbs. Part 1

Where? (at, in)	Hvor?	['vɒˀ]
here (adv)	her	['hɛˀɐ̯]
there (adv)	der	['dɛˀɐ̯]

| somewhere (to be) | et sted | [et 'stɛð] |
| nowhere (not anywhere) | ingen steder | ['eŋən ˌstɛːðʌ] |

| by (near, beside) | ved | [ve] |
| by the window | ved vinduet | [ve 'venduəð] |

Where (to)?	Hvorhen?	['vɒˀˌhɛn]
here (e.g., come ~!)	herhen	['hɛˀɐ̯ˌhɛn]
there (e.g., to go ~)	derhen	['dɛˀɐ̯ˌhɛn]
from here (adv)	herfra	['hɛˀɐ̯ˌfʁɑˀ]
from there (adv)	derfra	['dɛˀɐ̯ˌfʁɑˀ]

| close (adv) | nær | ['nɛˀɐ̯] |
| far (adv) | langt | ['laŋˀt] |

near (e.g., ~ Paris)	nær	['nɛˀɐ̯]
nearby (adv)	i nærheden	[i 'nɛɐ̯ˌheðˀən]
not far (adv)	ikke langt	['ekə 'laŋˀt]

left (adj)	venstre	['vɛnstʁʌ]
on the left	til venstre	[te 'vɛnstʁʌ]
to the left	til venstre	[te 'vɛnstʁʌ]

right (adj)	højre	['hʌjʁʌ]
on the right	til højre	[te 'hʌjʁʌ]
to the right	til højre	[te 'hʌjʁʌ]

in front (adv)	foran	['fɒːˈanˀ]
front (as adj)	for-, ante-	[fʌ-], [antə-]
ahead (the kids ran ~)	fremad	['fʁamˀˌað]

behind (adv)	bagved	['bæˀjˌve]
from behind	bagpå	['bæˀjˌpɔˀ]
back (towards the rear)	tilbage	[te'bæːjə]
middle	midte (f)	['metə]
in the middle	i midten	[i 'metən]

at the side	fra siden	[fʁɑ 'siðən]
everywhere (adv)	overalt	[ɒwʌ'alˀt]
around (in all directions)	rundtomkring	['ʁɔnˀdʌmˌkʁɛŋˀ]

from inside	indefra	['enəˌfʁɑˀ]
somewhere (to go)	et sted	[et 'stɛð]
straight (directly)	ligeud	['liːəˈuðˀ]
back (e.g., come ~)	tilbage	[teˈbæːjə]

| from anywhere | et eller andet sted fra | [ed 'ɛlʌ 'anəð stɛð fʁɑˀ] |
| from somewhere | fra et sted | [fʁɑ ed 'stɛð] |

firstly (adv)	for det første	[fʌ de 'fœɐ̯stə]
secondly (adv)	for det andet	[fʌ de 'anəð]
thirdly (adv)	for det tredje	[fʌ de 'tʁɛðjə]

suddenly (adv)	pludseligt	['plusəlit]
at first (in the beginning)	i begyndelsen	[i beˈgønˀəlsən]
for the first time	for første gang	[fʌ 'fœɐ̯stə gɑŋˀ]
long before …	længe før …	['lɛŋə føˀɐ̯ …]
anew (over again)	på ny	[pɔ 'nyˀ]
for good (adv)	for evigt	[fʌ 'eːvið]

never (adv)	aldrig	['aldʁi]
again (adv)	igen	[iˈgɛn]
now (adv)	nu	['nu]
often (adv)	ofte	['ʌftə]
then (adv)	da, dengang	['da], ['dɛnˀˌgɑŋˀ]
urgently (quickly)	omgående	['ʌmˌgɔˀənə]
usually (adv)	vanligvis	['væːnliˌviˀs]

by the way, …	for resten …	[fʌ 'ʁastən …]
possible (that is ~)	muligt, muligvis	['muːlit], ['muːliˌviˀs]
probably (adv)	sandsynligvis	[sanˈsyˀnliˌviˀs]
maybe (adv)	måske	[mɔˈskeˀ]
besides, …	desuden, …	[desˈuːðən, …]
that's why …	derfor …	['dɛˀɐ̯fʌ …]
in spite of …	på trods af …	[pɔ 'tʁʌs æˀ …]
thanks to …	takket være …	['takəð ˌvɛˀʌ …]

what (pron.)	hvad	['vað]
that (conj.)	at	[at]
something	noget	['nɔːəð]
anything (something)	noget	['nɔːəð]
nothing	ingenting	['eŋən'tɛŋˀ]

who (pron.)	hvem	['vɛmˀ]
someone	nogen	['noən]
somebody	nogen	['noən]

| nobody | ingen | ['eŋən] |
| nowhere (a voyage to ~) | ingen steder | ['eŋən ˌstɛːðʌ] |

nobody's	**ingens**	['eŋəns]
somebody's	**nogens**	['noens]
so (I'm ~ glad)	**så**	['sʌ]
also (as well)	**også**	['ʌsə]
too (as well)	**også**	['ʌsə]

6. Function words. Adverbs. Part 2

Why?	**Hvorfor?**	['vɔfʌ]
for some reason	**af en eller anden grund**	[a en 'ɛlʌ 'anən 'gʁɔn']
because ...	**fordi ...**	[fʌ'di' ...]
for some purpose	**af en eller anden grund**	[a en 'ɛlʌ 'anən 'gʁɔn']
and	**og**	[ʌ]
or	**eller**	[ɛlʌ]
but	**men**	['mɛn]
for (e.g., ~ me)	**for, til**	[fʌ], [tel]
too (~ many people)	**for, alt for**	[fʌ], ['al't fʌ]
only (exclusively)	**bare, kun**	['bɑːa], ['kɔn]
exactly (adv)	**præcis**	[pʁɛ'si's]
about (more or less)	**cirka**	['siɐka]
approximately (adv)	**omtrent**	[ʌm'tʁan't]
approximate (adj)	**omtrentlig**	[ʌm'tʁan'tli]
almost (adv)	**næsten**	['nɛstən]
the rest	**rest** (f)	['ʁast]
the other (second)	**den anden**	[dən 'anən]
other (different)	**andre**	['andʁʌ]
each (adj)	**hver**	['vɛ'ɐ̯]
any (no matter which)	**hvilken som helst**	['velkən sʌm 'hɛl'st]
many, much (a lot of)	**megen, meget**	['majən], ['mɑɑð]
many people	**mange**	['maŋə]
all (everyone)	**alle**	['alə]
in return for ...	**til gengæld for ...**	[tel 'gɛn,gɛl' fʌ ...]
in exchange (adv)	**i stedet for**	[i 'stɛðə fʌ]
by hand (made)	**i hånden**	[i 'hʌnən]
hardly (negative opinion)	**næppe**	['nɛpə]
probably (adv)	**sandsynligvis**	[san'sy'nli,vi's]
on purpose (intentionally)	**med vilje, forsætlig**	[mɛ 'viljə], [fʌ'sɛtli]
by accident (adv)	**tilfældigt**	[te'fɛl'dit]
very (adv)	**meget**	['mɑɑð]
for example (adv)	**for eksempel**	[fʌ ɛk'sɛm'pəl]
between	**imellem**	[i'mɛl'əm]
among	**blandt**	['blant]

| so much (such a lot) | **så meget** | ['sʌ 'mɑɑð] |
| especially (adv) | **særligt** | ['sæɛ̯lit] |

T&P BOOKS

NUMBERS. MISCELLANEOUS

T&P Books Publishing

0 zero	nul	['nɔl]
1 one	en	['en]
2 two	to	['toˀ]
3 three	tre	['tʁɛˀ]
4 four	fire	['fiˀʌ]
5 five	fem	['fɛmˀ]
6 six	seks	['sɛks]
7 seven	syv	['sywˀ]
8 eight	otte	['ɔːtə]
9 nine	ni	['niˀ]
10 ten	ti	['tiˀ]
11 eleven	elleve	['ɛlvə]
12 twelve	tolv	['tʌlˀ]
13 thirteen	tretten	['tʁatən]
14 fourteen	fjorten	['fjoʁtən]
15 fifteen	femten	['fɛmtən]
16 sixteen	seksten	['sɑjstən]
17 seventeen	sytten	['søtən]
18 eighteen	atten	['atən]
19 nineteen	nitten	['netən]
20 twenty	tyve	['tyːvə]
21 twenty-one	enogtyve	['eːnʌˌtyːvə]
22 twenty-two	toogtyve	['toːʌˌtyːvə]
23 twenty-three	treogtyve	['tʁɛːʌˌtyːvə]
30 thirty	tredive	['tʁaðvə]
31 thirty-one	enogtredive	['eːnʌˌtʁaðvə]
32 thirty-two	toogtredive	['toːʌˌtʁaðvə]
33 thirty-three	treogtredive	['tʁɛːʌˌtʁaðvə]
40 forty	fyrre	['fœʁʌ]
41 forty-one	enogfyrre	['eːnʌˌfœʁʌ]
42 forty-two	toogfyrre	['toːʌˌfœʁʌ]
43 forty-three	treogfyrre	['tʁɛːʌˌfœʁʌ]
50 fifty	halvtreds	[hal'tʁɛs]
51 fifty-one	enoghalvtreds	['eːnʌ halˌtʁɛs]
52 fifty-two	tooghalvtreds	['toːʌ halˌtʁɛs]
53 fifty-three	treoghalvtreds	['tʁɛːʌ halˌtʁɛs]
60 sixty	tres	['tʁɛs]

61 sixty-one	enogtres	['e:nʌˌtʁɛs]
62 sixty-two	toogtres	['to:ʌˌtʁɛs]
63 sixty-three	treogtres	['tʁɛːʌˌtʁɛs]

70 seventy	halvfjerds	[hal'fjæɐ̯s]
71 seventy-one	enoghalvfjerds	['e:nʌ hal'fjæɐ̯s]
72 seventy-two	tooghalvfjerds	['to:ʌ hal'fjæɐ̯s]
73 seventy-three	treoghalvfjerds	['tʁɛːʌ hal'fjæɐ̯s]

80 eighty	firs	['fiɐ̯ˀs]
81 eighty-one	enogfirs	['e:nʌˌfiɐ̯ˀs]
82 eighty-two	toogfirs	['to:ʌˌfiɐ̯ˀs]
83 eighty-three	treogfirs	['tʁɛːʌˌfiɐ̯ˀs]

90 ninety	halvfems	[hal'fɛmˀs]
91 ninety-one	enoghalvfems	['e:nʌ halˌfɛmˀs]
92 ninety-two	tooghalvfems	['to:ʌ halˌfɛmˀs]
93 ninety-three	treoghalvfems	['tʁɛːʌ halˌfɛmˀs]

8. Cardinal numbers. Part 2

100 one hundred	hundrede	['hunʌðə]
200 two hundred	tohundrede	['tɔwˌhunʌðə]
300 three hundred	trehundrede	['tʁɛˌhunʌðə]
400 four hundred	firehundrede	['fiɐ̯ˌhunʌðə]
500 five hundred	femhundrede	['fɛmˌhunʌðə]

600 six hundred	sekshundrede	['sɛksˌhunʌðə]
700 seven hundred	syvhundrede	['sywˌhunʌðə]
800 eight hundred	ottehundrede	['ɔːtəˌhunʌðə]
900 nine hundred	nihundrede	['niˌhunʌðə]

1000 one thousand	tusind	['tuˀsən]
2000 two thousand	totusind	['toˌtuˀsən]
3000 three thousand	tretusind	['tʁɛˌtuˀsən]
10000 ten thousand	titusind	['tiˌtuˀsən]
one hundred thousand	hundredetusind	['hunʌðəˌtuˀsən]
million	million (f)	[mili'oˀn]
billion	milliard (f)	[mili'ɑˀd]

9. Ordinal numbers

first (adj)	første	['fœɐ̯stə]
second (adj)	anden	['anən]
third (adj)	tredje	['tʁɛðjə]
fourth (adj)	fjerde	['fjɛːʌ]
fifth (adj)	femte	['fɛmtə]
sixth (adj)	sjette	['ɕɛːtə]

seventh (adj)	syvende	['syw'ənə]
eighth (adj)	ottende	['ʌtənə]
ninth (adj)	niende	['ni'ənə]
tenth (adj)	tiende	['ti'ənə]

T&P BOOKS

COLOURS. UNITS OF MEASUREMENT

T&P Books Publishing

10. Colors

color	**farve** (f)	['fɑ:və]
shade (tint)	**nuance** (f)	[ny'ɑŋsə]
hue	**farvetone** (f)	['fɑ:və‚to:nə]
rainbow	**regnbue** (f)	['ʁɑjn‚bu:ə]
white (adj)	**hvid**	['við']
black (adj)	**sort**	['soɐ̯t]
gray (adj)	**grå**	['gʁɔ']
green (adj)	**grøn**	['gʁœn']
yellow (adj)	**gul**	['gu'l]
red (adj)	**rød**	['ʁœð']
blue (adj)	**blå**	['blɔ']
light blue (adj)	**lyseblå**	['lysə‚blɔ']
pink (adj)	**rosa**	['ʁo:sa]
orange (adj)	**orange**	[o'ʁɑŋɕə]
violet (adj)	**violblå**	[vi'ol‚blɔ']
brown (adj)	**brun**	['bʁu'n]
golden (adj)	**guld-**	['gul-]
silvery (adj)	**sølv-**	['søl-]
beige (adj)	**beige**	['bɛ:ɕ]
cream (adj)	**cremefarvet**	['kʁɛ:m‚fɑ'vəð]
turquoise (adj)	**turkis**	[tyɐ̯'ki's]
cherry red (adj)	**kirsebærrød**	['kiɐ̯səbæɐ̯‚ʁœð']
lilac (adj)	**lilla**	['lela]
crimson (adj)	**hindbærrød**	['henbæɐ̯‚ʁœð']
light (adj)	**lys**	['ly's]
dark (adj)	**mørk**	['mœɐ̯k]
bright, vivid (adj)	**klar**	['klɑ']
colored (pencils)	**farve-**	['fɑ:və-]
color (e.g., ~ film)	**farve**	['fɑ:və]
black-and-white (adj)	**sort-hvid**	['soɐ̯t'við']
plain (one-colored)	**ensfarvet**	['ens‚fɑ'vəð]
multicolored (adj)	**mangefarvet**	['mɑŋə‚fɑ:vəð]

11. Units of measurement

weight	**vægt** (f)	['vɛgt]
length	**længde** (f)	['lɛŋ'də]

width	bredde (f)	['bʁɛˀdə]
height	højde (f)	['hʌjˀdə]
depth	dybde (f)	['dybdə]
volume	rumfang (i)	['ʁomˌfaŋˀ]
area	areal (i)	[ˌɑːe'æˀl]

gram	gram (i)	['gʁam˞]
milligram	milligram (i)	['miliˌgʁam˞]
kilogram	kilogram (i)	['kiloˌgʁam˞]
ton	ton (i, f)	['tʌnˀ]
pound	pund (i)	['punˀ]
ounce	ounce (f)	['awns]

meter	meter (f)	['meˀtʌ]
millimeter	millimeter (f)	['miliˌmeˀtʌ]
centimeter	centimeter (f)	['sɛntiˌmeˀtʌ]
kilometer	kilometer (f)	['kiloˌmeˀtʌ]
mile	mil (f)	['miˀl]

inch	tomme (f)	['tʌmə]
foot	fod (f)	['foˀð]
yard	yard (f)	['jɑːd]

square meter	kvadratmeter (f)	[kva'dʁaˀtˌmeˀtʌ]
hectare	hektar (f)	[hɛk'tɑˀ]
liter	liter (f)	['litʌ]
degree	grad (f)	['gʁɑˀð]
volt	volt (f)	['vʌlˀt]
ampere	ampere (f)	[ɑm'pɛːɐ̯]
horsepower	hestekraft (f)	['hɛstəˌkʁaft]

quantity	mængde (f)	['mɛŋˀdə]
a little bit of ...	lidt ...	['let ...]
half	halvdel (f)	['haldeˀl]
dozen	dusin (i)	[du'siˀn]
piece (item)	stykke (i)	['støkə]

| size | størrelse (f) | ['stœʁʌlsə] |
| scale (map ~) | målestok (f) | ['mɔːləˌstʌk] |

minimal (adj)	minimal	[mini'mæˀl]
the smallest (adj)	mindst	['menˀst]
medium (adj)	middel	['miðˀəl]
maximal (adj)	maksimal	[mɑksi'mæˀl]
the largest (adj)	størst	['stœʁst]

12. Containers

| canning jar (glass ~) | glaskrukke (f) | ['glasˌkʁɔkə] |
| can | dåse (f) | ['dɔːsə] |

bucket	**spand** (f)	['span']
barrel	**tønde** (f)	['tønə]
wash basin (e.g., plastic ~)	**balje** (f)	['baljə]
tank (100L water ~)	**tank** (f)	['taŋ'k]
hip flask	**lommelærke** (f)	['lʌmə‚læɐ̯kə]
jerrycan	**dunk** (f)	['dɔŋ'k]
tank (e.g., tank car)	**tank** (f)	['taŋ'k]
mug	**krus** (i)	['kʁu's]
cup (of coffee, etc.)	**kop** (f)	['kʌp]
saucer	**underkop** (f)	['ɔnʌ‚kʌp]
glass (tumbler)	**glas** (i)	['glas]
wine glass	**vinglas** (i)	['vi:n‚glas]
stock pot (soup pot)	**gryde** (f)	['gʁy:ðə]
bottle (~ of wine)	**flaske** (f)	['flaskə]
neck (of the bottle, etc.)	**flaskehals** (f)	['flaskə‚hal's]
carafe (decanter)	**karaffel** (f)	[ka'ʁafəl]
pitcher	**kande** (f)	['kanə]
vessel (container)	**beholder** (f)	[be'hʌl'ʌ]
pot (crock, stoneware ~)	**potte** (f)	['pʌtə]
vase	**vase** (f)	['væ:sə]
bottle (perfume ~)	**flakon** (f)	[fla'kʌn]
vial, small bottle	**flaske** (f)	['flaskə]
tube (of toothpaste)	**tube** (f)	['tu:bə]
sack (bag)	**sæk** (f)	['sɛk]
bag (paper ~, plastic ~)	**pose** (f)	['po:sə]
pack (of cigarettes, etc.)	**pakke** (f)	['pakə]
box (e.g., shoebox)	**æske** (f)	['ɛskə]
crate	**kasse** (f)	['kasə]
basket	**kurv** (f)	['kuɐ̯'w]

MAIN VERBS

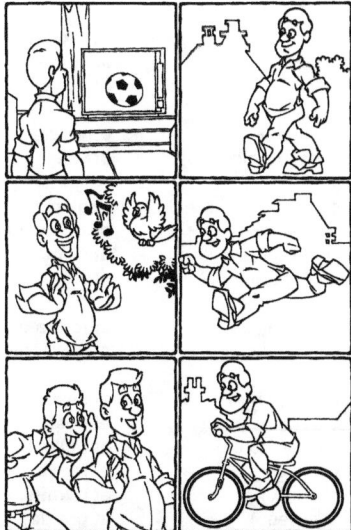

T&P Books Publishing

to advise (vt)	at råde	[ʌ 'ʁɔ:ðə]
to agree (say yes)	at samtykke	[ʌ 'sam,tykə]
to answer (vi, vt)	at svare	[ʌ 'svɑ:ɑ]
to apologize (vi)	at undskylde sig	[ʌ 'ɔn,skylʔə saj]
to arrive (vi)	at ankomme	[ʌ 'an,kʌmʔə]
to ask (~ oneself)	at spørge	[ʌ 'spœɐ̯ʌ]
to ask (~ sb to do sth)	at bede	[ʌ 'beʔðə]
to be (vi)	at være	[ʌ 'vɛ:ʌ]
to be afraid	at frygte	[ʌ 'fʁɶgtə]
to be hungry	at være sulten	[ʌ 'vɛ:ʌ 'sultən]
to be interested in ...	at interessere sig	[ʌ entʁə'seʔʌ saj]
to be needed	at være behøvet	[ʌ 'vɛ:ʌ be'høʔvəð]
to be surprised	at blive forundret	[ʌ 'bli:ə fʌ'ɔnʔdʁʌð]
to be thirsty	at være tørstig	[ʌ 'vɛ:ʌ 'tœɐ̯sti]
to begin (vt)	at begynde	[ʌ be'gønʔə]
to belong to ...	at tilhøre ...	[ʌ 'tel,hø'ʌ ...]
to boast (vi)	at prale	[ʌ 'pʁɑ:lə]
to break (split into pieces)	at bryde	[ʌ 'bʁy:ðə]
to call (~ for help)	at tilkalde	[ʌ 'tel,kalʔə]
can (v aux)	at kunne	[ʌ 'kunə]
to catch (vt)	at fange	[ʌ 'faŋə]
to change (vt)	at ændre	[ʌ 'ɛndʁʌ]
to choose (select)	at vælge	[ʌ 'vɛljə]
to come down (the stairs)	at gå ned	[ʌ gɔʔ 'neðʔ]
to compare (vt)	at sammenligne	[ʌ 'samən,liʔnə]
to complain (vi, vt)	at klage	[ʌ 'klæ:jə]
to confuse (mix up)	at forveksle	[ʌ fʌ'vɛkslə]
to continue (vt)	at fortsætte	[ʌ 'fɔ:t,sɛtə]
to control (vt)	at kontrollere	[ʌ kʌntʁo'le'ʌ]
to cook (dinner)	at lave	[ʌ 'læ:və]
to cost (vt)	at koste	[ʌ 'kʌstə]
to count (add up)	at tælle	[ʌ 'tɛlə]
to count on ...	at regne med ...	[ʌ 'ʁɑjnə mɛ ...]
to create (vt)	at oprette, at skabe	[ʌ 'ʌb,ʁatə], [ʌ 'skæ:bə]
to cry (weep)	at græde	[ʌ 'gʁa:ðə]

14. The most important verbs. Part 2

to deceive (vi, vt)	at snyde	[ʌ 'sny:ðə]
to decorate (tree, street)	at pryde	[ʌ 'pʁy:ðə]
to defend (a country, etc.)	at forsvare	[ʌ fʌ'svɑˀɑ]
to demand (request firmly)	at kræve	[ʌ 'kʁɛ:və]
to dig (vt)	at grave	[ʌ 'gʁɑ:və]
to discuss (vt)	at diskutere	[ʌ disku'teˀʌ]
to do (vt)	at gøre	[ʌ 'gœ:ʌ]
to doubt (have doubts)	at tvivle	[ʌ 'tviwlə]
to drop (let fall)	at tabe	[ʌ 'tæ:bə]
to enter (room, house, etc.)	at komme ind	[ʌ 'kʌmə ˌenˀ]
to excuse (forgive)	at tilgive	[ʌ 'telˌgiˀ]
to exist (vi)	at eksistere	[ʌ ɛksi'steˀʌ]
to expect (foresee)	at forudse	[ʌ 'fɒuðˌseˀ]
to explain (vt)	at forklare	[ʌ fʌ'klɑˀɑ]
to fall (vi)	at falde	[ʌ 'falə]
to find (vt)	at finde	[ʌ 'fenə]
to finish (vt)	at slutte	[ʌ 'slutə]
to fly (vi)	at flyve	[ʌ 'fly:və]
to follow ... (come after)	at følge efter ...	[ʌ 'føljə 'ɛftʌ ...]
to forget (vi, vt)	at glemme	[ʌ 'glɛmə]
to forgive (vt)	at tilgive	[ʌ 'telˌgiˀ]
to give (vt)	at give	[ʌ 'giˀ]
to give a hint	at give et vink	[ʌ 'giˀ et 'veŋˀk]
to go (on foot)	at gå	[ʌ 'gɔˀ]
to go for a swim	at bade	[ʌ 'bæˀðə]
to go out (for dinner, etc.)	at gå ud	[ʌ 'gɔˀ uðˀ]
to guess (the answer)	at gætte	[ʌ 'gɛtə]
to have (vt)	at have	[ʌ 'hæ:və]
to have breakfast	at spise morgenmad	[ʌ 'spi:sə 'mɒːɒnˌmað]
to have dinner	at spise aftensmad	[ʌ 'spi:sə 'ɑftənsˌmað]
to have lunch	at spise frokost	[ʌ 'spi:sə 'fʁɔkʌst]
to hear (vt)	at høre	[ʌ 'hø:ʌ]
to help (vt)	at hjælpe	[ʌ 'jɛlpə]
to hide (vt)	at gemme	[ʌ 'gɛmə]
to hope (vi, vt)	at håbe	[ʌ 'hɔ:bə]
to hunt (vi, vt)	at jage	[ʌ 'jæ:jə]
to hurry (vi)	at skynde sig	[ʌ 'skønə saj]

15. The most important verbs. Part 3

to inform (vt)	at informere	[ʌ enfɒ'me²ʌ]
to insist (vi, vt)	at insistere	[ʌ ensi'ste²ʌ]
to insult (vt)	at fornærme	[ʌ fʌ'næɐ̯'mə]
to invite (vt)	at indbyde, at invitere	[ʌ 'en‚by²ðə], [ʌ envi'te²ʌ]
to joke (vi)	at spøge	[ʌ 'spø:jə]

to keep (vt)	at beholde	[ʌ be'hʌl²ə]
to keep silent	at tie	[ʌ 'ti:ə]
to kill (vt)	at dræbe, at myrde	[ʌ 'dʁɛ:bə], [ʌ 'myɐ̯də]
to know (sb)	at kende	[ʌ 'kɛnə]
to know (sth)	at vide	[ʌ 'vi:ðə]
to laugh (vi)	at le, at grine	[ʌ 'le²], [ʌ 'gʁi:nə]

to liberate (city, etc.)	at befri	[ʌ be'fʁi²]
to like (I like ...)	at kunne lide	[ʌ 'kunə 'li:ðə]
to look for ... (search)	at søge ...	[ʌ 'sø:ə ...]
to love (sb)	at elske	[ʌ 'ɛlskə]
to make a mistake	at tage fejl	[ʌ 'tæ² faj²l]
to manage, to run	at styre, at lede	[ʌ 'sty:ʌ], [ʌ 'le:ðə]
to mean (signify)	at betyde	[ʌ be'ty²ðə]
to mention (talk about)	at omtale, at nævne	[ʌ 'ʌm‚tæ:lə], [ʌ 'nɛwnə]
to miss (school, etc.)	at forsømme	[ʌ fʌ'sœm²ə]
to notice (see)	at bemærke	[ʌ be'mæɐ̯kə]

to object (vi, vt)	at indvende	[ʌ 'en²‚vɛn²ə]
to observe (see)	at observere	[ʌ ʌbsæɐ̯'ve²ʌ]
to open (vt)	at åbne	[ʌ 'ɔ:bnə]
to order (meal, etc.)	at bestille	[ʌ be'stel²ə]
to order (mil.)	at beordre	[ʌ be'ɒ²dʁʌ]
to own (possess)	at besidde, at eje	[ʌ be'sið²ə], [ʌ 'ɑjə]
to participate (vi)	at deltage	[ʌ 'del‚tæ²]
to pay (vi, vt)	at betale	[ʌ be'tæ²lə]
to permit (vt)	at tillade	[ʌ 'te‚læ²ðə]
to plan (vt)	at planlægge	[ʌ 'plæ:n‚lɛgə]
to play (children)	at lege	[ʌ 'lɑjə]

to pray (vi, vt)	at bede	[ʌ 'be²ðə]
to prefer (vt)	at foretrække	[ʌ fɒ:ɒ'tʁakə]
to promise (vt)	at love	[ʌ 'lɔ:və]
to pronounce (vt)	at udtale	[ʌ 'uð‚tæ:lə]
to propose (vt)	at foreslå	[ʌ 'fɒ:ɒ‚slɔ²]
to punish (vt)	at straffe	[ʌ 'stʁɑfə]

16. The most important verbs. Part 4

| to read (vi, vt) | at læse | [ʌ 'lɛ:sə] |
| to recommend (vt) | at anbefale | [ʌ 'anbe‚fæ²lə] |

to refuse (vi, vt)	at vægre sig	[ʌ 'vɛːjʁʌ saj]
to regret (be sorry)	at beklage	[ʌ be'klæˀjə]
to rent (sth from sb)	at leje	[ʌ 'lajə]

to repeat (say again)	at gentage	[ʌ 'gɛnˌtæˀ]
to reserve, to book	at reservere	[ʌ ʁɛsæɐ̯'veˀʌ]
to run (vi)	at løbe	[ʌ 'løːbə]
to save (rescue)	at redde	[ʌ 'ʁɛðə]
to say (~ thank you)	at sige	[ʌ 'siː]

to scold (vt)	at skælde	[ʌ 'skɛlə]
to see (vt)	at se	[ʌ 'seˀ]
to sell (vt)	at sælge	[ʌ 'sɛljə]
to send (vt)	at sende	[ʌ 'sɛnə]
to shoot (vi)	at skyde	[ʌ 'skyːðə]

to shout (vi)	at skrige	[ʌ 'skʁiːə]
to show (vt)	at vise	[ʌ 'viːsə]
to sign (document)	at underskrive	[ʌ 'ɔnʌˌskʁiˀvə]
to sit down (vi)	at sætte sig	[ʌ 'sɛtə saj]

to smile (vi)	at smile	[ʌ 'smiːlə]
to speak (vi, vt)	at tale	[ʌ 'tæːlə]
to steal (money, etc.)	at stjæle	[ʌ 'stjɛːlə]
to stop (for pause, etc.)	at standse	[ʌ 'stansə]
to stop (please ~ calling me)	at stoppe, at slutte	[ʌ 'stʌpə], [ʌ 'slutə]

to study (vt)	at studere	[ʌ stu'deˀʌ]
to swim (vi)	at svømme	[ʌ 'svœmə]
to take (vt)	at tage	[ʌ 'tæˀ]
to think (vi, vt)	at tænke	[ʌ 'tɛŋkə]
to threaten (vt)	at true	[ʌ 'tʁuːə]

to touch (with hands)	at røre	[ʌ 'ʁœːʌ]
to translate (vt)	at oversætte	[ʌ 'ɔwʌˌsɛtə]
to trust (vt)	at stole på	[ʌ 'stoːlə pɔˀ]
to try (attempt)	at prøve	[ʌ 'pʁœːwə]
to turn (e.g., ~ left)	at svinge	[ʌ 'sveŋə]

to underestimate (vt)	at undervurdere	[ʌ 'ɔnʌvuɐ̯'deˀʌ]
to understand (vt)	at forstå	[ʌ fʌ'stɔˀ]
to unite (vt)	at forene	[ʌ fʌ'enə]
to wait (vt)	at vente	[ʌ 'vɛntə]

to want (wish, desire)	at ville	[ʌ 'vilə]
to warn (vt)	at advare	[ʌ 'aðˌvɑˀɑ]
to work (vi)	at arbejde	[ʌ 'ɑːˌbɑjˀdə]
to write (vt)	at skrive	[ʌ 'skʁiːvə]
to write down	at skrive ned	[ʌ 'skʁiːvə 'neðˀ]

T&P BOOKS

TIME. CALENDAR

T&P Books Publishing

Monday	mandag (f)	['man'da]
Tuesday	tirsdag (f)	['tiɐ̯'sda]
Wednesday	onsdag (f)	['ɔn'sda]
Thursday	torsdag (f)	['tɒ'sda]
Friday	fredag (f)	['fʁɛ'da]
Saturday	lørdag (f)	['lœɐ̯da]
Sunday	søndag (f)	['sœn'da]

today (adv)	i dag	[i 'dæ']
tomorrow (adv)	i morgen	[i 'mɒːɒn]
the day after tomorrow	i overmorgen	[i 'ɒwʌ,mɒːɒn]
yesterday (adv)	i går	[i 'gɒ']
the day before yesterday	i forgårs	[i 'fɒː,gɒ's]

day	dag (f)	['dæ']
working day	arbejdsdag (f)	['ɑːbɑjds,dæ']
public holiday	festdag (f)	['fɛst,dæ']
day off	fridag (f)	['fʁidæ']
weekend	weekend (f)	['wiː,kɛnd]

all day long	hele dagen	['heːlə 'dæ'ən]
the next day (adv)	næste dag	['nɛstə dæ']
two days ago	for to dage siden	[fʌ toʔ 'dæ'ə 'siðən]
the day before	dagen før	['dæ'ən fʌ]
daily (adj)	daglig	['dɑwli]
every day (adv)	hver dag	['vɛɐ̯ 'dæ']

week	uge (f)	['uːə]
last week (adv)	sidste uge	[i 'sistə 'uːə]
next week (adv)	i næste uge	[i 'nɛstə 'uːə]
weekly (adj)	ugentlig	['uːəntli]
every week (adv)	hver uge	['vɛɐ̯ 'uːə]
twice a week	to gange om ugen	['toː 'gɑŋə ɒm 'uːən]
every Tuesday	hver tirsdag	['vɛɐ̯ ,tiɐ̯'sda]

morning	morgen (f)	['mɒːɒn]
in the morning	om morgenen	[ʌm 'mɒːɒnən]
noon, midday	middag (f)	['meda]
in the afternoon	om eftermiddagen	[ʌm 'ɛftʌme,dæ'ən]
evening	aften (f)	['ɑftən]

in the evening	om aftenen	[ʌm 'ɑftənən]
night	nat (f)	['nat]
at night	om natten	[ʌm 'natən]
midnight	midnat (f)	['miðˌnat]

second	sekund (i)	[se'kɔnˀd]
minute	minut (i)	[me'nut]
hour	time (f)	['tiːmə]
half an hour	en halv time	[en 'halˀ 'tiːmə]
a quarter-hour	kvart (f)	['kvɑːt]
fifteen minutes	femten minutter	['fɛmtən me'nutʌ]
24 hours	døgn (i)	['dʌjˀn]

sunrise	solopgang (f)	['soːl 'ʌpˌgɑŋˀ]
dawn	daggry (i)	['dɑwˌgʁyː]
early morning	tidlig morgen (f)	['tiðli 'mɒːɒn]
sunset	solnedgang (f)	['soːl 'neðˌgɑŋˀ]

early in the morning	tidligt om morgenen	['tiðlit ʌm 'mɒːɒnən]
this morning	i morges	[i 'mɒːɒs]
tomorrow morning	i morgen tidlig	[i 'mɒːɒn 'tiðli]

this afternoon	i eftermiddag	[i 'ɛftʌmeˌdæˀ]
in the afternoon	om eftermiddagen	[ʌm 'ɛftʌmeˌdæˀən]
tomorrow afternoon	i morgen eftermiddag	[i 'mɒːɒn 'ɛftʌmeˌdæˀ]

| tonight (this evening) | i aften | [i 'ɑftən] |
| tomorrow night | i morgen aften | [i 'mɒːɒn 'ɑftən] |

at 3 o'clock sharp	klokken tre præcis	['klʌkən tʁɛ pʁɛ'siˀs]
about 4 o'clock	ved fire tiden	[ve 'fiˀʌ 'tiðən]
by 12 o'clock	ved 12-tiden	[ve 'tʌl 'tiðən]

in 20 minutes	om 20 minutter	[ʌm 'tyːve me'nutʌ]
in an hour	om en time	[ʌm en 'tiːmə]
on time (adv)	i tide	[i 'tiːðə]

a quarter of ...	kvart i ...	['kvɑːt i ...]
within an hour	inden for en time	['enənˀfʌ en 'tiːmə]
every 15 minutes	hvert 15 minut	['vɛˀɡt 'fɛmtən me'nut]
round the clock	døgnet rundt	['dʌjnəð 'ʁɔnˀt]

19. Months. Seasons

January	januar (f)	['januˌɑˀ]
February	februar (f)	['febʁuˌɑˀ]
March	marts (f)	['mɑːts]
April	april (f)	[a'pʁiˀl]
May	maj (f)	['mɑjˀ]
June	juni (f)	['juˀni]

July	juli (f)	['juˀli]
August	august (f)	[aw'gɔst]
September	september (f)	[sep'tɛmˀbʌ]
October	oktober (f)	[ok'toˀbʌ]
November	november (f)	[no'vɛmˀbʌ]
December	december (f)	[de'sɛmˀbʌ]

spring	forår (i)	['foːˌɒˀ]
in spring	om foråret	[ʌm 'foːˌɒˀð]
spring (as adj)	forårs-	['foːɒs-]

summer	sommer (f)	['sʌmʌ]
in summer	om sommeren	[ʌm 'sʌmʌən]
summer (as adj)	sommer-	['sʌmʌ-]

fall	efterår (i)	['ɛftʌˌɒˀ]
in fall	om efteråret	[ʌm 'ɛftʌˌɒˀð]
fall (as adj)	efterårs-	['ɛftʌˌɒs-]

winter	vinter (f)	['venˀtʌ]
in winter	om vinteren	[ʌm 'venˀtʌən]
winter (as adj)	vinter-	['ventʌ-]

month	måned (f)	['mɔːnəð]
this month	i denne måned	[i 'dɛnə 'mɔːnəð]
next month	næste måned	['nɛstə 'mɔːnəð]
last month	sidste måned	['sistə 'mɔːnəð]

a month ago	for en måned siden	[fʌ en 'mɔːnəð 'siðən]
in a month (a month later)	om en måned	[ʌm en 'mɔːnəð]
in 2 months (2 months later)	om 2 måneder	[ʌm to 'mɔːnəðʌ]
the whole month	en hel måned	[en 'heːl 'mɔːnəð]
all month long	hele måneden	['heːlə 'mɔːnəðən]

monthly (~ magazine)	månedlig	['mɔːnəðli]
monthly (adv)	månedligt	['mɔːnəðlit]
every month	hver måned	['vɛɐ̯ 'mɔːnəð]
twice a month	to gange om måneden	['toː 'gɑŋə ɒm 'mɔːnəðən]

year	år (i)	['ɒˀ]
this year	i år	[i 'ɒˀ]
next year	næste år	['nɛstə ɒˀ]
last year	i fjor	[i 'fjoˀɐ̯]

a year ago	for et år siden	[fʌ ed ɒˀ 'siðən]
in a year	om et år	[ʌm et 'ɒˀ]
in two years	om 2 år	[ʌm to 'ɒˀ]
the whole year	hele året	['heːlə 'ɒːɒð]
all year long	hele året	['heːlə 'ɒːɒð]
every year	hvert år	['vɛˀɐ̯t ɒˀ]
annual (adj)	årlig	['ɒːli]

annually (adv)	**årligt**	['ɒ:lit]
4 times a year	**fire gange om året**	['fiˀʌ 'gɑŋə ɒm 'ɒ:ɒð]
date (e.g., today's ~)	**dato** (f)	['dæ:to]
date (e.g., ~ of birth)	**dato** (f)	['dæ:to]
calendar	**kalender** (f)	[ka'lɛnˀʌ]
half a year	**et halvt år**	[et halˀt 'ɒˀ]
six months	**halvår** (i)	['halv‚ɒˀ]
season (summer, etc.)	**årstid** (f)	['ɒ:s‚tiðˀ]
century	**århundrede** (i)	[ɒ'hunʁʌðə]

TRAVEL. HOTEL

T&P Books Publishing

20. Trip. Travel

tourism, travel	**turisme** (f)	[tu'ʁismə]
tourist	**turist** (f)	[tu'ʁist]
trip, voyage	**rejse** (f)	['ʁɑjsə]
adventure	**eventyr** (i)	['ɛ:vənˌtyɐ̯ˀ]
trip, journey	**rejse** (f)	['ʁɑjsə]
vacation	**ferie** (f)	['feɐ̯ˀiə]
to be on vacation	**at holde ferie**	[ʌ 'hʌlə 'feɐ̯ˀiə]
rest	**ophold** (i), **hvile** (f)	['ʌpˌhʌlˀ], ['vi:lə]
train	**tog** (i)	['tɔˀw]
by train	**med tog**	[mɛ 'tɔˀw]
airplane	**fly** (i)	['flyˀ]
by airplane	**med fly**	[mɛ 'flyˀ]
by car	**med bil**	[mɛ 'biˀl]
by ship	**med skib**	[mɛ 'skiˀb]
luggage	**bagage** (f)	[ba'gæ:ɕə]
suitcase	**kuffert** (f)	['kɔfʌt]
luggage cart	**bagagevogn** (f)	[ba'gæ:ɕəˌvɒwˀn]
passport	**pas** (i)	['pas]
visa	**visum** (i)	['vi:sɔm]
ticket	**billet** (f)	[bi'lɛt]
air ticket	**flybillet** (f)	['fly bi'lɛt]
guidebook	**rejsehåndbog** (f)	['ʁɑjsəˌhʌnbɔˀw]
map (tourist ~)	**kort** (i)	['kɔ:t]
area (rural ~)	**område** (i)	['ʌmˌʁɔ:ðə]
place, site	**sted** (i)	['stɛð]
exotic (adj)	**eksotisk**	[ɛk'so'tisk]
amazing (adj)	**forunderlig**	[fʌ'ɔnˀʌli]
group	**gruppe** (f)	['gʁupə]
excursion, sightseeing tour	**udflugt** (f)	['uðˌflɔgt]
guide (person)	**guide** (f)	['gɑjd]

21. Hotel

hotel	**hotel** (i)	[ho'tɛlˀ]
motel	**motel** (i)	[mo'tɛlˀ]

three-star (~ hotel)	trestjernet	['tʁɛˌstjæɐ̯ˀnəð]
five-star	femstjernet	['fɛmˌstjæɐ̯ˀnəð]
to stay (in a hotel, etc.)	at bo	[ʌ 'boˀ]

room	værelse (i)	['væɐ̯ʌlsə]
single room	enkeltværelse (i)	['ɛŋˀkəltˌvæɐ̯ʌlsə]
double room	dobbeltværelse (i)	['dʌbəltˌvæɐ̯ʌlsə]
to book a room	at booke et værelse	[ʌ 'bukə et 'væɐ̯ʌlsə]

| half board | halvpension (f) | ['halˀ paŋ'ɕoˀn] |
| full board | helpension (f) | ['heˀl paŋ'ɕoˀn] |

with bath	med badekar	[mɛ 'bæːðəˌka]
with shower	med brusebad	[mɛ 'bʁuːsəˌbað]
satellite television	satellit-tv (i)	[satə'lit 'teˀˌveˀ]
air-conditioner	klimaanlæg (i)	['kliːmaˀanˌlɛˀg]
towel	håndklæde (i)	['hʌnˌklɛːðə]
key	nøgle (f)	['nʌjlə]

administrator	administrator (f)	[aðmini'stʁɑːtʌ]
chambermaid	stuepige (f)	['stuəˌpiːə]
porter, bellboy	drager (f)	['dʁɑːwʌ]
doorman	portier (f)	[pɒ'tje]

restaurant	restaurant (f)	[ʁɛsto'ʁɑŋ]
pub, bar	bar (f)	['baˀ]
breakfast	morgenmad (f)	['mɒːɒnˌmað]
dinner	aftensmad (f)	['ɑftənsˌmað]
buffet	buffet (f)	[by'fe]

| lobby | hall, lobby (f) | ['hɒːl], ['lʌbi] |
| elevator | elevator (f) | [ele'væːtʌ] |

| DO NOT DISTURB | VIL IKKE FORSTYRRES | ['vel 'ekə fʌ'styɐ̯ˀʌs] |
| NO SMOKING | RYGNING FORBUDT | ['ʁyːneŋ fʌ'byˀð] |

22. Sightseeing

monument	monument (i)	[monu'mɛnˀt]
fortress	fæstning (f)	['fɛstneŋ]
palace	palads (i)	[pa'las]
castle	slot (i), borg (f)	['slʌt], ['bɒˀw]
tower	tårn (i)	['tɒˀn]
mausoleum	mausoleum (i)	[mɑwso'lɛːɔm]

architecture	arkitektur (f)	[ɑkitɛk'tuɐ̯ˀ]
medieval (adj)	middelalderlig	['miðəlˌalˀʌli]
ancient (adj)	gammel	['gaməl]
national (adj)	national	[naɕo'næˀl]
famous (monument, etc.)	kendt, berømt	['kɛnˀt], [be'ʁœmˀt]

tourist	**turist** (f)	[tu'ʁist]
guide (person)	**guide** (f)	['gɑjd]
excursion, sightseeing tour	**udflugt** (f)	['uð̩ˌflɔgt]
to show (vt)	**at vise**	[ʌ 'vi:sə]
to tell (vt)	**at fortælle**	[ʌ fʌ'tɛlˀə]
to find (vt)	**at finde**	[ʌ 'fenə]
to get lost (lose one's way)	**at gå vild**	[ʌ gɔˀ 'vilˀ]
map (e.g., subway ~)	**kort** (i)	['kɒ:t]
map (e.g., city ~)	**kort** (i)	['kɒ:t]
souvenir, gift	**souvenir** (f)	[suvə'niːɐ̯]
gift shop	**souvenirforretning** (f)	[suvə'niːɐ̯ fʌ'ʁatnen]
to take pictures	**at fotografere**	[ʌ fotogʁɑ'feˀʌ]
to have one's picture taken	**at blive fotograferet**	[ʌ 'bli:ə fotogʁɑ:'feˀʌð]

T&P BOOKS

TRANSPORTATION

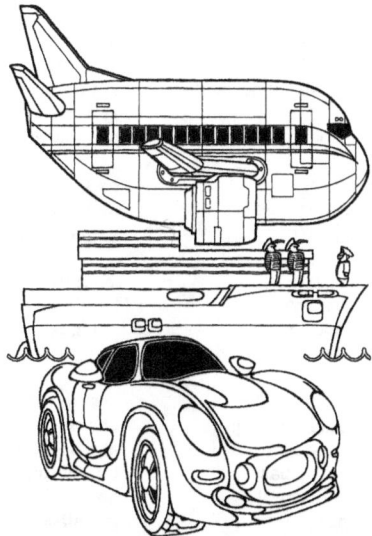

T&P Books Publishing

airport	**lufthavn** (f)	['lɔft̩haw'n]
airplane	**fly** (i)	['fly']
airline	**flyselskab** (i)	['fly'sɛl̩skæ'b]
air traffic controller	**flyveleder** (f)	['fly:və̩le:ðʌ]
departure	**afgang** (f)	['aw̩gaŋ']
arrival	**ankomst** (f)	['an̩kʌm'st]
to arrive (by plane)	**at ankomme**	[ʌ 'an̩kʌm'ə]
departure time	**afgangstid** (f)	['awgaŋs̩tið']
arrival time	**ankomsttid** (f)	['ankʌm'st̩tið]
to be delayed	**at blive forsinke**	[ʌ 'bli:ə fʌ'seŋ'kə]
flight delay	**afgangsforsinkelse** (f)	['aw̩gaŋs fʌ'seŋkəlsə]
information board	**informationstavle** (f)	[enfɒma'çons ̩tawlə]
information	**information** (f)	[enfɒma'çoʼn]
to announce (vt)	**at meddele**	[ʌ 'mɛð̩de'lə]
flight (e.g., next ~)	**flight** (f)	['flajt]
customs	**told** (f)	['tʌl']
customs officer	**toldbetjent** (f)	['tʌl be'tjɛn't]
customs declaration	**tolddeklaration** (f)	['tʌl deklaa̩çoʼn]
to fill out (vt)	**at udfylde**	[ʌ 'uð̩fyl'ə]
to fill out the declaration	**at udfylde en tolddeklaration**	[ʌ 'uð̩fyl'ə en 'tʌl'deklaa'çoʼn]
passport control	**paskontrol** (f)	['paskɔn̩tʁʌl']
luggage	**bagage** (f)	[ba'gæ:çə]
hand luggage	**håndbagage** (f)	['hʌn ba'gæ:çə]
luggage cart	**bagagevogn** (f)	[ba'gæ:çə̩vɒw'n]
landing	**landing** (f)	['laneŋ]
landing strip	**landingsbane** (f)	['laneŋs̩bæ:nə]
to land (vi)	**at lande**	[ʌ 'lanə]
airstairs	**trappe** (f)	['tʁapə]
check-in	**check-in** (f)	[tjɛk'en]
check-in counter	**check-in-skranke** (f)	[tjɛk'en̩skʁaŋkə]
to check-in (vi)	**at tjekke ind**	[ʌ 'tjɛkə 'en']
boarding pass	**boardingkort** (i)	['bɒ:deŋ̩kɒ:t]
departure gate	**gate** (f)	['gɛjt]
transit	**transit** (f)	[tʁan'sit]

to wait (vt)	**at vente**	[ʌ 'vɛntə]
departure lounge	**ventesal** (f)	['vɛntə‚sæˀl]
to see off	**at vinke farvel**	[ʌ 'veŋkə fɑ'vɛl]
to say goodbye	**at sige farvel**	[ʌ 'si: fɑ'vɛl]

24. Airplane

airplane	**fly** (i)	['flyˀ]
air ticket	**flybillet** (f)	['fly bi'lɛt]
airline	**flyselskab** (i)	['flyˀsɛl‚skæˀb]
airport	**lufthavn** (f)	['lɔft‚hɑwˀn]
supersonic (adj)	**overlyds-**	['ɒwʌ‚lyðs-]
captain	**kaptajn** (f)	[kɑp'tɑjˀn]
crew	**besætning** (f)	[be'sɛtneŋ]
pilot	**pilot** (f)	[pi'loˀt]
flight attendant (fem.)	**stewardesse** (f)	[stjuɑ'dɛsə]
navigator	**styrmand** (f)	['styɐ‚manˀ]
wings	**vinger** (f pl)	['veŋʌ]
tail	**hale** (f)	['hæ:lə]
cockpit	**cockpit** (i)	['kʌk‚pit]
engine	**motor** (f)	['mo:tʌ]
undercarriage (landing gear)	**landingshjul** (i)	['laneŋs‚juˀl]
turbine	**turbine** (f)	[tuɐ'bi:nə]
propeller	**propel** (f)	[pʁo'pɛlˀ]
black box	**sort boks** (f)	['soɐt 'bʌks]
yoke (control column)	**rat** (i)	['ʁat]
fuel	**brændstof** (i)	['bʁan‚stʌf]
safety card	**sikkerhedsinstruks** (f)	['sekʌ‚heðˀ en'stʁuks]
oxygen mask	**iltmaske** (f)	['ilt‚maskə]
uniform	**uniform** (f)	[uni'fɒˀm]
life vest	**redningsvest** (f)	['ʁɛðneŋs‚vɛst]
parachute	**faldskærm** (f)	['fal‚skæɐˀm]
takeoff	**start** (f)	['stɑˀt]
to take off (vi)	**at lette**	[ʌ 'lɛtə]
runway	**startbane** (f)	['stɑ:t‚bæ:nə]
visibility	**sigtbarhed** (f)	['segtbɑ‚heðˀ]
flight (act of flying)	**flyvning** (f)	['flywneŋ]
altitude	**højde** (f)	['hʌjˀdə]
air pocket	**lufthul** (i)	['lɔft‚hɔl]
seat	**plads** (f)	['plas]
headphones	**hovedtelefoner** (f pl)	['ho:əð telə'foˀnʌ]
folding tray (tray table)	**klapbord** (i)	['klɑp‚boˀɐ̯]

| airplane window | **vindue** (i) | ['vendu] |
| aisle | **midtergang** (f) | ['metʌˌgaŋˀ] |

25. Train

train	**tog** (i)	['tɔˀw]
commuter train	**lokaltog** (i)	[lo'kæˀlˌtɔˀw]
express train	**lyntog, eksprestog** (i)	['ly:nˌtɔˀw], [ɛks'pʁasˌtɔˀw]
diesel locomotive	**diesellokomotiv** (i)	['diˀsəl lokomo'tiwˀ]
steam locomotive	**damplokomotiv** (i)	['damp lokomo'tiwˀ]

| passenger car | **vogn** (f) | ['vɒwˀn] |
| dining car | **spisevogn** (f) | ['spi:səˌvɒwˀn] |

rails	**skinner** (f pl)	['skenʌ]
railroad	**jernbane** (f)	['jæɡˀnˌbæ:nə]
railway tie	**svelle** (f)	['svɛlə]

platform (railway ~)	**perron** (f)	[pa'ʁʌn]
track (~ 1, 2, etc.)	**spor** (i)	['spoˀɡ]
semaphore	**semafor** (f)	[sema'foˀɡ]
station	**station** (f)	[sta'ɕoˀn]

engineer (train driver)	**togfører** (f)	['tɔwˌføːʌ]
porter (of luggage)	**drager** (f)	['dʁɑ:wʌ]
car attendant	**togbetjent** (f)	['tɔw be'tjɛnˀt]
passenger	**passager** (f)	[pasa'ɕeˀɡ]
conductor (ticket inspector)	**kontrollør** (f)	[kʌntʁo'løˀɡ]

| corridor (in train) | **korridor** (f) | [kɒi'doˀɡ] |
| emergency brake | **nødbremse** (f) | ['nøðˌbʁamsə] |

compartment	**kupe, kupé** (f)	[ku'peˀ]
berth	**køje** (f)	['kʌjə]
upper berth	**overkøje** (f)	['ɒwʌˌkʌjə]
lower berth	**underkøje** (f)	['ɔnʌˌkʌjə]
bed linen, bedding	**sengetøj** (i)	['sɛŋəˌtʌj]

ticket	**billet** (f)	[bi'lɛt]
schedule	**køreplan** (f)	['køːʌˌplæˀn]
information display	**informationstavle** (f)	[enfɒma'ɕons ˌtɑwlə]

to leave, to depart	**at afgå**	[ʌ 'ɑwˌgɔˀ]
departure (of train)	**afgang** (f)	['ɑwˌgaŋˀ]
to arrive (ab. train)	**at ankomme**	[ʌ 'anˌkʌmˀə]
arrival	**ankomst** (f)	['anˌkʌmˀst]

| to arrive by train | **at ankomme med toget** | [ʌ 'anˌkʌmˀə mɛ 'tɔˀwəð] |
| to get on the train | **at stå på toget** | [ʌ 'sti:ə pɒ 'tɔˀwəð] |

to get off the train	at stå af toget	[ʌ 'stiːə a 'tɔʔwəð]
train wreck	togulykke (f)	['tɔw uˌløkə]
to derail (vi)	at afspore	[ʌ 'awˌspoʔʌ]

steam locomotive	damplokomotiv (i)	['damp lokomo'tiwʔ]
stoker, fireman	fyrbøder (f)	['fyɐ̯ˌbøðʌ]
firebox	fyrrum (i)	['fyɐ̯ˌʁɔmʔ]
coal	kul (i)	['kɔl]

26. Ship

| ship | skib (i) | ['skiʔb] |
| vessel | fartøj (i) | ['faːˌtʌj] |

steamship	dampskib (i)	['dampˌskiʔb]
riverboat	flodbåd (f)	['floðˌbɔʔð]
cruise ship	cruiseskib (i)	['kʁuːsˌskiʔb]
cruiser	krydser (f)	['kʁysʌ]

yacht	yacht (f)	['jagt]
tugboat	bugserbåd (f)	[bug'seɐ̯ˌbɔʔð]
barge	pram (f)	['pʁamʔ]
ferry	færge (f)	['fæɐ̯wə]

| sailing ship | sejlbåd (f) | ['sajlˌbɔʔð] |
| brigantine | brigantine (f) | [bʁigan'tiːnə] |

| ice breaker | isbryder (f) | ['isˌbʁyðʌ] |
| submarine | u-båd (f) | ['uʔˌbɔð] |

boat (flat-bottomed ~)	båd (f)	['bɔʔð]
dinghy	jolle (f)	['jʌlə]
lifeboat	redningsbåd (f)	['ʁɛðneŋsˌbɔʔð]
motorboat	motorbåd (f)	['moːtʌˌbɔʔð]

captain	kaptajn (f)	[kap'tajʔn]
seaman	matros (f)	[ma'tʁoʔs]
sailor	sømand (f)	['søˌmanʔ]
crew	besætning (f)	[be'sɛtneŋ]

boatswain	bådsmand (f)	['bɔðsˌmanʔ]
ship's boy	skibsdreng, jungmand (f)	['skibsˌdʁaŋʔ], ['jɔŋˌmanʔ]
cook	kok (f)	['kʌk]
ship's doctor	skibslæge (f)	['skibsˌlɛːjə]

deck	dæk (i)	['dɛk]
mast	mast (f)	['mast]
sail	sejl (i)	['sajʔl]
hold	lastrum (i)	['lastˌʁɔmʔ]
bow (prow)	bov (f)	['bɔwʔ]

stern	**agterende** (f)	['agtʌˌʁanə]
oar	**åre** (f)	['ɒːɒ]
screw propeller	**propel** (f)	[pʁoˈpɛlˀ]

cabin	**kahyt** (f)	[kaˈhyt]
wardroom	**officersmesse** (f)	[ʌfiˈseɡs ˌmɛsə]
engine room	**maskinrum** (i)	[maˈskiːnˌʁɔmˀ]
bridge	**kommandobro** (f)	[koˈmandoˌbʁoˀ]
radio room	**radiorum** (i)	['ʁadjoˌʁɔmˀ]
wave (radio)	**bølge** (f)	['bøljə]
logbook	**logbog** (f)	['lʌgˌbɔˀw]

spyglass	**kikkert** (f)	['kikʌt]
bell	**klokke** (f)	['klʌkə]
flag	**flag** (i)	['flæˀj]

| hawser (mooring ~) | **trosse** (f) | ['tʁʌsə] |
| knot (bowline, etc.) | **knob** (i) | ['knoˀb] |

| deckrails | **håndlister** (pl) | ['hʌnˌlestʌ] |
| gangway | **landgang** (f) | ['lanˌgaŋˀ] |

anchor	**anker** (i)	['aŋkʌ]
to weigh anchor	**at lette anker**	[ʌ 'lɛtə 'aŋkʌ]
to drop anchor	**at kaste anker**	[ʌ 'kastə 'aŋkʌ]
anchor chain	**ankerkæde** (f)	['aŋkʌˌkɛːðə]

port (harbor)	**havn** (f)	['hawˀn]
quay, wharf	**kaj** (f)	['kajˀ]
to berth (moor)	**at fortøje**	[ʌ fʌˈtʌjˀə]
to cast off	**at kaste los**	[ʌ 'kastə 'lʌs]

trip, voyage	**rejse** (f)	['ʁajsə]
cruise (sea trip)	**krydstogt** (i)	['kʁysˌtʌgt]
course (route)	**kurs** (f)	['kuɡˀs]
route (itinerary)	**rute** (f)	['ʁuːtə]

fairway (safe water channel)	**sejlrende** (f)	['sajlˌʁanə]
shallows	**grund** (f)	['gʁɔnˀ]
to run aground	**at gå på grund**	[ʌ 'gɔˀ pɔ 'gʁɔnˀ]

storm	**storm** (f)	['stɒˀm]
signal	**signal** (i)	[siˈnæˀl]
to sink (vi)	**at synke**	[ʌ 'søŋkə]
Man overboard!	**Mand over bord!**	['manˀ 'ɒwʌ ˌboˀɡ]
SOS (distress signal)	**SOS**	[ɛsoˈɛs]
ring buoy	**redningskrans** (f)	['ʁɛðneŋsˌkʁanˀs]

CITY

T&P Books Publishing

bus	**bus** (f)	['bus]
streetcar	**sporvogn** (f)	['spoɡ̊ˌvɒwˀn]
trolley bus	**trolleybus** (f)	['tʁʌliˌbus]
route (of bus, etc.)	**rute** (f)	['ʁuːtə]
number (e.g., bus ~)	**nummer** (i)	['nɔmˀʌ]

to go by ...	**at køre på ...**	[ʌ 'køːʌ 'pɔˀ ...]
to get on (~ the bus)	**at stå på ...**	[ʌ stɔˀ 'pɔˀ ...]
to get off ...	**at stå af ...**	[ʌ stɔˀ 'æˀ ...]

stop (e.g., bus ~)	**stop, stoppested** (i)	['stʌp], ['stʌpəstɛð]
next stop	**næste station** (f)	['nɛstə sta'ɕoˀn]
terminus	**endestation** (f)	['ɛnəsta'ɕoˀn]
schedule	**køreplan** (f)	['køːʌˌplæˀn]
to wait (vt)	**at vente**	[ʌ 'vɛntə]

ticket	**billet** (f)	[bi'lɛt]
fare	**billetpris** (f)	[bi'lɛtˌpʁiˀs]

cashier (ticket seller)	**kasserer** (f)	[ka'seˀʌ]
ticket inspection	**billetkontrol** (f)	[bi'lɛt kɔn'tʁʌlˀ]
ticket inspector	**kontrollør** (f)	[kʌntʁo'løˀɡ̊]

to be late (for ...)	**at komme for sent**	[ʌ 'kʌmə fʌ 'seˀnt]
to miss (~ the train, etc.)	**at komme for sent til ...**	[ʌ 'kʌmə fʌ 'seˀnt tel ...]
to be in a hurry	**at skynde sig**	[ʌ 'skønə saj]

taxi, cab	**taxi** (f)	['tɑksi]
taxi driver	**taxichauffør** (f)	['tɑksi ɕo'føˀɡ̊]
by taxi	**i taxi**	[i 'tɑksi]
taxi stand	**taxiholdeplads** (f)	['tɑksi 'hʌləˌplas]
to call a taxi	**at bestille en taxi**	[ʌ be'stelˀə en 'tɑksi]
to take a taxi	**at tage en taxi**	[ʌ 'tæˀ en 'tɑksi]

traffic	**trafik** (f)	[tʁɑ'fik]
traffic jam	**trafikprop** (f)	[tʁɑ'fikˌpʁʌp]
rush hour	**myldretid** (f)	['mylʁʌˌtiðˀ]
to park (vi)	**at parkere**	[ʌ pɑ'keˀʌ]
to park (vt)	**at parkere**	[ʌ pɑ'keˀʌ]
parking lot	**parkeringsplads** (f)	[pɑ'keˀɡ̊eŋsˌplas]

subway	**metro** (f)	['meːtʁo]
station	**station** (f)	[sta'ɕoˀn]
to take the subway	**at køre med metroen**	[ʌ 'køːʌ mɛ 'metʁoːən]

| train | tog (i) | ['tɔˀw] |
| train station | banegård (f) | ['bæːnəˌgɒˀ] |

28. City. Life in the city

city, town	by (f)	['byˀ]
capital city	hovedstad (f)	['hoːəðˌstað]
village	landsby (f)	['lansˌbyˀ]

city map	bykort (i)	['byˌkɒːt]
downtown	centrum (i) af byen	['sɛntʁɔm a 'byən]
suburb	forstad (f)	['fɒːˌstað]
suburban (adj)	forstads-	['fɒːˌstaðs-]

outskirts	udkant (f)	['uðˌkanˀt]
environs (suburbs)	omegne (f pl)	['ʌmˌɑjˀnə]
city block	kvarter (i)	[kvɑ'teˀɐ̯]
residential block (area)	boligkvarter (i)	['boːlikvɑ'teˀɐ̯]

traffic	trafik (f)	[tʁɑ'fik]
traffic lights	trafiklys (i)	[tʁɑ'fikˌlyˀs]
public transportation	offentlig transport (f)	['ʌfəntli tʁɑns'pɒːt]
intersection	kryds (i, f)	['kʁys]

crosswalk	fodgængerovergang (f)	['foðgɛŋʌ 'ɒwʌˌgɑŋˀ]
pedestrian underpass	gangtunnel (f)	['gɑŋtuˌnɛlˀ]
to cross (~ the street)	at gå over	[ʌ gɔˀ 'ɒwˀʌ]
pedestrian	fodgænger (f)	['foðˌgɛŋʌ]
sidewalk	fortov (i)	['fɒːˌtɒw]

bridge	bro (f)	['bʁoˀ]
embankment (river walk)	kaj (f)	['kɑjˀ]
fountain	springvand (i)	['spʁɛŋˌvanˀ]

allée (garden walkway)	alle (f)	[a'leˀ]
park	park (f)	['pɑːk]
boulevard	boulevard (f)	[buləˈvɑˀd]
square	torv (i)	['tɒˀw]
avenue (wide street)	avenue (f)	[avə'ny]
street	gade (f)	['gæːðə]
side street	sidegade (f)	['siːðəˌgæːðə]
dead end	blindgyde (f)	['blenˀˌgyːðə]

house	hus (i)	['huˀs]
building	bygning (f)	['bygnɛŋ]
skyscraper	skyskraber (f)	['skyˌskʁɑːbʌ]

facade	facade (f)	[fa'sæːðə]
roof	tag (i)	['tæˀj]
window	vindue (i)	['vendu]

115

arch	**bue** (f)	['bu:ə]
column	**søjle** (f)	['sʌjlə]
corner	**hjørne** (i)	['jœɐ̯ʔnə]

store window	**udstillingsvindue** (i)	['uð‚stelʔeŋs 'vendu]
signboard (store sign, etc.)	**skilt** (i)	['skelʔt]
poster	**plakat** (f)	[pla'kæʔt]
advertising poster	**reklameplakat** (f)	[ʁɛ'klæ:mə‚pla'kæʔt]
billboard	**reklameskilt** (i)	[ʁɛ'klæ:mə‚skelʔt]

garbage, trash	**affald** (i)	['ɑw‚falʔ]
trashcan (public ~)	**skraldespand** (f)	['skʁɑlə‚spanʔ]
to litter (vi)	**at smide affald**	[ʌ 'smi:ðə 'ɑw‚falʔ]
garbage dump	**losseplads** (f)	['lʌsə‚plas]

phone booth	**telefonboks** (f)	[telə'fo:n‚bʌks]
lamppost	**lygtepæl** (f)	['løgtə‚pɛʔl]
bench (park ~)	**bænk** (f)	['bɛnʔk]

police officer	**politibetjent** (f)	[poli'ti be'tjɛnʔt]
police	**politi** (i)	[poli'tiʔ]
beggar	**tigger** (f)	['tegʌ]
homeless (n)	**hjemløs** (f)	['jɛm‚løʔs]

29. Urban institutions

store	**forretning** (f), **butik** (f)	[fʌ'ʁatneŋ], [bu'tik]
drugstore, pharmacy	**apotek** (i)	[apo'teʔk]
eyeglass store	**optik** (f)	[ʌp'tik]
shopping mall	**indkøbscenter** (i)	['en‚køʔbs ‚sɛnʔtʌ]
supermarket	**supermarked** (i)	['su‚pʌ‚ma:kəð]

bakery	**bageri** (i)	[bæjʌ'ʁiʔ]
baker	**bager** (f)	['bæ:jʌ]
pastry shop	**konditori** (i)	[kʌnditʌ'ʁiʔ]
grocery store	**købmandsbutik** (f)	['kømans bu'tik]
butcher shop	**slagterbutik** (f)	['slagtʌ bu'tik]

produce store	**grønthandel** (f)	['gʁœnt‚hanʔəl]
market	**marked** (i)	['ma:kəð]

coffee house	**cafe, kaffebar** (f)	[ka'feʔ], ['kafə‚baʔ]
restaurant	**restaurant** (f)	[ʁɛsto'ʁaŋ]
pub, bar	**ølstue** (f)	['øl‚stu:ə]
pizzeria	**pizzeria** (i)	[pidsə'ʁi:a]

hair salon	**frisørsalon** (f)	[fʁi'søɐ̯ sa‚lʌn]
post office	**postkontor** (i)	['pʌst kɔn'toʔɐ̯]
dry cleaners	**renseri** (i)	[ʁansʌ'ʁiʔ]
photo studio	**fotoatelier** (i)	['foto atəl'je]

shoe store	skotøjsforretning (f)	['sko‚tʌjs fʌ'ʁatneŋ]
bookstore	boghandel (f)	['bɔw‚han'əl]
sporting goods store	sportsforretning (f)	['spɔːts fʌ'ʁatneŋ]

clothes repair shop	reparation (f) af tøj	[ʁɛpʁa'ɕoˀn a 'tʌj]
formal wear rental	udlejning (f) af tøj	['uð‚laj'neŋ a 'tʌj]
video rental store	filmleje (f)	['film‚lajə]

circus	cirkus (i)	['siɐ̯kus]
zoo	zoologisk have (f)	[soo'loˀisk 'hæːvə]
movie theater	biograf (f)	[bio'gʁɑˀf]
museum	museum (i)	[mu'sɛːɔm]
library	bibliotek (i)	[biblio'teˀk]

theater	teater (i)	[te'æˀtʌ]
opera (opera house)	opera (f)	['oˀpəʁa]
nightclub	natklub (f)	['nat‚klub]
casino	kasino (i)	[ka'siːno]

mosque	moske (f)	[mo'skeˀ]
synagogue	synagoge (f)	[syna'goːə]
cathedral	katedral (f)	[katə'dʁaˀl]
temple	tempel (i)	['tɛmˀpəl]
church	kirke (f)	['kiɐ̯kə]

college	institut (i)	[ensdi'tut]
university	universitet (i)	[univæɐ̯si'teˀt]
school	skole (f)	['skoːlə]

prefecture	præfektur (i)	[pʁɛfɛk'tuɐ̯ˀ]
city hall	rådhus (i)	['ʁɔð‚huˀs]
hotel	hotel (i)	[ho'tɛlˀ]
bank	bank (f)	['baŋˀk]

embassy	ambassade (f)	[ɑmba'sæːðə]
travel agency	rejsebureau (i)	['ʁajsə by‚ʁo]
information office	informationskontor (i)	[enfɔma'ɕons kɔn'toˀg̊]
currency exchange	vekselkontor (i)	['vɛksəl kɔn'toˀg̊]

| subway | metro (f) | ['meːtʁo] |
| hospital | sygehus (i) | ['syːə‚huˀs] |

| gas station | tankstation (f) | ['taŋk sta'ɕˀon] |
| parking lot | parkeringsplads (f) | [pɑ'keˀg̊eŋs‚plas] |

30. Signs

signboard (store sign, etc.)	skilt (i)	['skelˀt]
notice (door sign, etc.)	indskrift (f)	['en‚skʁɛft]
poster	poster (f)	['pɔwstʌ]

| direction sign | **vejviser** (f) | ['vɑjˌviːsʌ] |
| arrow (sign) | **pil** (f) | ['piʔl] |

caution	**advarsel** (f)	['aðˌvɑːsəl]
warning sign	**advarselsskilt** (i)	['aðˌvɑːsəls 'skelʔt]
to warn (vt)	**at advare**	[ʌ 'aðˌvɑʔɑ]

rest day (weekly ~)	**fridag** (f)	['fʁidæʔ]
timetable (schedule)	**køreplan** (f)	['køːʌˌplæʔn]
opening hours	**åbningstid** (f)	['ɔːbneŋsˌtiðʔ]

WELCOME!	**VELKOMMEN!**	['vɛlˌkʌmʔən]
ENTRANCE	**INDGANG**	['enˌgɑŋʔ]
EXIT	**UDGANG**	['uðˌgɑŋʔ]

PUSH	**TRYK**	['tʁœk]
PULL	**TRÆK**	['tʁak]
OPEN	**ÅBENT**	['ɔːbənt]
CLOSED	**LUKKET**	['lɔkəð]

| WOMEN | **KVINDE** | ['kvenə] |
| MEN | **MAND** | ['manʔ] |

| DISCOUNTS | **RABAT** | [ʁɑ'bat] |
| SALE | **UDSALG** | ['uðˌsalʔ] |

| NEW! | **NYHED!** | ['nyheðʔ] |
| FREE | **GRATIS** | ['gʁɑːtis] |

ATTENTION!	**PAS PÅ!**	['pas 'pɔ]
NO VACANCIES	**ingen ledige værelser**	['eŋən 'leːðiə 'væʁɐʌlsʌ]
RESERVED	**RESERVERET**	[ʁɛsæɐ'veʔʌð]

| ADMINISTRATION | **ADMINISTRATION** | [aðministʁɑ'ɕoʔn] |
| STAFF ONLY | **KUN FOR PERSONALE** | ['kɔn fʌ pæɐso'næːlə] |

BEWARE OF THE DOG!	**HER VOGTER JEG**	['hɛʔɐ 'vʌgtʌ 'jɑj]
NO SMOKING	**RYGNING FORBUDT**	['ʁyːneŋ fʌ'byʔð]
DO NOT TOUCH!	**MÅ IKKE BERØRES!**	[mɔ 'ekə be'ʁœʔʌs]

DANGEROUS	**FARLIG**	['fɑːli]
DANGER	**FARE**	['fɑːɑ]
HIGH VOLTAGE	**HØJSPÆNDING**	['hʌjˌspɛneŋ]

| NO SWIMMING! | **BADNING FORBUDT** | ['bæːðneŋ fʌ'byʔð] |
| OUT OF ORDER | **UDE AF DRIFT** | ['uːðə a 'dʁɛft] |

FLAMMABLE	**BRANDFARLIG**	['bʁɑnˌfɑːli]
FORBIDDEN	**FORBUDT**	[fʌ'byʔt]
NO TRESPASSING!	**ADGANG FORBUDT**	['aðˌgɑŋʔ fʌ'byʔð]
WET PAINT	**NYMALET**	['nyˌmæʔləð]

31. Shopping

to buy (purchase)	at købe	[ʌ 'kø:bə]
purchase	indkøb (i)	['enˌkøˀb]
to go shopping	at gå på indkøb	[ʌ gɔˀ pɔ 'enˌkøˀb]
shopping	shopping (f)	['ɕʌpeŋ]

| to be open (ab. store) | at være åben | [ʌ 'vɛ:ʌ 'ɔ:bən] |
| to be closed | at være lukket | [ʌ 'vɛ:ʌ 'lɔkəð] |

footwear, shoes	sko (f)	['skoˀ]
clothes, clothing	klæder (i pl)	['klɛ:ðʌ]
cosmetics	kosmetik (f)	[kʌsmə'tik]
food products	madvarer (f pl)	['maðvɑ:ʌ]
gift, present	gave (f)	['gæ:və]

| salesman | sælger (f) | ['sɛljʌ] |
| saleswoman | sælger (f) | ['sɛljʌ] |

check out, cash desk	kasse (f)	['kasə]
mirror	spejl (i)	['spɑjˀl]
counter (store ~)	disk (f)	['disk]
fitting room	prøverum (i)	['pʁœ:wəˌʁɔmˀ]

to try on	at prøve	[ʌ 'pʁœ:wə]
to fit (ab. dress, etc.)	at passe	[ʌ 'pasə]
to like (I like ...)	at kunne lide	[ʌ 'kunə 'li:ðə]

price	pris (f)	['pʁiˀs]
price tag	prismærke (i)	['pʁisˌmæʁkə]
to cost (vt)	at koste	[ʌ 'kʌstə]
How much?	Hvor meget?	[vɒˀ 'mɑɑð]
discount	rabat (f)	[ʁɑ'bat]

inexpensive (adj)	billig	['bili]
cheap (adj)	billig	['bili]
expensive (adj)	dyr	['dyɐ̯ˀ]
It's expensive	Det er dyrt	[de 'æɐ̯ 'dyɐ̯ˀt]

rental (n)	leje (f)	['lɑjə]
to rent (~ a tuxedo)	at leje	[ʌ 'lɑjə]
credit (trade credit)	kredit (f)	[kʁɛ'dit]
on credit (adv)	på kredit	[pɔ kʁɛ'dit]

T&p BOOKS

CLOTHING & ACCESSORIES

T&P Books Publishing

clothes	**tøj** (i), **klæder** (i pl)	['tʌj], ['klɛ:ðʌ]
outerwear	**overtøj** (i)	['ɒwʌˌtʌj]
winter clothing	**vintertøj** (i)	['ventʌˌtʌj]

coat (overcoat)	**frakke** (f)	['fʁakə]
fur coat	**pels** (f), **pelskåbe** (f)	['pɛlˀs], ['pɛlsˌkɔ:bə]
fur jacket	**pelsjakke** (f)	['pɛlsˌjakə]
down coat	**dynejakke** (f)	['dy:nəˌjakə]

jacket (e.g., leather ~)	**jakke** (f)	['jakə]
raincoat (trenchcoat, etc.)	**regnfrakke** (f)	['ʁajnˌfʁakə]
waterproof (adj)	**vandtæt**	['vanˌtɛt]

shirt (button shirt)	**skjorte** (f)	['skjoʁtə]
pants	**bukser** (pl)	['bɒksʌ]
jeans	**jeans** (pl)	['dji:ns]
suit jacket	**jakke** (f)	['jakə]
suit	**jakkesæt** (i)	['jakəˌsɛt]

dress (frock)	**kjole** (f)	['kjo:lə]
skirt	**nederdel** (f)	['neðʌˌdeˀl]
blouse	**bluse** (f)	['blu:sə]
knitted jacket (cardigan, etc.)	**strikket trøje** (f)	['stʁɛkəð 'tʁʌjə]
jacket (of woman's suit)	**blazer** (f)	['blɛjsʌ]

T-shirt	**t-shirt** (f)	['ti:ˌɕœ:t]
shorts (short trousers)	**shorts** (pl)	['ɕɒ:ts]
tracksuit	**træningsdragt** (f)	['tʁɛ:neŋsˌdʁagt]
bathrobe	**badekåbe** (f)	['bæ:ðəˌkɔ:bə]
pajamas	**pyjamas** (f)	[py'jæ:mas]

| sweater | **sweater** (f) | ['swɛtʌ] |
| pullover | **pullover** (f) | [pul'ɔwʌ] |

vest	**vest** (f)	['vɛst]
tailcoat	**kjolesæt** (i)	['kjo:ləˌsɛt]
tuxedo	**smoking** (f)	['smo:keŋ]
uniform	**uniform** (f)	[uni'fɒˀm]
workwear	**arbejdstøj** (i)	['a:bajdsˌtʌj]

| overalls | kedeldragt, overall (f) | ['keðəlˌdʁɑgt], ['ɒwɒˌɒːl] |
| coat (e.g., doctor's smock) | kittel (f) | ['kitəl] |

34. Clothing. Underwear

underwear	undertøj (i)	['ɔnʌˌtʌj]
boxers, briefs	boxershorts (pl)	['bʌgsʌˌɕɒːʦ]
panties	trusser (pl)	['tʁusʌ]
undershirt (A-shirt)	undertrøje (f)	['ɔnʌˌtʁʌjə]
socks	sokker (f pl)	['sʌkʌ]

nightgown	natkjole (f)	['natˌkjoːlə]
bra	bh (f), brystholder (f)	[beˈhɔʔ], ['bʁœstˌhʌlʔʌ]
knee highs (knee-high socks)	knæstrømper (f pl)	['knɛˌstʁœmpʌ]
pantyhose	strømpebukser (pl)	['stʁœmbəˌbɔksʌ]
stockings (thigh highs)	strømper (f pl)	['stʁœmpʌ]
bathing suit	badedragt (f)	['bæːðəˌdʁɑgt]

35. Headwear

hat	hue (f)	['huːə]
fedora	hat (f)	['hat]
baseball cap	baseballkasket (f)	['bɛjsˌbɒːl kaˈskɛt]
flatcap	kasket (f)	[kaˈskɛt]

beret	baskerhue (f)	['bɑːskʌˌhuːə]
hood	hætte (f)	['hɛtə]
panama hat	panamahat (f)	['panˈamaˌhat]
knit cap (knitted hat)	strikhue (f)	['stʁɛkˌhuə]

| headscarf | tørklæde (i) | ['tœʁˌklɛːðə] |
| women's hat | hat (f) | ['hat] |

hard hat	hjelm (f)	['jɛlʔm]
garrison cap	skråhue (f)	['skʁʌˌhuːə]
helmet	hjelm (f)	['jɛlʔm]

| derby | bowlerhat (f) | ['bɒwlʌˌhat] |
| top hat | høj hat (f) | ['hʌj 'hat] |

36. Footwear

footwear	sko (f)	['skoʔ]
shoes (men's shoes)	støvler (f pl)	['stœwlʌ]
shoes (women's shoes)	damesko (f pl)	['dæːməˌskoː]

| boots (e.g., cowboy ~) | **støvler** (f pl) | ['stœwlʌ] |
| slippers | **hjemmesko** (f pl) | ['jɛmə‚skoˀ] |

tennis shoes (e.g., Nike ~)	**tennissko, kondisko** (f pl)	['tɛnis‚skoˀ], ['kʌndi‚skoˀ]
sneakers (e.g., Converse ~)	**kanvas sko** (f pl)	['kanvas ‚skoˀ]
sandals	**sandaler** (f pl)	[san'dæˀlʌ]

cobbler (shoe repairer)	**skomager** (f)	['sko‚mæˀjʌ]
heel	**hæl** (f)	['hɛˀl]
pair (of shoes)	**par** (i)	['pɑ]

| shoestring | **snøre** (f) | ['snœːʌ] |
| to lace (vt) | **at snøre** | [ʌ 'snœːʌ] |

| shoehorn | **skohorn** (i) | ['sko‚hoɐ̯ˀn] |
| shoe polish | **skocreme** (f) | ['sko‚kʁɛˀm] |

37. Personal accessories

gloves	**handsker** (f pl)	['hanskʌ]
mittens	**vanter** (f pl)	['vanˀtʌ]
scarf (muffler)	**halstørklæde** (i)	['hals ˈtœɐ̯‚klɛːðə]

glasses (eyeglasses)	**briller** (pl)	['bʁɛlʌ]
frame (eyeglass ~)	**brillestel** (i)	['bʁɛlə‚stɛlˀ]
umbrella	**paraply** (f)	[pɑɑ'plyˀ]
walking stick	**stok** (f)	['stʌk]

| hairbrush | **hårbørste** (f) | ['hɒ‚bœɐ̯stə] |
| fan | **vifte** (f) | ['veftə] |

| tie (necktie) | **slips** (i) | ['sleps] |
| bow tie | **butterfly** (f) | ['bʌtʌ‚flɑj] |

| suspenders | **seler** (f pl) | ['seːlʌ] |
| handkerchief | **lommetørklæde** (i) | ['lʌmə‚tœɐ̯klɛːðə] |

| comb | **kam** (f) | ['kɑmˀ] |
| barrette | **hårspænde** (i) | ['hɒː‚spɛnə] |

| hairpin | **hårnål** (f) | ['hɒː‚nɔˀl] |
| buckle | **spænde** (i) | ['spɛnə] |

| belt | **bælte** (i) | ['bɛltə] |
| shoulder strap | **rem** (f) | ['ʁamˀ] |

bag (handbag)	**taske** (f)	['taskə]
purse	**dametaske** (f)	['dæːme‚taskə]
backpack	**rygsæk** (f)	['ʁœg‚sɛk]

38. Clothing. Miscellaneous

fashion	mode (f)	['mo:ðə]
in vogue (adj)	moderigtig	['mo:ðəˌʁɛgti]
fashion designer	modedesigner (f)	['mo:ðə de'sajnʌ]
collar	krave (f)	['kʁɑ:və]
pocket	lomme (f)	['lʌmə]
pocket (as adj)	lomme-	['lʌmə-]
sleeve	ærme (i)	['æəmə]
hanging loop	strop (f)	['stʁʌp]
fly (on trousers)	gylp (f)	['gyl'p]
zipper (fastener)	lynlås (f)	['lynˌlɔ's]
fastener	hægte, lukning (f)	['hɛgtə], ['lɔknen]
button	knap (f)	['knap]
buttonhole	knaphul (i)	['knapˌhɔl]
to come off (ab. button)	at falde af	[ʌ 'falə 'æ']
to sew (vi, vt)	at sy	[ʌ sy']
to embroider (vi, vt)	at brodere	[ʌ bʁo'de'ʌ]
embroidery	broderi (i)	[bʁodʌ'ʁi']
sewing needle	synål (f)	['syˌnɔ'l]
thread	tråd (f)	['tʁɔ'ð]
seam	søm (f)	['sœm']
to get dirty (vi)	at smudse sig til	[ʌ 'smusə sɑ 'tel]
stain (mark, spot)	plet (f)	['plɛt]
to crease, crumple (vi)	at blive krøllet	[ʌ 'bli:ə 'kʁœləð]
to tear, to rip (vt)	at rive	[ʌ 'ʁi:və]
clothes moth	møl (i)	['møl]

39. Personal care. Cosmetics

toothpaste	tandpasta (f)	['tanˌpasta]
toothbrush	tandbørste (f)	['tanˌbœɐstə]
to brush one's teeth	at børste tænder	[ʌ 'bœɐstə 'tɛnʌ]
razor	skraber (f)	['skʁɑ:bʌ]
shaving cream	barbercreme (f)	[ba'be'ɐ̯ˌkʁɛ'm]
to shave (vi)	at barbere sig	[ʌ ba'be'ʌ saj]
soap	sæbe (f)	['sɛ:bə]
shampoo	shampoo (f)	['çæ:mˌpu:]
scissors	saks (f)	['saks]
nail file	neglefil (f)	['najləˌfi'l]
nail clippers	neglesaks (f)	['najləˌsaks]
tweezers	pincet (f)	[pen'sɛt]

cosmetics	kosmetik (f)	[kʌsmə'tik]
face mask	ansigtsmaske (f)	['ansegts 'maskə]
manicure	manicure (f)	[mani'ky:ʌ]
to have a manicure	at få manicure	[ʌ 'fɔʔ mani'ky:ʌ]
pedicure	pedicure (f)	[pedi'ky:ʌ]

make-up bag	kosmetiktaske (f)	[kʌsmə'tik,taskə]
face powder	pudder (i)	['puðʔʌ]
powder compact	pudderdåse (f)	['puðʌ,dɔ:sə]
blusher	rouge (f)	['ʁu:ɕ]

perfume (bottled)	parfume (f)	[pɑ'fy:mə]
toilet water (lotion)	eau de toilette (f)	[,odətoa'lɛt]
lotion	lotion (f)	['lɔwɕən]
cologne	eau de cologne (f)	[odəko'lʌnjə]

eyeshadow	øjenskygge (f)	['ʌjən,skygə]
eyeliner	eyeliner (f)	['ɑ:j,lɑjnʌ]
mascara	mascara (f)	[ma'skɑ:ɑ]

lipstick	læbestift (f)	['lɛ:bə,steft]
nail polish, enamel	neglelak (f)	['nɑjlə,lɑk]
hair spray	hårspray (f)	['hɒːˌspʁɛj]
deodorant	deodorant (f)	[deodo'ʁɑnʔt]

cream	creme (f)	['kʁɛʔm]
face cream	ansigtscreme (f)	['ansegts 'kʁɛʔm]
hand cream	håndcreme (f)	['hʌn,kʁɛʔm]
anti-wrinkle cream	antirynke creme (f)	[antə'ʁœŋkə 'kʁɛʔm]
day cream	dagcreme (f)	['dɑw,kʁɛʔm]
night cream	natcreme (f)	['nat,kʁɛʔm]
day (as adj)	dag-	['dɑw-]
night (as adj)	nat-	['nat-]

tampon	tampon (f)	[tɑm'pʌn]
toilet paper (toilet roll)	toiletpapir (i)	[toa'lɛt pa'piɐ̯ʔ]
hair dryer	hårtørrer (f)	['hɒːˌtœɐ̯ʌ]

40. Watches. Clocks

watch (wristwatch)	armbåndsur (i)	['ɑ:mbʌns,uɐ̯ʔ]
dial	urskive (f)	['uɐ̯,ski:və]
hand (of clock, watch)	viser (f)	['vi:sʌ]
metal watch band	armbånd (i)	['ɑ:m,bʌnʔ]
watch strap	urrem (f)	['uɐ̯,ʁam']

battery	batteri (i)	[batʌ'ʁiʔ]
to be dead (battery)	at blive afladet	[ʌ 'bli:ə 'ɑw,læʔðəð]
to change a battery	at skifte et batteri	[ʌ 'skiftə et batʌ'ʁiʔ]
to run fast	at gå for hurtigt	[ʌ gɔʔ fʌ 'hoɐ̯tit]

to run slow	**at gå for langsomt**	[ʌ gɔˀ fʌ ˈlɑŋˌsʌmt]
wall clock	**vægur** (i)	[ˈvɛːgˌuɐ̯ˀ]
hourglass	**timeglas** (i)	[ˈtiːməˌglas]
sundial	**solur** (i)	[ˈsoːlˌuɐ̯ˀ]
alarm clock	**vækkeur** (i)	[ˈvɛkəˌuɐ̯ˀ]
watchmaker	**urmager** (f)	[ˈuɐ̯ˌmæˀjʌ]
to repair (vt)	**at reparere**	[ʌ ʁɛpəˈʁɛˀʌ]

BOOKS

EVERYDAY EXPERIENCE

T&P Books Publishing

41. Money

money	**penge** (pl)	['pɛŋə]
currency exchange	**veksling** (f)	['vɛkslen]
exchange rate	**kurs** (f)	['kuɐ̯'s]
ATM	**pengeautomat** (f)	['pɛŋə awto'mæˀt]
coin	**mønt** (f)	['mønˀt]
dollar	**dollar** (f)	['dʌlʌ]
euro	**euro** (f)	['œwʁo]
lira	**lire** (f)	['liːʌ]
Deutschmark	**mark** (f)	['mɑːk]
franc	**franc** (f)	['fʁɑŋˀk]
pound sterling	**engelske pund** (i)	['ɛŋˀəlskə punˀ]
yen	**yen** (f)	['jɛn]
debt	**gæld** (f)	['gɛlˀ]
debtor	**skyldner** (f)	['skylnʌ]
to lend (money)	**at låne ud**	[ʌ 'lɔːnə ˌuðˀ]
to borrow (vi, vt)	**at låne**	[ʌ 'lɔːnə]
bank	**bank** (f)	['bɑŋˀk]
account	**konto** (f)	['kʌnto]
to deposit (vt)	**at indsætte**	[ʌ 'enˌsɛtə]
to deposit into the account	**at sætte ind på kontoen**	[ʌ 'sɛtə 'enˀ pɔ 'kʌntoːən]
to withdraw (vt)	**at hæve fra kontoen**	[ʌ 'hɛːvə fʁɑ 'kʌntoːən]
credit card	**kreditkort** (i)	[kʁɛ'dit kɒːt]
cash	**kontanter** (pl)	[kɔn'tanˀtʌ]
check	**check** (f)	['ɕɛk]
to write a check	**at skrive en check**	[ʌ 'skʁiːvə en 'ɕɛk]
checkbook	**checkhæfte** (i)	['ɕɛkˌhɛftə]
wallet	**tegnebog** (f)	['tajnəˌbɔˀw]
change purse	**pung** (f)	['pɔŋˀ]
safe	**pengeskab** (i)	['pɛŋəˌskæˀb]
heir	**arving** (f)	['ɑːven]
inheritance	**arv** (f)	['ɑˀw]
fortune (wealth)	**formue** (f)	['fɒːˌmuːə]
lease	**leje** (f)	['lajə]
rent (money)	**husleje** (f)	['husˌlajə]
to rent (sth from sb)	**at leje**	[ʌ 'lajə]
price	**pris** (f)	['pʁiˀs]

| cost | omkostning (f) | ['ʌmˌkʌstneŋ] |
| sum | sum (f) | ['sɔmˀ] |

to spend (vt)	at bruge	[ʌ 'bʁuːə]
expenses	udgifter (f pl)	['uðˌgiftʌ]
to economize (vi, vt)	at spare	[ʌ 'spɑːɑ]
economical	sparsommelig	[spɑ'sʌmˀəli]

to pay (vi, vt)	at betale	[ʌ be'tæˀlə]
payment	betaling (f)	[be'tæˀleŋ]
change (give the ~)	byttepenge (pl)	['bytəˌpɛŋə]

tax	skat (f)	['skat]
fine	bøde (f)	['bøːðə]
to fine (vt)	at give bødestraf	[ʌ 'giˀ 'bøːðəˌstʁɑf]

42. Post. Postal service

post office	postkontor (i)	['pʌst kɔn'toˀg̊]
mail (letters, etc.)	post (f)	['pʌst]
mailman	postbud (i)	['pʌstˌbuð]
opening hours	åbningstid (f)	['ɔːbneŋsˌtiðˀ]

letter	brev (i)	['bʁɛwˀ]
registered letter	rekommanderet brev (i)	[ʁɛkɔman'deˀʌð 'bʁɛwˀ]
postcard	postkort (i)	['pʌstˌkɒːt]
telegram	telegram (i)	[telə'gʁɑmˀ]
package (parcel)	postpakke (f)	['pʌstˌpɑkə]
money transfer	pengeoverførsel (f)	['pɛŋə 'ɒwʌˌføg̊ˀsəl]

to receive (vt)	at modtage	[ʌ 'moðˌtæˀ]
to send (vt)	at sende	[ʌ 'sɛnə]
sending	afsendelse (f)	['awˌsɛnˀəlsə]
address	adresse (f)	[a'dʁasə]
ZIP code	postnummer (i)	['pʌstˌnɔmˀʌ]
sender	afsender (f)	['awˌsɛnˀʌ]
receiver	modtager (f)	['moðˌtæˀjʌ]

| name (first name) | fornavn (i) | ['fɔːˌnɑwˀn] |
| surname (last name) | efternavn (i) | ['ɛftʌˌnɑwˀn] |

postage rate	tarif (f)	[tɑ'ʁif]
standard (adj)	vanlig	['væˀnli]
economical (adj)	økonomisk	[øko'noˀmisk]

weight	vægt (f)	['vɛgt]
to weigh (~ letters)	at veje	[ʌ 'vɑjə]
envelope	konvolut, kuvert (f)	[kɔnvo'lut], [ku'væg̊t]
postage stamp	frimærke (i)	['fʁiˌmæg̊kə]
to stamp an envelope	at frankere	[ʌ fʁɑŋ'keˀʌ]

43. Banking

bank	bank (f)	['baŋˀk]
branch (of bank, etc.)	afdeling (f)	['aw̩deˀleŋ]
bank clerk, consultant	konsulent (f)	[kʌnsu'lɛnˀt]
manager (director)	forretningsfører (f)	[fʌ'ʁatneŋs̩føːʌ]
bank account	bankkonto (f)	['baŋˀk̩kʌnto]
account number	kontonummer (i)	['kʌnto̩nɔmˀʌ]
checking account	checkkonto (f)	['ɕɛk̩kʌnto]
savings account	opsparingskonto (f)	['ʌp̩spaˀeŋs ̩kʌnto]
to open an account	at åbne en konto	[ʌ 'ɔːbnə en 'kʌnto]
to close the account	at lukke kontoen	[ʌ 'lɔkə 'kʌntoːən]
to deposit into the account	at sætte ind på kontoen	[ʌ 'sɛtə 'enˀ pɔ 'kʌntoːən]
to withdraw (vt)	at hæve fra kontoen	[ʌ 'hɛːvə fʁa 'kʌntoːən]
deposit	indskud (i)	['en̩skuð]
to make a deposit	at indsætte	[ʌ 'en̩sɛtə]
wire transfer	overførelse (f)	['ɒwʌ̩føːʌlsə]
to wire, to transfer	at overføre	[ʌ 'ɒwʌ̩føˀʌ]
sum	sum (f)	['sɔmˀ]
How much?	Hvor meget?	[vɒˀ 'maɑð]
signature	signatur, underskrift (f)	[sina'tuɐ̯ˀ], ['ɔnʌ̩skʁɛft]
to sign (vt)	at underskrive	[ʌ 'ɔnʌ̩skʁiˀvə]
credit card	kreditkort (i)	[kʁɛ'dit kɒːt]
code (PIN code)	kode (f)	['koːðə]
credit card number	kreditkortnummer (i)	[kʁɛ'dit koːt 'nɔmˀʌ]
ATM	pengeautomat (f)	['pɛŋə awto'mæˀt]
check	check (f)	['ɕɛk]
to write a check	at skrive en check	[ʌ 'skʁiːvə en 'ɕɛk]
checkbook	checkhæfte (i)	['ɕɛk̩hɛftə]
loan (bank ~)	lån (i)	['lɔˀn]
to apply for a loan	at ansøge om lån	[ʌ 'an̩søːə ɒm 'lɔˀn]
to get a loan	at få et lån	[ʌ 'fɔˀ et 'lɔˀn]
to give a loan	at yde et lån	[ʌ 'y:ðə et 'lɔˀn]
guarantee	garanti (f)	[gaan'tiˀ]

44. Telephone. Phone conversation

telephone	telefon (f)	[telə'foˀn]
cell phone	mobiltelefon (f)	[mo'bil telə'foˀn]
answering machine	telefonsvarer (f)	[telə'foːn̩svaːɑ]

| to call (by phone) | at ringe | [ʌ 'ʁɛŋə] |
| phone call | telefonsamtale (f) | [teləˈfoːn 'sɑmˌtæːlə] |

to dial a number	at taste et nummer	[ʌ 'tastə et 'nɔmˀʌ]
Hello!	Hallo!	[ha'lo]
to ask (vt)	at spørge	[ʌ 'spœʁʌ]
to answer (vi, vt)	at svare	[ʌ 'svɑːɑ]

to hear (vt)	at høre	[ʌ 'høːʌ]
well (adv)	godt	['gʌt]
not well (adv)	dårligt	['dɒːlit]
noises (interference)	støj (f)	['stʌjˀ]

receiver	telefonrør (i)	[teləˈfoːnˌʁœˀʁ]
to pick up (~ the phone)	at tage telefonen	[ʌ 'tæˀ teləˈfoˀnən]
to hang up (~ the phone)	at lægge på	[ʌ 'lɛgə pɔˀ]

busy (engaged)	optaget	['ʌpˌtæˀj]
to ring (ab. phone)	at ringe	[ʌ 'ʁɛŋə]
telephone book	telefonbog (f)	[teləˈfoːnˌbɔˀw]

local (adj)	lokal-	[loˈkæl-]
local call	lokalopkald (i)	[loˈkæˀl 'ʌpˌkalˀ]
long distance (~ call)	fjern-	['fjæʁn-]
long-distance call	fjernopkald (i)	['fjæʁn 'ʌpˌkalˀ]
international (adj)	international	['entʌnaɕoˌnæˀl]
international call	internationalt opkald (i)	['entʌnaɕoˌnæˀlt 'ʌpˌkalˀ]

45. Cell phone

cell phone	mobiltelefon (f)	[moˈbil teləˈfoˀn]
display	skærm (f)	['skæʁˀm]
button	knap (f)	['knɑp]
SIM card	SIM-kort (i)	['semˌkɒːt]

battery	batteri (i)	[batʌˈʁiˀ]
to be dead (battery)	at blive afladet	[ʌ 'bliːə 'awˌlæˀðəð]
charger	oplader (f)	['ʌplˌlæˀðʌ]

menu	menu (f)	[meˈny]
settings	indstillinger (f pl)	['enˌstelˀeŋʌ]
tune (melody)	melodi (f)	[meloˈdiˀ]
to select (vt)	at vælge	[ʌ 'vɛljə]

calculator	lommeregner (f)	['lʌməˌʁɑjnʌ]
voice mail	telefonsvarer (f)	[teləˈfoːnˌsvɑːɑ]
alarm clock	vækkeur (i)	['vɛkəˌuʁˀ]
contacts	kontakter (f pl)	[kɔnˈtaktʌ]
SMS (text message)	SMS (f)	[ɛsɛmˈɛs]
subscriber	abonnent (f)	[aboˈnɛnˀt]

46. Stationery

ballpoint pen	**kuglepen** (f)	['ku:lə‚pɛnˀ]
fountain pen	**fyldepen** (f)	['fylə‚pɛnˀ]
pencil	**blyant** (f)	['bly:‚anˀt]
highlighter	**mærkepen** (f)	[mɑ'køɡ‚pɛnˀ]
felt-tip pen	**tuschpen** (f)	['tuɕ‚pɛnˀ]
notepad	**notesblok** (f)	['no:təs‚blʌk]
agenda (diary)	**dagbog** (f)	['dɑw‚bɔˀw]
ruler	**lineal** (f)	[line'æˀl]
calculator	**regnemaskine** (f)	['ʁajnə ma'ski:nə]
eraser	**viskelæder** (i)	['veskə‚lɛðˀʌ]
thumbtack	**tegnestift** (f)	['tajnə‚steft]
paper clip	**clips** (i)	['kleps]
glue	**lim** (f)	['liˀm]
stapler	**hæftemaskine** (f)	['hɛfta ma'ski:nə]
hole punch	**hullemaskine** (f)	['hɔlə ma'ski:nə]
pencil sharpener	**blyantspidser** (f)	['bly:ant‚spesʌ]

47. Foreign languages

language	**sprog** (i)	['spʁɔˀw]
foreign (adj)	**fremmed-**	['fʁaməð-]
foreign language	**fremmedsprog** (i)	['fʁaməð'spʁɔˀw]
to study (vt)	**at studere**	[ʌ stu'deˀʌ]
to learn (language, etc.)	**at lære**	[ʌ 'lɛ:ʌ]
to read (vi, vt)	**at læse**	[ʌ 'lɛ:sə]
to speak (vi, vt)	**at tale**	[ʌ 'tæ:lə]
to understand (vt)	**at forstå**	[ʌ fʌ'stɔˀ]
to write (vt)	**at skrive**	[ʌ 'skʁi:və]
fast (adv)	**hurtigt**	['hoɡtit]
slowly (adv)	**langsomt**	['lɑŋ‚sʌmt]
fluently (adv)	**flydende**	['fly:ðənə]
rules	**regler** (f pl)	['ʁejlʌ]
grammar	**grammatik** (f)	[gʁama'tik]
vocabulary	**ordforråd** (i)	['oɡfɔ‚ʁɔˀð]
phonetics	**fonetik** (f)	[fonə'tik]
textbook	**lærebog** (f)	['lɛ:ʌ‚bɔˀw]
dictionary	**ordbog** (f)	['oɡ‚bɔˀw]
teach-yourself book	**lærebog** (f) **til selvstudium**	['lɛ:ʌ‚bɔˀw tel 'sɛl‚stuˀdjɔm]

phrasebook	parlør (f)	[pɑ'lœ:ɐ̯]
cassette, tape	kassette (f)	[ka'sɛtə]
videotape	videokassette (f)	['viˀdjo ka'sɛtə]
CD, compact disc	cd (f)	[se'deˀ]
DVD	dvd (f)	[deve'deˀ]

alphabet	alfabet (i)	[alfa'beˀt]
to spell (vt)	at stave	[ʌ 'stæ:və]
pronunciation	udtale (f)	['uð,tæ:lə]

accent	accent (f)	[ɑk'sɑŋ]
with an accent	med accent	[mɛ ɑk'sɑŋ]
without an accent	uden accent	['uðən ɑk'sɑŋ]

| word | ord (i) | ['oˀɐ̯] |
| meaning | betydning (f) | [be'tyðˀnen] |

course (e.g., a French ~)	kursus (i)	['kuɐ̯sʌ]
to sign up	at indmelde sig	[ʌ 'enl,mɛlˀə saj]
teacher	lærer (f)	['lɛ:ʌ]

translation (process)	oversættelse (f)	['ɒwʌ,sɛtəlsə]
translation (text, etc.)	oversættelse (f)	['ɒwʌ,sɛtəlsə]
translator	oversætter (f)	['ɒwʌ,sɛtʌ]
interpreter	tolk (f)	['tʌlˀk]

| polyglot | polyglot (f) | [poly'glʌt] |
| memory | hukommelse (f) | [hu'kʌmˀəlsə] |

T&P BOOKS

MEALS. RESTAURANT

T&P Books Publishing

48. Table setting

spoon	ske (f)	[' skeˀ]
knife	kniv (f)	['kniwˀ]
fork	gaffel (f)	['gɑfəl]

cup (e.g., coffee ~)	kop (f)	['kʌp]
plate (dinner ~)	tallerken (f)	[ta'læɐ̯kən]
saucer	underkop (f)	['ɔnʌˌkʌp]
napkin (on table)	serviet (f)	[sæɐ̯vi'ɛt]
toothpick	tandstikker (f)	['tanˌstekʌ]

49. Restaurant

restaurant	restaurant (f)	[ʁɛsto'ʁɑŋ]
coffee house	cafe, kaffebar (f)	[ka'feˀ], ['kɑfəˌbɑˀ]
pub, bar	bar (f)	['bɑˀ]
tearoom	tesalon (f)	['teˀsa'lʌŋ]

waiter	tjener (f)	['tjɛːnʌ]
waitress	servitrice (f)	[sæɐ̯vi'tʁiːsə]
bartender	bartender (f)	['bɑːˌtɛndʌ]
menu	menu (f)	[me'ny]
wine list	vinkort (i)	['viːnˌkɔːt]
to book a table	at bestille et bord	[ʌ be'stelˀə ed 'boˀɐ̯]

course, dish	ret (f)	['ʁat]
to order (meal)	at bestille	[ʌ be'stelˀə]
to make an order	at bestille	[ʌ be'stelˀə]
aperitif	aperitif (f)	[apeɐ̯i'tif]
appetizer	forret (f)	['foːʁat]
dessert	dessert (f)	[de'sɛɐ̯ˀt]

check	regning (f)	['ʁajnɛŋ]
to pay the check	at betale regningen	[ʌ be'tæˀlə 'ʁɑjneŋən]
to give change	at give tilbage	[ʌ 'giˀ te'bæːjə]
tip	drikkepenge (pl)	['dʁɛkəˌpɛŋə]

50. Meals

| food | mad (f) | ['mɑð] |
| to eat (vi, vt) | at spise | [ʌ 'spiːsə] |

breakfast	morgenmad (f)	['mɒːɒnˌmað]
to have breakfast	at spise morgenmad	[ʌ 'spiːsə 'mɒːɒnˌmað]
lunch	frokost (f)	['fʁɔkʌst]
to have lunch	at spise frokost	[ʌ 'spiːsə 'fʁɔkʌst]
dinner	aftensmad (f)	['ɑftənsˌmað]
to have dinner	at spise aftensmad	[ʌ 'spiːsə 'ɑftənsˌmað]
appetite	appetit (f)	[ɑpə'tit]
Enjoy your meal!	Velbekomme!	['vɛlbə'kʌmˀə]
to open (~ a bottle)	at åbne	[ʌ 'ɔ:bnə]
to spill (liquid)	at spilde	[ʌ 'spilə]
to spill out (vi)	at spildes ud	[ʌ 'spiləs uðˀ]
to boil (vi)	at koge	[ʌ 'kɔ:wə]
to boil (vt)	at koge	[ʌ 'kɔ:wə]
boiled (~ water)	kogt	['kʌgt]
to chill, cool down (vt)	at afkøle	[ʌ 'ɑwˌkøˀlə]
to chill (vi)	at afkøles	[ʌ 'ɑwˌkøˀləs]
taste, flavor	smag (f)	['smæˀj]
aftertaste	bismag (f)	['bismæˀj]
to slim down (lose weight)	at være på diæt	[ʌ 'vɛːʌ pɔˀ di'ɛˀt]
diet	diæt (f)	[di'ɛˀt]
vitamin	vitamin (i)	[vita'miˀn]
calorie	kalorie (f)	[ka'loɐˀjə]
vegetarian (n)	vegetar, vegetarianer (f)	[vegə'tɑˀ], [vegətai'æˀnʌ]
vegetarian (adj)	vegetarisk	[vegə'tɑˀisk]
fats (nutrient)	fedt (i)	['fet]
proteins	proteiner (i pl)	[pʁotə'iˀnʌ]
carbohydrates	kulhydrater (i pl)	['kɔlhyˌdʁɑˀdʌ]
slice (of lemon, ham)	skive (f)	['skiːvə]
piece (of cake, pie)	stykke (i)	['støkə]
crumb (of bread, cake, etc.)	krumme (f)	['kʁɔmə]

51. Cooked dishes

course, dish	ret (f)	['ʁat]
cuisine	køkken (i)	['køkən]
recipe	opskrift (f)	['ʌpˌskʁɛft]
portion	portion (f)	[pɒ'ɕoˀn]
salad	salat (f)	[sa'læˀt]
soup	suppe (f)	['sɔpə]
clear soup (broth)	bouillon (f)	[bul'jʌŋ]
sandwich (bread)	smørrebrød (i)	['smœɐʌˌbʁœðˀ]

fried eggs	spejlæg (i)	['spɑjlˌɛˀg]
hamburger (beefburger)	hamburger (f)	['hæːmˌbœːgʌ]
beefsteak	bøf (f)	['bøf]

side dish	tilbehør (i)	['telbeˌhøˀɐ̯]
spaghetti	spaghetti (f)	[spa'gɛti]
mashed potatoes	kartoffelmos (f)	[kɑ'tʌfəlˌmɔs]
pizza	pizza (f)	['pidsa]
porridge (oatmeal, etc.)	grød (f)	['gʁœðˀ]
omelet	omelet (f)	[omə'lɛt]

boiled (e.g., ~ beef)	kogt	['kʌgt]
smoked (adj)	røget	['ʁʌjəð]
fried (adj)	stegt	['stɛgt]
dried (adj)	tørret	['tœɐ̯ʌð]
frozen (adj)	frossen	['fʁɔsən]
pickled (adj)	syltet	['syltəð]

sweet (sugary)	sød	['søðˀ]
salty (adj)	saltet	['saltəð]
cold (adj)	kold	['kʌlˀ]
hot (adj)	hed, varm	['heðˀ], ['vɑˀm]
bitter (adj)	bitter	['betʌ]
tasty (adj)	lækker	['lɛkʌ]

to cook in boiling water	at koge	[ʌ 'kɔːwə]
to cook (dinner)	at lave	[ʌ 'læːvə]
to fry (vt)	at stege	[ʌ 'stɑjə]
to heat up (food)	at varme op	[ʌ 'vɑːmə ʌp]

to salt (vt)	at salte	[ʌ 'saltə]
to pepper (vt)	at pebre	[ʌ 'pewʁʌ]
to grate (vt)	at rive	[ʌ 'ʁiːvə]
peel (n)	skal, skræl (f)	['skalˀ], ['skʁalˀ]
to peel (vt)	at skrælle	[ʌ 'skʁalə]

52. Food

meat	kød (i)	['køð]
chicken	høne (f)	['hœːnə]
Rock Cornish hen (poussin)	kylling (f)	['kyleŋ]
duck	and (f)	['anˀ]
goose	gås (f)	['gɔˀs]
game	vildt (i)	['vilˀt]
turkey	kalkun (f)	[kal'kuˀn]

pork	flæsk (i)	['flɛsk]
veal	kalvekød (i)	['kalvəˌkøð]
lamb	lammekød (i)	['lɑməˌkøð]

beef	oksekød (i)	['ʌksə‚køð]
rabbit	kanin (f)	[ka'niʔn]

sausage (bologna, pepperoni, etc.)	pølse (f)	['pølsə]
vienna sausage (frankfurter)	wienerpølse (f)	['viʔnʌ‚pølsə]
bacon	bacon (i, f)	['bɛjkʌn]
ham	skinke (f)	['skeŋkə]
gammon	skinke (f)	['skeŋkə]

pâté	pate, paté (f)	[pa'te]
liver	lever (f)	['lewʔʌ]
hamburger (ground beef)	kødfars (f)	['køð‚faʔs]
tongue	tunge (f)	['tɔŋə]

egg	æg (i)	['ɛʔg]
eggs	æg (i pl)	['ɛʔg]
egg white	hvide (f)	['viːðə]
egg yolk	blomme (f)	['blʌmə]

fish	fisk (f)	['fesk]
seafood	fisk og skaldyr	[fesk 'ɒw 'skaldyɐ̯ʔ]
crustaceans	krebsdyr (i pl)	['kʁabs‚dyɐ̯ʔ]
caviar	kaviar (f)	['kavi‚ɑʔ]

crab	krabbe (f)	['kʁabə]
shrimp	reje (f)	['ʁɑjə]
oyster	østers (f)	['østʌs]
spiny lobster	languster (f)	[lɑŋ'gustʌ]
octopus	blæksprutte (f)	['blɛk‚spʁutə]
squid	blæksprutte (f)	['blɛk‚spʁutə]

sturgeon	stør (f)	['støʔɐ̯]
salmon	laks (f)	['laks]
halibut	helleflynder (f)	['hɛlə‚flønʌ]

cod	torsk (f)	['tɔːsk]
mackerel	makrel (f)	[mɑ'kʁalʔ]
tuna	tunfisk (f)	['tuːn‚fesk]
eel	ål (f)	['ɔʔl]

trout	ørred (f)	['œɐ̯ʌð]
sardine	sardin (f)	[sɑ'diʔn]
pike	gedde (f)	['geðə]
herring	sild (f)	['silʔ]

bread	brød (i)	['bʁœðʔ]
cheese	ost (f)	['ɔst]
sugar	sukker (i)	['sɔkʌ]
salt	salt (i)	['salʔt]
rice	ris (f)	['ʁiʔs]

| pasta (macaroni) | **pasta** (f) | ['pasta] |
| noodles | **nudler** (f pl) | ['nuð'lʌ] |

butter	**smør** (i)	['smœɡ]
vegetable oil	**vegetabilsk olie** (f)	[vegəta'bi'lsk 'oljə]
sunflower oil	**solsikkeolie** (f)	['so:lˌsekə ˌoljə]
margarine	**margarine** (f)	[maga'ʁi:nə]

| olives | **oliven** (f pl) | [o'li'vən] |
| olive oil | **olivenolie** (f) | [o'li'vənˌoljə] |

milk	**mælk** (f)	['mɛl'k]
condensed milk	**kondenseret mælk** (f)	[kʌndən'se'ʌð mɛl'k]
yogurt	**yoghurt** (f)	['joˌguʁ't]
sour cream	**cremefraiche,**	[kʁɛ:m'fʁɛ:ɕ],
	syrnet fløde (f)	['syɡnəð 'flø:ðə]
cream (of milk)	**fløde** (f)	['flø:ðə]

| mayonnaise | **mayonnaise** (f) | [majo'nɛ:s] |
| buttercream | **creme** (f) | ['kʁɛ'm] |

cereal grains (wheat, etc.)	**gryn** (i)	['gʁy'n]
flour	**mel** (i)	['me'l]
canned food	**konserves** (f)	[kɔn'sæɡvəs]

cornflakes	**cornflakes** (pl)	['koɡnˌflɛks]
honey	**honning** (f)	['hʌneŋ]
jam	**syltetøj** (i)	['syltəˌtʌj]
chewing gum	**tyggegummi** (i)	['tygəˌgomi]

53. Drinks

water	**vand** (i)	['van']
drinking water	**drikkevand** (i)	['dʁɛkəˌvan']
mineral water	**mineralvand** (i)	[minə'ʁalˌvan']

still (adj)	**uden brus**	['uðən 'bʁu's]
carbonated (adj)	**med kulsyre**	[mɛ 'bʁu's]
sparkling (adj)	**med brus**	[mɛ 'bʁu's]
ice	**is** (f)	['i's]
with ice	**med is**	[mɛ 'i's]

non-alcoholic (adj)	**alkoholfri**	['alkohʌlˌfʁi']
soft drink	**alkoholfri drik** (f)	['alkohʌlˌfʁi' 'dʁɛk]
refreshing drink	**læskedrik** (f)	['lɛskəˌdʁɛk]
lemonade	**limonade** (f)	[limo'næ:ðə]

liquors	**alkoholiske drikke** (f pl)	[alko'ho'liskə 'dʁɛkə]
wine	**vin** (f)	['vi'n]
white wine	**hvidvin** (f)	['við ˌvi'n]

red wine	rødvin (f)	['ʁœð‚vi²n]
liqueur	likør (f)	[li'kø²g̊]
champagne	champagne (f)	[ɕam'panjə]
vermouth	vermouth (f)	['væɐ̯mut]

whiskey	whisky (f)	['wiski]
vodka	vodka (f)	['vʌdka]
gin	gin (f)	['djen]
cognac	cognac, konjak (f)	['kʌn²jɑg]
rum	rom (f)	['ʁʌm²]

coffee	kaffe (f)	['kɑfə]
black coffee	sort kaffe (f)	['soɡ̊t 'kɑfə]
coffee with milk	kaffe (f) med mælk	['kɑfə mɛ 'mɛl²k]
cappuccino	cappuccino (f)	[kɑpu'tji:no]
instant coffee	pulverkaffe (f)	['pɔlvʌ‚kɑfə]

milk	mælk (f)	['mɛl²k]
cocktail	cocktail (f)	['kʌk‚tɛjl]
milkshake	milkshake (f)	['milk‚ɕɛjk]

juice	juice (f)	['dʒu:s]
tomato juice	tomatjuice (f)	[to'mæ:t‚dʒu:s]
orange juice	appelsinjuice (f)	[ɑpəl'si²n 'dʒu:s]
freshly squeezed juice	friskpresset juice (f)	['fʁɛsk‚pʁasəð 'dʒu:s]

beer	øl (i)	['øl]
light beer	lyst øl (i)	['lyst ‚øl]
dark beer	mørkt øl (i)	['mɶg̊kt ‚øl]

tea	te (f)	['te²]
black tea	sort te (f)	['soɡ̊t ‚te²]
green tea	grøn te (f)	['gʁœn² ‚te²]

54. Vegetables

| vegetables | grøntsager (pl) | ['gʁœnt‚sæ²jʌ] |
| greens | grønt (i) | ['gʁœn²t] |

tomato	tomat (f)	[to'mæ²t]
cucumber	agurk (f)	[a'gug̊k]
carrot	gulerod (f)	['gulə‚ʁo²ð]
potato	kartoffel (f)	[kɑ't̥ʌfəl]
onion	løg (i)	['lʌj²]
garlic	hvidløg (i)	['við‚lʌj²]

cabbage	kål (f)	['kɔ²l]
cauliflower	blomkål (f)	['blʌm‚kɔ²l]
Brussels sprouts	rosenkål (f)	['ʁo:sən‚kɔ²l]
broccoli	broccoli (f)	['bʁʌkoli]

143

beetroot	**rødbede** (f)	[ʁœð'beːðə]
eggplant	**aubergine** (f)	[obæɡ'ɕiːn]
zucchini	**squash, zucchini** (f)	['sgwʌɕ], [su'kiːni]
pumpkin	**græskar** (i)	['gʁaskɑ]
turnip	**majroe** (f)	['mɑjˌʁoːə]
parsley	**persille** (f)	[pæɡ'selə]
dill	**dild** (f)	['dilʔ]
lettuce	**salat** (f)	[sa'læʔt]
celery	**selleri** (f)	['selʌˌʁiʔ]
asparagus	**asparges** (f)	[a'spɑʔs]
spinach	**spinat** (f)	[spi'næʔt]
pea	**ærter** (f pl)	['æɡʔtʌ]
beans	**bønner** (f pl)	['bœnʌ]
corn (maize)	**majs** (f)	['mɑjʔs]
kidney bean	**bønne** (f)	['bœnə]
bell pepper	**peber** (i, f)	['pewʌ]
radish	**radiser** (f pl)	[ʁa'disə]
artichoke	**artiskok** (f)	[ˌɑːti'skʌk]

55. Fruits. Nuts

fruit	**frugt** (f)	['fʁɔgt]
apple	**æble** (i)	['ɛʔblə]
pear	**pære** (f)	['pɛʔʌ]
lemon	**citron** (f)	[si'tʁoʔn]
orange	**appelsin** (f)	[ɑpəl'siʔn]
strawberry (garden ~)	**jordbær** (i)	['joɡˌbæɡ]
mandarin	**mandarin** (f)	[mandɑ'ʁiʔn]
plum	**blomme** (f)	['blʌmə]
peach	**fersken** (f)	['fæɡskən]
apricot	**abrikos** (f)	[abʁi'koʔs]
raspberry	**hindbær** (i)	['henˌbæɡ]
pineapple	**ananas** (f)	['ananas]
banana	**banan** (f)	[ba'næʔn]
watermelon	**vandmelon** (f)	['van me'loʔn]
grape	**drue** (f)	['dʁuːə]
sour cherry	**kirsebær** (i)	['kiɡsəˌbæɡ]
sweet cherry	**morel** (f)	[mo'ʁælʔ]
melon	**melon** (f)	[me'loʔn]
grapefruit	**grapefrugt** (f)	['gʁɛjpˌfʁɔgt]
avocado	**avokado** (f)	[avo'kæːdo]
papaya	**papaja** (f)	[pa'pɑja]
mango	**mango** (f)	['mɑŋgo]
pomegranate	**granatæble** (i)	[gʁɑ'næʔtˌɛːblə]

redcurrant	ribs (i, f)	['ʁɛbs]
blackcurrant	solbær (i)	['so:lˌbæɡ]
gooseberry	stikkelsbær (i)	['stekəlsˌbæɡ]
bilberry	blåbær (i)	['blɔˀˌbæɡ]
blackberry	brombær (i)	['bʁɔmˌbæɡ]

raisin	rosin (f)	[ʁoˈsiˀn]
fig	figen (f)	['fi:ən]
date	daddel (f)	['daðˀəl]

peanut	jordnød (f)	['joɡˌnøðˀ]
almond	mandel (f)	['manˀəl]
walnut	valnød (f)	['valˌnøðˀ]
hazelnut	hasselnød (f)	['hasəlˌnøðˀ]
coconut	kokosnød (f)	['ko:kosˌnøðˀ]
pistachios	pistacier (f pl)	[piˈstæːɕʌ]

56. Bread. Candy

bakers' confectionery (pastry)	konditorvarer (f pl)	[kʌnˈditʌˌvɑːɑ]
bread	brød (i)	['bʁœðˀ]
cookies	småkager (f pl)	['smʌˌkæːjʌ]

chocolate (n)	chokolade (f)	[ɕokoˈlæːðə]
chocolate (as adj)	chokolade-	[ɕokoˈlæːðə-]
candy (wrapped)	konfekt, karamel (f)	[kɔnˈfɛkt], [kɑɑˈmɛlˀ]
cake (e.g., cupcake)	kage (f)	['kæːjə]
cake (e.g., birthday ~)	lagkage (f)	['lɑwˌkæːjə]

pie (e.g., apple ~)	pie (f)	['pɑːj]
filling (for cake, pie)	fyld (i, f)	['fylˀ]

jam (whole fruit jam)	syltetøj (i)	['syltəˌtʌj]
marmalade	marmelade (f)	[mɑməˈlæːðə]
waffles	vaffel (f)	['vɑfəl]
ice-cream	is (f)	['iˀs]
pudding	budding (f)	['buðeŋ]

57. Spices

salt	salt (i)	['salˀt]
salty (adj)	saltet	['saltəð]
to salt (vt)	at salte	[ʌ 'saltə]

black pepper	sort peber (i, f)	['soɡt 'pewʌ]
red pepper (milled ~)	rød peber (i, f)	['ʁœð 'pewʌ]
mustard	sennep (f)	['senʌp]

horseradish	peberrod (f)	['pewʌˌʁoˀð]
condiment	krydderi (i)	[kʁyðʌ'ʁiˀ]
spice	krydderi (i)	[kʁyðʌ'ʁiˀ]
sauce	sovs, sauce (f)	['sɒwˀs]
vinegar	eddike (f)	['ɛðikə]
anise	anis (f)	['anis]
basil	basilikum (f)	[ba'silˀikɔm]
cloves	nellike (f)	['nelˀekə]
ginger	ingefær (f)	['enəˌfæɡ]
coriander	koriander (f)	[kɒi'anˀdʌ]
cinnamon	kanel (i, f)	[ka'neˀl]
sesame	sesam (f)	['se:sɑm]
bay leaf	laurbærblad (i)	['lɑwʌbæɡˌblað]
paprika	paprika (f)	['pɑpʁika]
caraway	kommen (f)	['kʌmən]
saffron	safran (i, f)	[sa'fʁɑˀn]

PERSONAL INFORMATION. FAMILY

T&P Books Publishing

name (first name)	**navn** (i)	['nɑwˀn]
surname (last name)	**efternavn** (i)	['ɛftʌˌnɑwˀn]
date of birth	**fødselsdato** (f)	['føsəlsˌdæ:to]
place of birth	**fødested** (i)	['fø:ðəˌstɛð]
nationality	**nationalitet** (f)	[naɕonali'teˀt]
place of residence	**bopæl** (i)	['boˌpɛˀl]
country	**land** (i)	['lanˀ]
profession (occupation)	**fag** (i), **profession** (f)	['fæˀj], [pʁofə'ɕoˀn]
gender, sex	**køn** (i)	['kœnˀ]
height	**højde** (f)	['hʌjˀdə]
weight	**vægt** (f)	['vɛgt]

mother	**mor** (f), **moder** (f)	['moɐ̯], ['mo:ðʌ]
father	**far** (f), **fader** (f)	['fɑ:], ['fæ:ðʌ]
son	**søn** (f)	['sœn]
daughter	**datter** (f)	['datʌ]
younger daughter	**yngste datter** (f)	['øŋˀstə 'datʌ]
younger son	**yngste søn** (f)	['øŋˀstə 'sœn]
eldest daughter	**ældste datter** (f)	['ɛlˀstə 'datʌ]
eldest son	**ældste søn** (f)	['ɛlˀstə sœn]
brother	**bror** (f)	['bʁoɐ̯]
elder brother	**storebror** (f)	['stoɐ̯ˌbʁoɐ̯]
younger brother	**lillebror** (f)	['liləˌbʁoɐ̯]
sister	**søster** (f)	['søstʌ]
elder sister	**storesøster** (f)	['stoɐ̯ˌsøstʌ]
younger sister	**lillesøster** (f)	['liləˌsøstʌ]
cousin (masc.)	**fætter** (f)	['fɛtʌ]
cousin (fem.)	**kusine** (f)	[ku'si:nə]
mom, mommy	**mor** (f)	['moɐ̯]
dad, daddy	**papa, far** (f)	['papa], ['fɑ:]
parents	**forældre** (pl)	[fʌ'ɛlˀdʁʌ]
child	**barn** (i)	['baˀn]
children	**børn** (pl)	['bœɐ̯ˀn]
grandmother	**bedstemor** (f)	['bɛstəˌmoɐ̯]
grandfather	**bedstefar** (f)	['bɛstəˌfɑ:]

grandson	**barnebarn** (i)	['bɑ:nə,bɑʔn]
granddaughter	**barnebarn** (i)	['bɑ:nə,bɑʔn]
grandchildren	**børnebørn** (pl)	['bœɐ̯nə,bœɐ̯ʔn]

uncle	**onkel** (f)	['ɔŋʔkəl]
aunt	**tante** (f)	['tantə]
nephew	**nevø** (f)	[ne'vø]
niece	**niece** (f)	[ni'ɛ:sə]

mother-in-law (wife's mother)	**svigermor** (f)	['sviʔʌ,moɐ̯]
father-in-law (husband's father)	**svigerfar** (f)	['sviʔʌ,fɑ:]
son-in-law (daughter's husband)	**svigersøn** (f)	['sviʔʌ,sœn]
stepmother	**stedmor** (f)	['stɛð,moɐ̯]
stepfather	**stedfar** (f)	['stɛð,fɑ:]

infant	**spædbarn** (i)	['spɛð,bɑʔn]
baby (infant)	**spædbarn** (i)	['spɛð,bɑʔn]
little boy, kid	**lille barn** (i)	['lilə 'bɑʔn]

wife	**kone** (f)	['ko:nə]
husband	**mand** (f)	['manʔ]
spouse (husband)	**ægtemand** (f)	['ɛgtə,manʔ]
spouse (wife)	**hustru** (f)	['hustʁu]

married (masc.)	**gift**	['gift]
married (fem.)	**gift**	['gift]
single (unmarried)	**ugift**	['u,gift]
bachelor	**ungkarl** (f)	['ɔŋ,kæʔl]
divorced (masc.)	**fraskilt**	['fʁɑ,skelʔt]
widow	**enke** (f)	['ɛŋkə]
widower	**enkemand** (f)	['ɛŋkə,manʔ]

relative	**slægtning** (f)	['slɛgtneŋ]
close relative	**nær slægtning** (f)	['nɛʔɐ̯ 'slɛgtneŋ]
distant relative	**fjern slægtning** (f)	['fjæɐ̯ʔn 'slɛgtneŋ]
relatives	**slægtninge** (pl)	['slɛgtneŋə]

orphan (boy or girl)	**forældreløst barn** (i)	[fʌ'ɛlʔdʁʌlø:st bɑʔn]
guardian (of a minor)	**formynder** (f)	['fɔ:,mønʔʌ]
to adopt (a boy)	**at adoptere**	[ʌ adʌp'teʔʌ]
to adopt (a girl)	**at adoptere**	[ʌ adʌp'teʔʌ]

60. Friends. Coworkers

friend (masc.)	**ven** (f)	['vɛn]
friend (fem.)	**veninde** (f)	[vɛn'enə]
friendship	**venskab** (i)	['vɛn,skæʔb]

to be friends	at være venner	[ʌ 'vɛːʌ 'vɛnʌ]
buddy (masc.)	ven (f)	['vɛn]
buddy (fem.)	veninde (f)	[vɛn'enə]
partner	partner (f)	['pɑːtnʌ]

chief (boss)	chef (f)	['ɕɛˀf]
superior (n)	overordnet (f)	['ɒwʌˌpˀdnəð]
owner, proprietor	ejer (f)	['ɑjʌ]
subordinate (n)	underordnet (f)	['ɔnʌˌpˀdnəð]
colleague	kollega (f)	[ko'leːga]

acquaintance (person)	bekendt (f)	[be'kɛnˀt]
fellow traveler	medrejsende (f)	['mɛðˌʁɑjˀsənə]
classmate	klassekammerat (f)	['klasə kamə'ʁɑːt]

neighbor (masc.)	nabo (f)	['næːbo]
neighbor (fem.)	nabo (f)	['næːbo]
neighbors	naboer (pl)	['næːboˀʌ]

T&P BOOKS

HUMAN BODY. MEDICINE

T&P Books Publishing

head	hoved (i)	['ho:əð]
face	ansigt (i)	['ansegt]
nose	næse (f)	['nɛ:sə]
mouth	mund (f)	['mɔnʔ]

eye	øje (i)	['ʌjə]
eyes	øjne (i pl)	['ʌjnə]
pupil	pupil (f)	[pu'pilʔ]
eyebrow	øjenbryn (i)	['ʌjən‚bʁyʔn]
eyelash	øjenvippe (f)	['ʌjən‚vepə]
eyelid	øjenlåg (i)	['ʌjən‚lɔʔw]

tongue	tunge (f)	['tɔŋə]
tooth	tand (f)	['tanʔ]
lips	læber (f pl)	['lɛ:bʌ]
cheekbones	kindben (i pl)	['ken‚beʔn]
gum	tandkød (i)	['tan‚køð]
palate	gane (f)	['gæ:nə]

nostrils	næsebor (i pl)	['nɛ:sə‚boʔɐ̯]
chin	hage (f)	['hæ:jə]
jaw	kæbe (f)	['kɛ:bə]
cheek	kind (f)	['kenʔ]

forehead	pande (f)	['panə]
temple	tinding (f)	['tenəŋ]
ear	øre (i)	['ø:ʌ]
back of the head	nakke (f)	['nakə]
neck	hals (f)	['halʔs]
throat	strube, hals (f)	['stʁu:bə], ['halʔs]

hair	hår (i pl)	['hɔʔ]
hairstyle	frisure (f)	[fʁi'sy'ʌ]
haircut	klipning (f)	['klepnəŋ]
wig	paryk (f)	[pa'ʁœk]

mustache	moustache (f)	[mu'stæ:ɕ]
beard	skæg (i)	['skɛʔg]
to have (a beard, etc.)	at have	[ʌ 'hæ:və]
braid	fletning (f)	['flɛtnəŋ]
sideburns	bakkenbart (f)	['bakən‚baʔt]

| red-haired (adj) | rødhåret | ['ʁœð‚hɒʔɒð] |
| gray (hair) | grå | ['gʁɔʔ] |

| bald (adj) | skaldet | ['skaləð] |
| bald patch | skaldet plet (f) | ['skaləð‚plɛt] |

| ponytail | hestehale (f) | ['hɛstə‚hæ:lə] |
| bangs | pandehår (i) | ['panə‚hɒˀ] |

62. Human body

| hand | hånd (f) | ['hʌnˀ] |
| arm | arm (f) | ['ɑˀm] |

finger	finger (f)	['feŋˀʌ]
toe	tå (f)	['tɔˀ]
thumb	tommel (f)	['tʌməl]
little finger	lillefinger (f)	['lilə‚feŋˀʌ]
nail	negl (f)	['nɑjˀl]

fist	knytnæve (f)	['knyt‚nɛ:və]
palm	håndflade (f)	['hʌn‚flæ:ðə]
wrist	håndled (i)	['hʌn‚leð]
forearm	underarm (f)	['ɔnʌ‚ɑ:m]
elbow	albue (f)	['al‚bu:ə]
shoulder	skulder (f)	['skulʌ]

leg	ben (i)	['beˀn]
foot	fod (f)	['foˀð]
knee	knæ (i)	['knɛˀ]
calf (part of leg)	læg (f)	['lɛˀg]
hip	hofte (f)	['hʌftə]
heel	hæl (f)	['hɛˀl]

body	krop (f)	['kʁʌp]
stomach	mave (f)	['mæ:və]
chest	bryst (i)	['bʁœst]
breast	bryst (i)	['bʁœst]

flank	side (f)	['si:ðə]
back	ryg (f)	['ʁœg]
lower back	lænderyg (f)	['lɛnə‚ʁœg]
waist	midje, talje (f)	['miðjə], ['taljə]

navel (belly button)	navle (f)	['nɑwlə]
buttocks	baller, balder (f pl)	['balʌ]
bottom	bag (f)	['bæˀj]

| beauty mark | skønhedsplet (f) | ['skœnheðs‚plɛt] |
| birthmark (café au lait spot) | modermærke (i) | ['mo:ð ʌ'mæʁkə] |

| tattoo | tatovering (f) | [tato've ˀʁeŋ] |
| scar | ar (i) | ['ɑˀ] |

63. Diseases

sickness	sygdom (f)	['sy:ˌdʌmˀ]
to be sick	at være syg	[ʌ 'vɛːʌ syˀ]
health	helse, sundhed (f)	['hɛlsə], ['sɔnˌheðˀ]

runny nose (coryza)	snue (f)	['snuːə]
tonsillitis	angina (f)	[aŋ'giːna]
cold (illness)	forkølelse (f)	[fʌ'køˀləlsə]
to catch a cold	at blive forkølet	[ʌ 'bliːə fʌ'køˀləð]

bronchitis	bronkitis (f)	[bʁʌŋ'kitis]
pneumonia	lungebetændelse (f)	['lɔŋə be'tɛnˀəlsə]
flu, influenza	influenza (f)	[enflu'ɛnsa]

nearsighted (adj)	nærsynet	['næɐ̯ˌsyˀnəð]
farsighted (adj)	langsynet	['laŋˌsyˀnəð]
strabismus (crossed eyes)	skeløjethed (f)	['skelˌʌjəðˌheðˀ]
cross-eyed (adj)	skeløjet	['skelˌʌjˀəð]
cataract	grå stær (f)	['gʁɔˀ 'stɛˀɐ̯]
glaucoma	glaukom (i), grøn stær (f)	[glaw'koˀm], ['gʁœnˀ 'stɛˀɐ̯]

stroke	hjerneblødning (f)	['jæɐ̯nəˌbløðneŋ]
heart attack	infarkt (i, f)	[en'faːkt]
myocardial infarction	hjerteinfarkt (i, f)	['jæɐ̯tə en'faːkt]
paralysis	lammelse (f)	['laməlsə]
to paralyze (vt)	at lamme, at paralysere	[ʌ 'lamə], [ʌ paaly'seˀʌ]

allergy	allergi (f)	[alæɐ̯'giˀ]
asthma	astma (f)	['astma]
diabetes	diabetes (f)	[dia'beːtəs]

| toothache | tandpine (f) | ['tanˌpiːnə] |
| caries | caries, karies (f) | ['kaˀiəs] |

diarrhea	diarre (f)	[dia'ʁɛ]
constipation	forstoppelse (f)	[fʌ'stʌpəlsə]
stomach upset	mavebesvær (i)	['mæːvəˌbe'svɛˀɐ̯]
food poisoning	madforgiftning (f)	['maðfʌˌgiftneŋ]
to get food poisoning	at få madforgiftning	[ʌ 'fɔˀ 'maðfʌˌgiftəˀ]

arthritis	artritis (f)	[a'tʁitis]
rickets	rakitis (f)	[ʁa'kitis]
rheumatism	reumatisme (f)	[ʁʌjma'tismə]
atherosclerosis	arterieforkalkning (f)	[a'teˀɐ̯iə fʌ'kalˀkneŋ]

gastritis	gastritis (f)	[ga'stʁitis]
appendicitis	appendicit (f)	[apɛndi'sit]
cholecystitis	galdeblærebetændelse (f)	['galəˌblɛːʌ be'tɛnˀəlsə]
ulcer	mavesår (i)	['mæːvəˌsɔˀ]
measles	mæslinger (pl)	['mɛsˌleŋˀʌ]

rubella (German measles)	røde hunde (f)	['ʁœːðə 'hunə]
jaundice	gulsot (f)	['gulˌso'ʔt]
hepatitis	hepatitis (f)	[hepa'titis]
schizophrenia	skizofreni (f)	[skidsofʁɛ'ni'ʔ]
rabies (hydrophobia)	rabies (f)	['ʁɑ'ʔbjɛs]
neurosis	neurose (f)	[nœw'ʁoːsə]
concussion	hjernerystelse (f)	['jæɡnəˌʁœstəlsə]
cancer	kræft (f), cancer (f)	['kʁaft], ['kan'sʌ]
sclerosis	sklerose (f)	[skləˈʁoːsə]
multiple sclerosis	multipel sklerose (f)	[mul'ti'ʔpəl skle'ʁoːsə]
alcoholism	alkoholisme (f)	[alkoho'lismə]
alcoholic (n)	alkoholiker (f)	[alko'ho'ʔlikʌ]
syphilis	syfilis (f)	['syfilis]
AIDS	AIDS (f)	['ɛjds]
tumor	svulst, tumor (f)	['svul'st], ['tuːmɒ]
malignant (adj)	ondartet, malign	['ɔnˌɑ'ʔdəð], [ma'li'ʔn]
benign (adj)	godartet, benign	['goðˌɑ'ʔtəð], [be'ni'ʔn]
fever	feber (f)	['fe'ʔbʌ]
malaria	malaria (f)	[ma'lɑ'ʔia]
gangrene	koldbrand (f)	['kʌlˌbʁɑn'ʔ]
seasickness	søsyge (f)	['søˌsy:ə]
epilepsy	epilepsi (f)	[epilɛp'si'ʔ]
epidemic	epidemi (f)	[epedə'mi'ʔ]
typhus	tyfus (f)	['tyfus]
tuberculosis	tuberkulose (f)	[tubæɡku'loːsə]
cholera	kolera (f)	['ko'ʔləʁɑ]
plague (bubonic ~)	pest (f)	['pɛst]

64. Symptoms. Treatments. Part 1

symptom	symptom (i)	[sym'to'ʔm]
temperature	temperatur (f)	[tɛmpʁɑ'tuɐ̯'ʔ]
high temperature (fever)	høj temperatur, feber (f)	['hʌj tɛmpʁɑ'tuɐ̯'ʔ], ['fe'ʔbʌ]
pulse	puls (f)	['pul'ʔs]
dizziness (vertigo)	svimmelhed (f)	['svem'ʔəlˌheð'ʔ]
hot (adj)	varm	['vɑ'ʔm]
shivering	gysen (f)	['gy:sən]
pale (e.g., ~ face)	bleg	['blɑj'ʔ]
cough	hoste (f)	['hoːstə]
to cough (vi)	at hoste	[ʌ 'hoːstə]
to sneeze (vi)	at nyse	[ʌ 'nyːsə]
faint	besvimelse (f)	[be'svi'ʔməlsə]
to faint (vi)	at besvime	[ʌ be'svi'ʔmə]

bruise (hématome)	blåt mærke (i)	['blʌt 'mæɐ̯kə]
bump (lump)	bule (f)	['buːlə]
to bang (bump)	at slå sig	[ʌ 'slɔʔ saj]
contusion (bruise)	blåt mærke (i)	['blʌt 'mæɐ̯kə]
to get a bruise	at støde sig	[ʌ 'sdøːðə saj]
to limp (vi)	at halte	[ʌ 'haltə]
dislocation	forvridning (f)	[fʌ'vʁiðˀneŋ]
to dislocate (vt)	at forvride	[ʌ fʌ'vʁiðˀə]
fracture	brud (i), fraktur (f)	['bʁuð], [fʁak'tuɐ̯ʔ]
to have a fracture	at få et brud	[ʌ 'fɔʔ ed 'bʁuð]
cut (e.g., paper ~)	snitsår (i)	['snitˌsɒʔ]
to cut oneself	at skære sig	[ʌ 'skɛːʌ saj]
bleeding	blødning (f)	['bløðneŋ]
burn (injury)	brandsår (i)	['bʁanˌsɒʔ]
to get burned	at brænde sig	[ʌ 'bʁanə saj]
to prick (vt)	at stikke	[ʌ 'stekə]
to prick oneself	at stikke sig	[ʌ 'stekə saj]
to injure (vt)	at skade	[ʌ 'skæːðə]
injury	skade (f)	['skæːðə]
wound	sår (i)	['sɒʔ]
trauma	traume, trauma (i)	['tʁawmə], ['tʁawma]
to be delirious	at tale i vildelse	[ʌ 'tæːlə i 'vilelsə]
to stutter (vi)	at stamme	[ʌ 'stamə]
sunstroke	solstik (i)	['soːlˌstek]

65. Symptoms. Treatments. Part 2

pain, ache	smerte (f)	['smæɐ̯tə]
splinter (in foot, etc.)	splint (f)	['splenʔt]
sweat (perspiration)	sved (f)	['sveð']
to sweat (perspire)	at svede	[ʌ 'sveːðə]
vomiting	opkastning (f)	['ʌpˌkastneŋ]
convulsions	kramper (f pl)	['kʁampʌ]
pregnant (adj)	gravid	[gʁa'viðˀ]
to be born	at fødes	[ʌ 'føːðəs]
delivery, labor	fødsel (f)	['føsəl]
to deliver (~ a baby)	at føde	[ʌ 'føːðə]
abortion	abort (f)	[a'bɒʔt]
breathing, respiration	åndedræt (i)	['ʌnəˌdʁat]
in-breath (inhalation)	indånding (f)	['enˌʌnʔeŋ]
out-breath (exhalation)	udånding (f)	['uðˌʌnʔeŋ]
to exhale (breathe out)	at ånde ud	[ʌ 'ʌnə uð]

to inhale (vi)	at ånde ind	[ʌ 'ʌnə en']
disabled person	handikappet person (f)	['handi,kapəð pæɐ'so'n]
cripple	krøbling (f)	['kʁœblen]
drug addict	narkoman (f)	[nɑko'mæ'n]

deaf (adj)	døv	['dø'w]
mute (adj)	stum	['stɔm']
deaf mute (adj)	døvstum	['døw,stɔm']

mad, insane (adj)	gal, sindssyg	['gæ'l], ['sen',sy']
madman (demented person)	gal mand (f)	['gæ'l 'man']
madwoman	gal kvinde (f)	['gæ'l 'kvenə]
to go insane	at blive sindssyg	[ʌ 'bli:ə 'sen',sy']

gene	gen (i)	['ge'n]
immunity	immunitet (f)	[imuni'te't]
hereditary (adj)	arvelig	['ɑ:vəli]
congenital (adj)	medfødt	['mɛð,fø't]

virus	virus (i, f)	['vi:ʁus]
microbe	mikrobe (f)	[mi'kʁo:bə]
bacterium	bakterie (f)	[bak'teɐ'iə]
infection	infektion (f)	[enfɛk'ɕo'n]

66. Symptoms. Treatments. Part 3

| hospital | sygehus (i) | ['sy:ə,hu's] |
| patient | patient (f) | [pa'ɕɛn't] |

diagnosis	diagnose (f)	[dia'gno:sə]
cure	kur, behandling (f)	['kuɐ'], [be'han'len]
medical treatment	behandling (f)	[be'han'len]
to get treatment	at blive behandlet	[ʌ 'bli:ə be'han'ləð]
to treat (~ a patient)	at behandle	[ʌ be'han'lə]
to nurse (look after)	at pleje	[ʌ 'plajə]
care (nursing ~)	pleje (f)	['plajə]

operation, surgery	operation (f)	[opəʁa'ɕo'n]
to bandage (head, limb)	at forbinde	[ʌ fʌ'ben'ə]
bandaging	forbinding (f)	[fʌ'ben'en]

vaccination	vaccination (f)	[vagsina'ɕo'n]
to vaccinate (vt)	at vaccinere	[ʌ vaksi'ne'ʌ]
injection, shot	injektion (f)	[enjɛk'ɕo'n]
to give an injection	at give en sprøjte	[ʌ 'gi' en 'spʁʌjtə]

attack	anfald (i)	['an,fal']
amputation	amputation (f)	[amputa'ɕo'n]
to amputate (vt)	at amputere	[ʌ ampu'te'ʌ]

coma	koma (f)	['ko:ma]
to be in a coma	at ligge i koma	[ʌ 'legə i 'ko:ma]
intensive care	intensivafdeling (f)	['entən,siw' 'ɑw,de'len]

to recover (~ from flu)	at blive rask	[ʌ 'bli:ə 'ʁɑsk]
condition (patient's ~)	tilstand (f)	['tel,stan']
consciousness	bevidsthed (f)	[be'vest,heð']
memory (faculty)	hukommelse (f)	[hu'kʌm'əlsə]

to pull out (tooth)	at trække ud	[ʌ 'tʁakə uð']
filling	plombe (f)	['plɔmbə]
to fill (a tooth)	at plombere	[ʌ plɔm'be'ʌ]

| hypnosis | hypnose (f) | [hyp'no:sə] |
| to hypnotize (vt) | at hypnotisere | [ʌ hypnoti'se'ʌ] |

67. Medicine. Drugs. Accessories

medicine, drug	medicin (f)	[medi'si'n]
remedy	middel (i)	['miðʼəl]
to prescribe (vt)	at ordinere	[ʌ ɔdi'ne'ʌ]
prescription	recept (f)	[ʁɛ'sɛpt]

tablet, pill	tablet (f), pille (f)	[tab'lɛt], ['pelə]
ointment	salve (f)	['salvə]
ampule	ampul (f)	[ɑm'pul']
mixture	mikstur (f)	[meks'tuɐ̯']
syrup	sirup (f)	['si'ʁɔp]
pill	pille (f)	['pelə]
powder	pulver (i)	['pɔl'vʌ]

gauze bandage	gazebind (i)	['gæ:sə,ben']
cotton wool	vat (i)	['vat]
iodine	jod (i, f)	['jo'ð]

| Band-Aid | plaster (i) | ['plastʌ] |
| eyedropper | pipette (f) | [pi'pɛtə] |

| thermometer | termometer (i) | [tæɡmo'me'tʌ] |
| syringe | sprøjte (f) | ['spʁʌjtə] |

| wheelchair | kørestol (f) | ['kø:ʌ,sto'l] |
| crutches | krykker (f pl) | ['kʁœkə] |

painkiller	smertestillende medicin (i)	['smæɡdə,stelənə medi'si'n]
laxative	laksativ (i)	[lɑksa'tiw']
spirits (ethanol)	sprit (f)	['spʁit]
medicinal herbs	lægeurter (f pl)	['lɛ:jə,uɐ̯'tʌ]
herbal (~ tea)	urte-	['uɐ̯tə-]

T&P BOOKS

APARTMENT

T&P Books Publishing

apartment	**lejlighed** (f)	['lɑjliˌheð']
room	**rum, værelse** (i)	['ʁɔm'], ['væɐ̯ʌlsə]
bedroom	**soveværelse** (i)	['sɒwəˌvæɐ̯ʌlsə]
dining room	**spisestue** (f)	['spiːsəˌstuːə]
living room	**dagligstue** (f)	['dɑwliˌstuːə]
study (home office)	**arbejdsværelse** (i)	['ɑːbɑjdsˌvæɐ̯ʌlsə]
entry room	**entre** (f), **forstue** (f)	[ɑŋ'tʁɛ], ['fɒˌstuːə]
bathroom (room with a bath or shower)	**badeværelse** (i)	['bæːðəˌvæɐ̯ʌlsə]
half bath	**toilet** (i)	[toa'lɛt]
ceiling	**loft** (i)	['lʌft]
floor	**gulv** (i)	['gɔl]
corner	**hjørne** (i)	['jœɐ̯'nə]

furniture	**møbler** (pl)	['møˀblʌ]
table	**bord** (i)	['boˀɐ̯]
chair	**stol** (f)	['stoˀl]
bed	**seng** (f)	['sɛŋ']
couch, sofa	**sofa** (f)	['soːfa]
armchair	**lænestol** (f)	['lɛːnəˌstoˀl]
bookcase	**bogskab** (i)	['bɔwˌskæːb]
shelf	**hylde** (f)	['hylə]
wardrobe	**klædeskab** (i)	['klɛːðəˌskæˀb]
coat rack (wall-mounted ~)	**knagerække** (f)	['knæːjəˌʁakə]
coat stand	**stumtjener** (f)	['stɔmˌtjɛːnʌ]
bureau, dresser	**kommode** (f)	[ko'moːðə]
coffee table	**sofabord** (i)	['soːfaˌboˀɐ̯]
mirror	**spejl** (i)	['spɑjˀl]
carpet	**tæppe** (i)	['tɛpə]
rug, small carpet	**lille tæppe** (i)	['lilə 'tɛpə]
fireplace	**pejs** (f), **kamin** (f)	['pɑjˀs], [ka'miˀn]
candle	**lys** (i)	['lyˀs]
candlestick	**lysestage** (f)	['lysəˌstæːjə]

drapes	gardiner (i pl)	[gɑ'di'nʌ]
wallpaper	tapet (i)	[ta'pe't]
blinds (jalousie)	persienne (f)	[pæɡ'ɕɛnə]

table lamp	bordlampe (f)	['boɡˌlɑmpə]
wall lamp (sconce)	væglampe (f)	['vɛgˌlɑmpə]
floor lamp	standerlampe (f)	['stanʌˌlɑmpə]
chandelier	lysekrone (f)	['lysəˌkʁoːnə]

leg (of chair, table)	ben (i)	['beʔn]
armrest	armlæn (i)	['ɑ'mˌlɛʔn]
back (backrest)	ryg (f), ryglæn (i)	['ʁœg], ['ʁœgˌlɛʔn]
drawer	skuffe (f)	['skɔfə]

70. Bedding

bedclothes	sengetøj (i)	['sɛŋəˌtʌj]
pillow	pude (f)	['puːðə]
pillowcase	pudebetræk (i)	['puːðə be'tʁak]
duvet, comforter	dyne (f)	['dyːnə]
sheet	lagen (i)	['læjʔən]
bedspread	sengetæppe (i)	['sɛŋəˌtɛpə]

71. Kitchen

kitchen	køkken (i)	['køkən]
gas	gas (f)	['gas]
gas stove (range)	gaskomfur (i)	['gasˌkɔm'fuɡʔ]
electric stove	elkomfur (i)	['ɛlˌkɔm'fuɡʔ]
oven	bageovn (f)	['bæːjəˌɒwʔn]
microwave oven	mikroovn (f)	['mikʁoˌɒwʔn]

refrigerator	køleskab (i)	['køːləˌskæʔb]
freezer	fryser (f)	['fʁyːsʌ]
dishwasher	opvaskemaskine (f)	[ʌp'vaskə ma'skiːnə]

meat grinder	kødhakker (f)	['køðˌhɑkʌ]
juicer	juicepresser (f)	['dʒuːsˌpʁasʌ]
toaster	brødrister, toaster (f)	['bʁœðˌʁɛstʌ], ['tɔwstʌ]
mixer	mikser, mixer (f)	['meksʌ]

coffee machine	kaffemaskine (f)	['kɑfə ma'skiːnə]
coffee pot	kaffekande (f)	['kɑfəˌkanə]
coffee grinder	kaffekværn (f)	['kɑfəˌkvæɡʔn]

kettle	kedel (f)	['keðəl]
teapot	tekande (f)	['teˌkanə]
lid	låg (i)	['lɔʔw]

tea strainer	**tesi** (f)	['te'ˌsi']
spoon	**ske** (f)	['ske']
teaspoon	**teske** (f)	['te'ˌske']
soup spoon	**spiseske** (f)	['spi:səˌske']
fork	**gaffel** (f)	['gɑfəl]
knife	**kniv** (f)	['kniw']

tableware (dishes)	**service** (i)	[sæɡ'vi:sə]
plate (dinner ~)	**tallerken** (f)	[ta'læɡkən]
saucer	**underkop** (f)	['ɔnʌˌkʌp]

shot glass	**shotglas** (i)	['ɕʌtˌglas]
glass (tumbler)	**glas** (i)	['glas]
cup	**kop** (f)	['kʌp]

sugar bowl	**sukkerskål** (f)	['sɔkʌˌskɔ'l]
salt shaker	**saltbøsse** (f)	['saltˌbøsə]
pepper shaker	**peberbøsse** (f)	['pewʌˌbøsə]
butter dish	**smørskål** (f)	['smœɡˌskɔ'l]

stock pot (soup pot)	**gryde** (f)	['gʁy:ðə]
frying pan (skillet)	**stegepande** (f)	['stɑjəˌpanə]
ladle	**slev** (f)	['slew']
colander	**dørslag** (i)	['dɑɡˌslæ'j]
tray (serving ~)	**bakke** (f)	['bɑkə]

bottle	**flaske** (f)	['flaskə]
jar (glass)	**glasdåse** (f)	['glasˌdɔ:sə]
can	**dåse** (f)	['dɔ:sə]

bottle opener	**oplukker** (f)	['ʌpˌlɔkʌ]
can opener	**dåseåbner** (f)	['dɔ:səˌɔ:bnʌ]
corkscrew	**proptrækker** (f)	['pʁʌpˌtʁakʌ]
filter	**filter** (i)	['fil'tʌ]
to filter (vt)	**at filtrere**	[ʌ fil'tʁɛ'ʌ]

trash, garbage (food waste, etc.)	**affald, skrald** (i)	['ɑwˌfal'], ['skʁal']
trash can (kitchen ~)	**skraldespand** (f)	['skʁɑləˌspan']

72. Bathroom

bathroom	**badeværelse** (i)	['bæ:ðəˌvæɡʌlsə]
water	**vand** (i)	['van']
faucet	**hane** (f)	['hæ:nə]
hot water	**varmt vand** (i)	['vɑ'mt van']
cold water	**koldt vand** (i)	['kʌlt van']

toothpaste	**tandpasta** (f)	['tanˌpasta]
to brush one's teeth	**at børste tænder**	[ʌ 'bœɡstə 'tɛnʌ]

toothbrush	tandbørste (f)	['tanˌbœɐ̯stə]
to shave (vi)	at barbere sig	[ʌ bɑ'be'ʌ sɑj]
shaving foam	barberskum (i)	[bɑ'be'g̊ˌskɔm']
razor	skraber (f)	['skʁɑːbʌ]

to wash (one's hands, etc.)	at vaske	[ʌ 'vaskə]
to take a bath	at vaske sig	[ʌ 'vaskə sɑj]
shower	brusebad (i)	['bʁuːsəˌbað]
to take a shower	at tage brusebad	[ʌ 'tæ' 'bʁuːsəˌbað]

bathtub	badekar (i)	['bæːðəˌkɑ]
toilet (toilet bowl)	toiletkumme (f)	[toa'lɛt 'kɔmə]
sink (washbasin)	håndvask (f)	['hʌn'ˌvask]

| soap | sæbe (f) | ['sɛːbə] |
| soap dish | sæbeskål (f) | ['sɛːbəˌskɔ'l] |

sponge	svamp (f)	['svɑm'p]
shampoo	shampoo (f)	['ɕæːmˌpuː]
towel	håndklæde (i)	['hʌnˌklɛːðə]
bathrobe	badekåbe (f)	['bæːðəˌkɔːbə]

laundry (process)	vask (f)	['vask]
washing machine	vaskemaskine (f)	['vaskə ma'skiːnə]
to do the laundry	at vaske tøj	[ʌ 'vaskə 'tʌj]
laundry detergent	vaskepulver (i)	['vaskəˌpɔl'vʌ]

73. Household appliances

TV set	tv, fjernsyn (i)	['te'ˌve'], ['fjæɐ̯nˌsy'n]
tape recorder	båndoptager (f)	['bɔnˌʌbtæ'ʌ]
VCR (video recorder)	video (f)	['vi'djo]
radio	radio (i)	['ʁɑ'djo]
player (CD, MP3, etc.)	afspiller (f)	['awˌspel'ʌ]

video projector	projektor (f)	[pʁo'ɕɛktʌ]
home movie theater	hjemmebio (f)	['jɛməˌbiːo]
DVD player	dvd-afspiller (f)	[deve'de' aw'spel'ʌ]
amplifier	forstærker (f)	[fʌ'stæɐ̯kʌ]
video game console	spillekonsol (f)	['spelə kɔn'sʌl']

video camera	videokamera (i)	['vi'djo ˌkæ'məʁɑ]
camera (photo)	kamera (i)	['kæ'məʁɑ]
digital camera	digitalkamera (i)	[digi'tæ'l ˌkæ'məʁɑ]

vacuum cleaner	støvsuger (f)	['støwˌsu'ʌ]
iron (e.g., steam ~)	strygejern (i)	['stʁyəˌjæɐ̯'n]
ironing board	strygebræt (i)	['stʁyəˌbʁat]
telephone	telefon (f)	[telə'fo'n]
cell phone	mobiltelefon (f)	[mo'bil telə'fo'n]

typewriter	**skrivemaskine** (f)	['skʁiːvə ma'skiːnə]
sewing machine	**symaskine** (f)	['syma͵skiːnə]
microphone	**mikrofon** (f)	[mikʁo'foˀn]
headphones	**hovedtelefoner** (f pl)	['hoːəð telə'foˀnʌ]
remote control (TV)	**fjernbetjening** (f)	['fjæɡn be'tjɛˀneŋ]
CD, compact disc	**cd** (f)	[se'deˀ]
cassette, tape	**kassette** (f)	[ka'sɛtə]
vinyl record	**plade** (f)	['plæːðə]

T&P BOOKS

THE EARTH. WEATHER

T&P Books Publishing

space	rummet, kosmos (i)	['ʁɔmet], ['kʌsmʌs]
space (as adj)	rum-	['ʁɔm-]
outer space	ydre rum (i)	['yðʁʌ ʁɔmʔ]

world	verden (f)	['væɡdən]
universe	univers (i)	[uni'væɡs]
galaxy	galakse (f)	[ga'lɑksə]

star	stjerne (f)	['stjæɡnə]
constellation	stjernebillede (i)	['stjæɡnə,beləðə]
planet	planet (f)	[pla'neʔt]
satellite	satellit (f)	[satə'lit]

meteorite	meteorit (f)	[meteo'ʁit]
comet	komet (f)	[ko'meʔt]
asteroid	asteroide (f)	[astəʁo'iːðə]

orbit	bane (f)	['bæːnə]
to revolve (~ around the Earth)	at rotere	[ʌ ʁo'teʔʌ]
atmosphere	atmosfære (f)	[atmo'sfɛːʌ]

the Sun	Solen	['soːlən]
solar system	solsystem (i)	['soːl sy'steʔm]
solar eclipse	solformørkelse (f)	['soːl fʌ'mæɡkəlsə]

the Earth	Jorden	['joʔɡən]
the Moon	Månen	['mɔːnən]

Mars	Mars	['mɑʔs]
Venus	Venus	['veːnus]
Jupiter	Jupiter	['jupitʌ]
Saturn	Saturn	['sæ,tuɡn]

Mercury	Merkur	[mæɡ'kuɡʔ]
Uranus	Uranus	[u'ʁɑnus]
Neptune	Neptun	[nɛp'tuʔn]
Pluto	Pluto	['pluto]

Milky Way	Mælkevejen	['mɛlkə,vajən]
Great Bear (Ursa Major)	Store Bjørn	['stoɡ ,bjæɡʔn]
North Star	Polarstjernen	[po'lɑ,stjæɡnən]
Martian	marsboer (f)	['mɑʔs,boʔʌ]
extraterrestrial (n)	ikkejordisk væsen (i)	[,ekə'joɡdisk ,vɛʔsən]

| alien | rumvæsen (i) | ['ʁɔmˌvɛʔsən] |
| flying saucer | flyvende tallerken (f) | ['fly:vənə ta'læɡkən] |

spaceship	rumskib (i)	['ʁɔmˌskiʔb]
space station	rumstation (f)	['ʁɔm sta'ɕoʔn]
blast-off	start (f)	['stɑʔt]

engine	motor (f)	['mo:tʌ]
nozzle	dyse (f)	['dysə]
fuel	brændsel (i)	['bʁanʔsəl]

cockpit, flight deck	cockpit (i)	['kʌkˌpit]
antenna	antenne (f)	[an'tɛnə]
porthole	koøje (i)	['koˌʌjə]
solar panel	solbatteri (i)	['so:lbatʌ'ʁiʔ]
spacesuit	rumdragt (f)	['ʁɔmˌdʁɑgt]

| weightlessness | vægtløshed (f) | ['vɛgtlø:sˌheð'] |
| oxygen | ilt (f), oxygen (i) | ['ilʔt], [ʌgsy'geʔn] |

| docking (in space) | dokning (f) | ['dʌknen] |
| to dock (vi, vt) | at dokke | [ʌ 'dʌkə] |

observatory	observatorium (i)	[ʌbsæɡva'toɡʔjɔm]
telescope	teleskop (i)	[telə'sko:p]
to observe (vt)	at observere	[ʌ ʌbsæɡ've'ʌ]
to explore (vt)	at udforske	[ʌ 'uðˌfɔ:skə]

75. The Earth

the Earth	Jorden	['joʔɡən]
the globe (the Earth)	jordklode (f)	['joɡˌklo:ðə]
planet	planet (f)	[pla'neʔt]

atmosphere	atmosfære (f)	[atmo'sfɛ:ʌ]
geography	geografi (f)	[geogʁɑ'fiʔ]
nature	natur (f)	[na'tuɡʔ]

globe (table ~)	globus (f)	['glo:bus]
map	kort (i)	['kɔ:t]
atlas	atlas (i)	['atlas]

Europe	Europa	[œw'ʁo:pa]
Asia	Asien	['æʔɕən]
Africa	Afrika	['afʁika]
Australia	Australien	[aw'stʁɑʔljən]

America	Amerika	[ɑ'meʁika]
North America	Nordamerika	['noɡ ɑ'meʁika]
South America	Sydamerika	['syð ɑ'meʁika]

Antarctica	**Antarktis**	[an'tɑˀktis]
the Arctic	**Arktis**	['ɑˀktis]

76. Cardinal directions

north	**nord** (i)	['noˀɡ]
to the north	**mod nord**	[moð 'noˀɡ]
in the north	**i nord**	[i 'noˀɡ]
northern (adj)	**nordlig**	['noɡli]

south	**syd** (f)	['syð]
to the south	**mod syd**	[moð 'syð]
in the south	**i syd**	[i 'syð]
southern (adj)	**sydlig**	['syðli]

west	**vest** (f)	['vɛst]
to the west	**mod vest**	[moð 'vɛst]
in the west	**i vest**	[i 'vɛst]
western (adj)	**vestlig**	['vɛstli]

east	**øst** (f)	['øst]
to the east	**mod øst**	[moð 'øst]
in the east	**i øst**	[i 'øst]
eastern (adj)	**østlig**	['østli]

77. Sea. Ocean

sea	**hav** (i)	['hɑw]
ocean	**ocean** (i)	[osə'æˀn]
gulf (bay)	**bugt** (f)	['bɔgt]
straits	**stræde** (i), **sund** (i)	['stʁɛːðə], ['sɔnˀ]

land (solid ground)	**land** (i)	['lanˀ]
continent (mainland)	**fastland, kontinent** (i)	['fastˌlanˀ], [kʌnti'nɛnˀt]
island	**ø** (f)	['øˀ]
peninsula	**halvø** (f)	['halˌøˀ]
archipelago	**øhav, arkipelag** (i)	['øˌhɑw], [ɑkipe'læˀj]

bay, cove	**bugt** (f)	['bɔgt]
harbor	**havn** (f)	['hɑwˀn]
lagoon	**lagune** (f)	[la'guːnə]
cape	**kap** (i)	['kɑp]

atoll	**atol** (f)	[a'tʌlˀ]
reef	**rev** (i)	['ʁɛw]
coral	**koral** (f)	[ko'ʁalˀ]
coral reef	**koralrev** (i)	[ko'ʁalˌʁɛw]
deep (adj)	**dyb**	['dyˀb]

depth (deep water)	**dybde** (f)	['dybdə]
abyss	**afgrund** (f), **dyb** (i)	['ɑwˌɡʁɔn²], ['dy²b]
trench (e.g., Mariana ~)	**oceangrav** (f)	[osəˌæn 'ɡʁɑ²w]
current (Ocean ~)	**strøm** (f)	['stʁœm²]
to surround (bathe)	**at omgive**	[ʌ 'ʌmˌgi²]
shore	**kyst** (f)	['køst]
coast	**kyst** (f)	['køst]
flow (flood tide)	**flod** (f)	['flo²ð]
ebb (ebb tide)	**ebbe** (i)	['ɛbə]
shoal	**sandbanke** (f)	['sanˌbɑŋkə]
bottom (~ of the sea)	**bund** (f)	['bɔn²]
wave	**bølge** (f)	['bøljə]
crest (~ of a wave)	**bølgekam** (f)	['bøljəˌkam²]
spume (sea foam)	**skum** (i)	['skɔm²]
storm (sea storm)	**storm** (f)	['stɑ²m]
hurricane	**orkan** (f)	[ɒ'kæ²n]
tsunami	**tsunami** (f)	[tsu'nɑ:mi]
calm (dead ~)	**stille** (i)	['stelə]
quiet, calm (adj)	**stille**	['stelə]
pole	**pol** (f)	['po²l]
polar (adj)	**polar-**	[po'lɑ-]
latitude	**bredde** (f)	['bʁɛ²də]
longitude	**længde** (f)	['lɛŋ²də]
parallel	**breddegrad** (f)	['bʁɛ²dəˌɡʁɑ²ð]
equator	**ækvator** (f)	[ɛ'kvæ:tʌ]
sky	**himmel** (f)	['heməl]
horizon	**horisont** (f)	[hɒi'sʌn²t]
air	**luft** (f)	['lɔft]
lighthouse	**fyr** (i)	['fyɐ̯²]
to dive (vi)	**at dykke**	[ʌ 'døkə]
to sink (ab. boat)	**at synke**	[ʌ 'søŋkə]
treasures	**skatte** (f pl)	['skatə]

78. Seas' and Oceans' names

Atlantic Ocean	**Atlanterhavet**	[at'lan²tʌˌhæ²vəð]
Indian Ocean	**Det Indiske Ocean**	[de 'en²diskə osə'æ²n]
Pacific Ocean	**Stillehavet**	['stelǝˌhæ²vəð]
Arctic Ocean	**Polarhavet**	[po'lɑˌhæ²vəð]
Black Sea	**Sortehavet**	['soɐ̯təˌhæ²vəð]
Red Sea	**Rødehavet**	['ʁœ:ðəˌhæ²vəð]

| Yellow Sea | Det Gule hav | [de 'gulə 'hɑw] |
| White Sea | Hvidehavet | ['vi:ðəˌhæˀvəð] |

Caspian Sea	Det Kaspiske Hav	[de 'kaspi:skə 'hɑw]
Dead Sea	Dødehavet	['dø:ðəˌhæˀvəð]
Mediterranean Sea	Middelhavet	['miðəlˌhæˀvəð]

| Aegean Sea | Ægæerhavet | [ɛ'gɛˀɛʌ 'hæˀvəð] |
| Adriatic Sea | Adriaterhavet | [æˀdʁi'æˀtʌ 'hæˀvəð] |

Arabian Sea	Arabiahavet	[ɑ'ʁɑˀbia 'hæˀvəð]
Sea of Japan	Det Japanske Hav	[de ja'pæˀnskə 'hɑw]
Bering Sea	Beringshavet	['be:ʁeŋsˌhæˀvəð]
South China Sea	Det Sydkinesiske Hav	[de 'syðkiˌne:siskə 'hɑw]

Coral Sea	Koralhavet	[ko'ʁalˌhæˀvəð]
Tasman Sea	Det Tasmanske hav	[de tas'manskə 'hɑw]
Caribbean Sea	Det Caribiske Hav	[de kɑ'ʁibiskə ˌhɑw]

| Barents Sea | Barentshavet | ['bɑːæntsˌhæˀvəð] |
| Kara Sea | Karahavet | ['kɑɑˌhæˀvəð] |

North Sea	Nordsøen	['noʁˌsøˀən]
Baltic Sea	Østersøen	['østʌˌsøˀən]
Norwegian Sea	Norskehavet	['nɒ:skəˌhæˀvəð]

79. Mountains

mountain	bjerg (i)	['bjæɡˀw]
mountain range	bjergkæde (f)	['bjæɡwˌkɛ:ðə]
mountain ridge	bjergryg (f)	['bjæɡwˌʁœg]

summit, top	top (f), bjergtop (f)	['tʌp], ['bjæɡwˌtʌp]
peak	tinde (f)	['tenə]
foot (~ of the mountain)	fod (f)	['fo'ð]
slope (mountainside)	skråning (f)	['skʁɔˀneŋ]

volcano	vulkan (f)	[vul'kæˀn]
active volcano	aktiv vulkan (f)	['akˌtiwˀ vul'kæˀn]
dormant volcano	udslukt vulkan (f)	['uðˌslɔkt vul'kæˀn]

eruption	udbrud (i)	['uðˌbʁuð]
crater	krater (i)	['kʁɑˀtʌ]
magma	magma (i, f)	['mɑwma]
lava	lava (f)	['læ:va]
molten (~ lava)	glødende	['glø:ðənə]

canyon	canyon (f)	['kanjʌn]
gorge	kløft (f)	['kløft]
crevice	revne (f)	['ʁawnə]

abyss (chasm)	afgrund (f)	['ɑwˌɡʁɔnˀ]
pass, col	pas (i)	['pas]
plateau	plateau (i)	[pla'to]
cliff	klippe (f)	['klepə]
hill	bakke (f)	['bɑkə]

glacier	gletsjer (f)	['glɛtɕʌ]
waterfall	vandfald (i)	['vanˌfalˀ]
geyser	gejser (f)	['gɑjˀsʌ]
lake	sø (f)	['søˀ]

plain	slette (f)	['slɛtə]
landscape	landskab (i)	['lanˌskæˀb]
echo	ekko (i)	['ɛko]

alpinist	alpinist (f)	[alpi'nist]
rock climber	bjergbestiger (f)	['bjæɡwbe'stiˀə]
to conquer (in climbing)	at erobre	[ʌ e'ʁoˀbʁʌ]
climb (an easy ~)	bestigning (f)	[be'stiˀnen]

80. Mountains names

The Alps	Alperne	['alpɒnə]
Mont Blanc	Mont Blanc	[ˌmɒn'blʌn]
The Pyrenees	Pyrenæerne	[pyɡˀnɛːɡnə]

The Carpathians	Karpaterne	[kɑ:'pætɒnə]
The Ural Mountains	Uralbjergene	[u:'ʁæˀl 'bjæɡˀwənə]
The Caucasus Mountains	Kaukasus	['kɑukasus]
Mount Elbrus	Elbrus	[ɛl'bʁu:s]

The Altai Mountains	Altaj	[al'tɑj]
The Tian Shan	Tien-Shan	[ti'enˌɕæn]
The Pamir Mountains	Pamir	[pæ'miɡˀ]
The Himalayas	Himalaya	[hima'lɑja]
Mount Everest	Everest	['ɛ:vʁɛst]

The Andes	Andesbjergene	['anəs 'bjæɡˀwənə]
Mount Kilimanjaro	Kilimanjaro	[kiliman'dʒaʁo:]

81. Rivers

river	flod (f)	['floˀð]
spring (natural source)	kilde (f)	['kilə]
riverbed (river channel)	flodseng (f)	['floðˌsɛŋˀ]
basin (river valley)	flodbassin (i)	['floð ba'sɛŋ]
to flow into ...	at munde ud ...	[ʌ 'mɔnə uðˀ ...]
tributary	biflod (f)	['biˌfloˀð]

bank (of river)	**bred** (f)	['bʁɛð']
current (stream)	**strøm** (f)	['stʁœmˀ]
downstream (adv)	**nedstrøms**	['neð,stʁœmˀs]
upstream (adv)	**opstrøms**	['ʌp,stʁœmˀs]
inundation	**oversvømmelse** (f)	['ɒwʌ,svœmˀəlsə]
flooding	**flom** (f)	['flʌmˀ]
to overflow (vi)	**at flyde over**	[ʌ 'fly:ðə 'ɒwˀʌ]
to flood (vt)	**at oversvømme**	[ʌ 'ɒwʌ,svœmˀə]
shallow (shoal)	**grund** (f)	['gʁɔnˀ]
rapids	**strømfald** (i)	['stʁœm,falˀ]
dam	**dæmning** (f)	['dɛmneŋ]
canal	**kanal** (f)	[ka'næˀl]
reservoir (artificial lake)	**reservoir** (i)	[ʁɛsæɐ̯vo'ɑ:]
sluice, lock	**sluse** (f)	['slu:sə]
water body (pond, etc.)	**vandområde** (i)	['van 'ʌm,ʁɔ:ðə]
swamp (marshland)	**sump, mose** (f)	['sɔmˀp], ['mo:sə]
bog, marsh	**hængesæk** (f)	['hɛŋə,sɛk]
whirlpool	**strømhvirvel** (f)	['stʁœm,viɐ̯ˀwəl]
stream (brook)	**bæk** (f)	['bɛk]
drinking (ab. water)	**drikke-**	['dʁɛkə-]
fresh (~ water)	**ferske**	['fæɐ̯skə]
ice	**is** (f)	['iˀs]
to freeze over	**at fryse til**	[ʌ 'fʁy:sə tel]
(ab. river, etc.)		

82. Rivers' names

Seine	**Seinen**	['sɛ:nən]
Loire	**Loire**	[lu'ɒ:ʁ]
Thames	**Themsen**	['tɛmsən]
Rhine	**Rhinen**	['ʁi:nən]
Danube	**Donau**	[do'nɑu]
Volga	**Volga**	['vɔlga]
Don	**Don**	['dɔn]
Lena	**Lena**	['le:na]
Yellow River	**Huang He**	[hu,ang'he:]
Yangtze	**Yangtze**	['jɑŋtsə]
Mekong	**Mekong**	[me'kɒŋ]
Ganges	**Ganges**	['gɑ:ŋəs]
Nile River	**Nilen**	['ni:lən]
Congo River	**Congo**	['kʌngo]

Okavango River	**Okavango**	[ɔka'vɑngo]
Zambezi River	**Zambezi**	[sɑm'bɛsi]
Limpopo River	**Limpopo**	[li:mpopo]
Mississippi River	**Mississippi**	['misisi:pi]

83. Forest

| forest, wood | **skov** (f) | ['skɒwˀ] |
| forest (as adj) | **skov-** | ['skɒw-] |

thick forest	**tæt skov** (f)	['tɛt ˌskɒwˀ]
grove	**lund** (f)	['lɔnˀ]
forest clearing	**lysning** (f)	['lysnen]

| thicket | **tæt krat** (i) | ['tɛt 'kʁɑt] |
| scrubland | **buskads** (i) | [bu'skæˀs] |

| footpath (troddenpath) | **sti** (f) | ['stiˀ] |
| gully | **ravine** (f) | [ʁɑ'vi:nə] |

tree	**træ** (i)	['tʁɛˀ]
leaf	**blad** (i)	['blað]
leaves (foliage)	**løv** (i)	['løˀw]

fall of leaves	**løvfald** (i)	['løwˌfalˀ]
to fall (ab. leaves)	**at falde**	[ʌ 'falə]
top (of the tree)	**trætop** (f)	['tʁɛˌtʌp]

branch	**kvist** (f)	['kvest]
bough	**gren** (f)	['gʁɛˀn]
bud (on shrub, tree)	**knop** (f)	['knɔp]
needle (of pine tree)	**nål** (f)	['nɔˀl]
pine cone	**kogle** (f)	['kɒwlə]

hollow (in a tree)	**træhul** (i)	['tʁɛˌhɔl]
nest	**rede** (f)	['ʁɛːðə]
burrow (animal hole)	**hule** (f)	['hu:lə]

trunk	**stamme** (f)	['stɑmə]
root	**rod** (f)	['ʁoˀð]
bark	**bark** (f)	['bɑːk]
moss	**mos** (i)	['mɔs]

to uproot (remove trees or tree stumps)	**at rykke op med rode**	[ʌ 'ʁœkə ʌp mɛ 'ʁoːðə]
to chop down	**at fælde**	[ʌ 'fɛlə]
to deforest (vt)	**at hugge ned**	[ʌ 'hɔgə 'neðˀ]
tree stump	**træstub** (f)	['tʁɛˌstub]
campfire	**bål** (i)	['bɔˀl]
forest fire	**skovbrand** (f)	['skɒwˌbʁɑnˀ]

to extinguish (vt)	at slukke	[ʌ 'slɔkə]
forest ranger	skovløber (f)	['skɒwˌløːbʌ]
protection	værn (i), beskyttelse (f)	['væɡʼn], [be'skøtəlsə]
to protect (~ nature)	at beskytte	[ʌ be'skøtə]
poacher	krybskytte (f)	['kʁybˌskøtə]
steel trap	saks (f), fælde (f)	['sɑks], ['fɛlə]

| to gather, to pick (vt) | at plukke | [ʌ 'plɔkə] |
| to lose one's way | at fare vild | [ʌ 'faːɑ 'vilʼ] |

84. Natural resources

natural resources	naturressourcer (f pl)	[na'tuɡ ʁɛ'suɡsʌ]
minerals	mineraler (i pl)	[minə'ʁɑʼlʌ]
deposits	forekomster (f pl)	['fɒːɒˌkʌmʼstʌ]
field (e.g., oilfield)	felt (i)	['fɛlʼt]

to mine (extract)	at udvinde	[ʌ 'uðˌvenʼə]
mining (extraction)	udvinding (f)	['uðˌvenɛŋ]
ore	malm (f)	['malʼm]
mine (e.g., for coal)	mine (f)	['miːnə]
shaft (mine ~)	mineskakt (f)	['minəˌskɑkt]
miner	minearbejder (f)	['miːnəʼɑːˌbɑjʼdʌ]

| gas (natural ~) | gas (f) | ['gas] |
| gas pipeline | gasledning (f) | ['gasˌleðnɛŋ] |

oil (petroleum)	olie (f)	['oljə]
oil pipeline	olieledning (f)	['oljəˌleðnɛŋ]
oil well	oliebrønd (f)	['oljəˌbʁœnʼ]
derrick (tower)	boretårn (i)	['boːʌˌtɒʼn]
tanker	tankskib (i)	['tɑŋkˌskiʼb]

sand	sand (i)	['sanʼ]
limestone	kalksten (f)	['kalkˌsteʼn]
gravel	grus (i)	['gʁuʼs]
peat	tørv (f)	['tœɡʼw]
clay	ler (i)	['leʼɡ]
coal	kul (i)	['kɔl]

iron (ore)	jern (i)	['jæɡʼn]
gold	guld (i)	['gul]
silver	sølv (i)	['søl]
nickel	nikkel (i)	['nekəl]
copper	kobber (i)	['kɒwʼʌ]

zinc	zink (i, f)	['senʼk]
manganese	mangan (i)	[mɑŋ'gæʼn]
mercury	kviksølv (i)	['kvikˌsøl]
lead	bly (i)	['blyʼ]

mineral	mineral (i)	[minə'ʁɑˀl]
crystal	krystal (i, f)	[kʁy'stalˀ]
marble	marmor (i)	['mɑˀmoɐ̯]
uranium	uran (i, f)	[u'ʁɑˀn]

85. Weather

weather	vejr (i)	['vɛˀɐ̯]
weather forecast	vejrudsigt (f)	['vɛɐ̯ˌuðsegt]
temperature	temperatur (f)	[tɛmpʁɑ'tuɐ̯ˀ]
thermometer	termometer (i)	[tæɐ̯mo'meˀtʌ]
barometer	barometer (i)	[bɑo'meˀtʌ]

humid (adj)	fugtig	['fɔgti]
humidity	fugtighed (f)	['fɔgtiˌheð]
heat (extreme ~)	hede (f)	['he:ðə]
hot (torrid)	hed	['heðˀ]
it's hot	det er hedt	[de 'æɐ̯ 'heðˀ]

it's warm	det er varmt	[de 'æɐ̯ 'vɑˀmt]
warm (moderately hot)	varm	['vɑˀm]
it's cold	det er koldt	[de 'æɐ̯ 'kʌlt]
cold (adj)	kold	['kʌlˀ]

sun	sol (f)	['soˀl]
to shine (vi)	at skinne	[ʌ 'skenə]
sunny (day)	solrig	['soːlˌʁiˀ]
to come up (vi)	at stå op	[ʌ stɔˀ 'ʌp]
to set (vi)	at gå ned	[ʌ gɔˀ 'neðˀ]

cloud	sky (f)	['skyˀ]
cloudy (adj)	skyet	['sky:əð]
rain cloud	regnsky (f)	['ʁajnˌskyˀ]
somber (gloomy)	mørk	['mœɐ̯k]

rain	regn (f)	['ʁajˀn]
it's raining	det regner	[de 'ʁajnʌ]
rainy (~ day, weather)	regnvejrs-	['ʁajnˌvɛɐ̯s-]
to drizzle (vi)	at småregne	[ʌ 'smɒʁajnə]

pouring rain	øsende regn (f)	['øːsənə ˌʁajˀn]
downpour	styrtregn (f)	['styɐ̯tˌʁajˀn]
heavy (e.g., ~ rain)	kraftig, heftig	['kʁɑfti], ['hɛfti]
puddle	vandpyt (f)	['vanˌpyt]
to get wet (in rain)	at blive våd	[ʌ 'bliːə 'vɔˀð]

fog (mist)	tåge (f)	['tɔːwə]
foggy	tåget	['tɔːwəð]
snow	sne (f)	['sneˀ]
it's snowing	det sner	[de 'sneˀʌ]

86. Severe weather. Natural disasters

thunderstorm	tordenvejr (i)	['toɡdən,vɛ'ɡ]
lightning (~ strike)	lyn (i)	['ly'n]
to flash (vi)	at glimte	[ʌ 'glemtə]
thunder	torden (f)	['toɡdən]
to thunder (vi)	at tordne	[ʌ 'toɡdnə]
it's thundering	det tordner	[de 'toɡdnʌ]
hail	hagl (i)	['hɑw'l]
it's hailing	det hagler	[de 'hɑwlɡ]
to flood (vt)	at oversvømme	[ʌ 'ɒwʌ,svɑem'ə]
flood, inundation	oversvømmelse (f)	['ɒwʌ,svɑem'əlsə]
earthquake	jordskælv (i)	['joɡ,skɛl'v]
tremor, quake	skælv (i)	['skɛl'v]
epicenter	epicenter (i)	[epi'sɛn'tʌ]
eruption	udbrud (i)	['uð,bʁuð]
lava	lava (f)	['læ:va]
twister	skypumpe (f)	['sky,pɒmpə]
tornado	tornado (f)	[tɒ'næ:do]
typhoon	tyfon (f)	[ty'fo'n]
hurricane	orkan (f)	[ɒ'kæ'n]
storm	storm (f)	['stɒ'm]
tsunami	tsunami (f)	[tsu'nɑ:mi]
cyclone	cyklon (f)	[sy'klo'n]
bad weather	uvejr (i)	['u,vɛ'ɡ]
fire (accident)	brand (f)	['bʁɑn']
disaster	katastrofe (f)	[kata'stʁo:fə]
meteorite	meteorit (f)	[meteo'ʁit]
avalanche	lavine (f)	[la'vi:nə]
snowslide	sneskred (i)	['sne,skʁɛð]
blizzard	snefog (i)	['sne,fow']
snowstorm	snestorm (f)	['sne,stɒ'm]

T&P BOOKS

FAUNA

T&P Books Publishing

predator	**rovdyr** (i)	['ʁɒwˌdyɐ̯ˀ]
tiger	**tiger** (f)	['tiːʌ]
lion	**løve** (f)	['løːvə]
wolf	**ulv** (f)	['ulˀv]
fox	**ræv** (f)	['ʁɛˀw]
jaguar	**jaguar** (f)	[jaguˈɑˀ]
leopard	**leopard** (f)	[leoˈpɑˀd]
cheetah	**gepard** (f)	[geˈpɑˀd]
black panther	**panter** (f)	['panˀtʌ]
puma	**puma** (f)	['puːma]
snow leopard	**sneleopard** (f)	['sne leoˈpɑˀd]
lynx	**los** (f)	['lʌs]
coyote	**coyote, prærieulv** (f)	[koˈjoːtə], ['pʁɛ̞ʁjəˌulˀv]
jackal	**sjakal** (f)	[ɕaˈkæˀl]
hyena	**hyæne** (f)	[hyˈɛːnə]

animal	**dyr** (i)	['dyɐ̯ˀ]
beast (animal)	**bæst** (i), **udyr** (i)	['bɛˀst], ['uˌdyɐ̯ˀ]
squirrel	**egern** (i)	['eˀjʌn]
hedgehog	**pindsvin** (i)	['penˌsviˀn]
hare	**hare** (f)	['haːɑ]
rabbit	**kanin** (f)	[kaˈniˀn]
badger	**grævling** (f)	['gʁawleŋ]
raccoon	**vaskebjørn** (f)	['vaskəˌbjœɡ̊ˀn]
hamster	**hamster** (f)	['hamˀstʌ]
marmot	**murmeldyr** (i)	['muɐ̯ˀməlˌdyɐ̯ˀ]
mole	**muldvarp** (f)	['mulˌvaːp]
mouse	**mus** (f)	['muˀs]
rat	**rotte** (f)	['ʁʌtə]
bat	**flagermus** (f)	['flawʌˌmuˀs]
ermine	**hermelin** (f)	[hæɡ̊məˈliˀn]
sable	**zobel** (f)	['soˀbəl]
marten	**mår** (f)	['mɒˀ]

| weasel | brud (f) | ['bʁuð] |
| mink | mink (f) | ['meŋˀk] |

| beaver | bæver (f) | ['bɛˀvʌ] |
| otter | odder (f) | ['ʌðˀʌ] |

horse	hest (f)	['hɛst]
moose	elg (f)	['ɛlˀj]
deer	hjort (f)	['jɔ:t]
camel	kamel (f)	[ka'meˀl]

bison	bison (f)	['bisʌn]
aurochs	urokse (f)	['uʁˌʌksə]
buffalo	bøffel (f)	['bøfəl]

zebra	zebra (f)	['se:bʁɑ]
antelope	antilope (f)	[anti'lo:pə]
roe deer	rådyr (i), rå (f)	['ʁʌˌdyɡ̊ˀ], ['ʁɔˀ]
fallow deer	dådyr (i)	['dʌˌdyɡ̊ˀ]
chamois	gemse (f)	['gɛmsə]
wild boar	vildsvin (i)	['vilˌsviˀn]

whale	hval (f)	['væˀl]
seal	sæl (f)	['sɛˀl]
walrus	hvalros (f)	['valˌʁʌs]
fur seal	pelssæl (f)	['pɛlsˌsɛˀl]
dolphin	delfin (f)	[dɛl'fiˀn]

bear	bjørn (f)	['bjœɡ̊ˀn]
polar bear	isbjørn (f)	['isˌbjœɡ̊ˀn]
panda	panda (f)	['panda]

monkey	abe (f)	['æ:bə]
chimpanzee	chimpanse (f)	[ɕim'pansə]
orangutan	orangutang (f)	[o'ʁɑŋguˌtaŋˀ]
gorilla	gorilla (f)	[go'ʁila]
macaque	makak (f)	[mæ'kɑk]
gibbon	gibbon (f)	['gibʌn]

| elephant | elefant (f) | [elə'fanˀt] |
| rhinoceros | næsehorn (i) | ['nɛ:səˌhoɡ̊ˀn] |

| giraffe | giraf (f) | [gi'ʁɑf] |
| hippopotamus | flodhest (f) | ['floðˌhɛst] |

| kangaroo | kænguru (f) | [kɛŋgu:ʁu] |
| koala (bear) | koala (f) | [ko'æ:la] |

mongoose	mangust (f)	[mɑŋ'gust]
chinchilla	chinchilla (f)	[tjen'tjila]
skunk	skunk (f)	['skɔŋˀk]
porcupine	hulepindsvin (i)	['hu:lə 'penˌsviˀn]

89. Domestic animals

cat	kat (f)	['kat]
tomcat	hankat (f)	['han‚kat]
dog	hund (f)	['hunˀ]

horse	hest (f)	['hɛst]
stallion (male horse)	hingst (f)	['heŋˀst]
mare	hoppe (f)	['hʌpə]

cow	ko (f)	['koˀ]
bull	tyr (f)	['tyɡ̊ˀ]
ox	okse (f)	['ʌksə]

sheep (ewe)	får (i)	['fɑ:]
ram	vædder (f)	['vɛðˀʌ]
goat	ged (f)	['geðˀ]
billy goat, he-goat	gedebuk (f)	['ge:ðə‚bɔk]

donkey	æsel (i)	['ɛˀsəl]
mule	muldyr (i)	['mul‚dyɡ̊ˀ]

pig, hog	svin (i)	['sviˀn]
piglet	gris (f)	['gʁiˀs]
rabbit	kanin (f)	[ka'niˀn]

hen (chicken)	høne (f)	['hœ:nə]
rooster	hane (f)	['hæ:nə]

duck	and (f)	['anˀ]
drake	andrik (f)	['anˀdʁɛk]
goose	gås (f)	['gɔˀs]

tom turkey, gobbler	kalkun hane (f)	[kal'kuˀn 'hæ:nə]
turkey (hen)	kalkun (f)	[kal'kuˀn]

domestic animals	husdyr (i pl)	['hus‚dyɡ̊ˀ]
tame (e.g., ~ hamster)	tam	['tɑmˀ]
to tame (vt)	at tæmme	[ʌ 'tɛmə]
to breed (vt)	at avle, at opdrætte	[ʌ 'awlə], [ʌ 'ʌp‚dʁatə]

farm	farm (f)	['fɑˀm]
poultry	fjerkræ (i)	['fjeɡ̊‚kʁɛˀ]
cattle	kvæg (i)	['kvɛˀj]
herd (cattle)	hjord (f)	['jɒˀd]

stable	stald (f)	['stalˀ]
pigpen	svinesti (f)	['svinə‚stiˀ]
cowshed	kostald (f)	['ko‚stalˀ]
rabbit hutch	kaninbur (i)	[ka'nin‚buɡ̊ˀ]
hen house	hønsehus (i)	['hœnsə‚huˀs]

90. Birds

bird	fugl (f)	['fuˀl]
pigeon	due (f)	['du:ə]
sparrow	spurv (f)	['spuɐ̯ˀw]
tit (great tit)	musvit (f)	[mu'svit]
magpie	skade (f)	['skæ:ðə]

raven	ravn (f)	['ʁawˀn]
crow	krage (f)	['kʁɑ:wə]
jackdaw	kaie (f)	['kɑjə]
rook	råge (f)	['ʁɔ:wə]

duck	and (f)	['anˀ]
goose	gås (f)	['gɔˀs]
pheasant	fasan (f)	[fa'sæˀn]

eagle	ørn (f)	['œɐ̯ˀn]
hawk	høg (f)	['høˀj]
falcon	falk (f)	['falˀk]
vulture	grib (f)	['gʁiːb]
condor (Andean ~)	kondor (f)	[kʌn'doˀɐ̯]

swan	svane (f)	['svæ:nə]
crane	trane (f)	['tʁɑ:nə]
stork	stork (f)	['stɒːk]

parrot	papegøje (f)	[papə'gʌjə]
hummingbird	kolibri (f)	[koli'bʁiˀ]
peacock	påfugl (f)	['pʌˌfuˀl]

ostrich	struds (f)	['stʁus]
heron	hejre (f)	['hɑjʁʌ]
flamingo	flamingo (f)	[fla'meŋgo]
pelican	pelikan (f)	[peli'kæˀn]

nightingale	nattergal (f)	['natʌˌgæˀl]
swallow	svale (f)	['svæ:lə]

thrush	drossel, sjagger (f)	['dʁʌsəl], ['ɕagʌ]
song thrush	sangdrossel (f)	['saŋˌdʁʌsəl]
blackbird	solsort (f)	['soːlˌsoɐ̯t]

swift	mursejler (f)	['muɐ̯ˌsɑjlʌ]
lark	lærke (f)	['læɐ̯kə]
quail	vagtel (f)	['vagtəl]

woodpecker	spætte (f)	['spɛtə]
cuckoo	gøg (f)	['gøˀj]
owl	ugle (f)	['u:lə]
eagle owl	hornugle (f)	['hoɐ̯nˌu:lə]

wood grouse	tjur (f)	['tjuɐˀ]
black grouse	urfugl (f)	['uɐˌfuˀl]
partridge	agerhøne (f)	['æˀjʌˌhœːnə]

starling	stær (f)	['stɛˀɐ̯]
canary	kanariefugl (f)	[ka'naˀjəˌfuˀl]
hazel grouse	hjerpe, jærpe (f)	['jæɐ̯pə]
chaffinch	bogfinke (f)	['bɔwˌfeŋkə]
bullfinch	dompap (f)	['dɔmˌpap]

seagull	måge (f)	['mɔːwə]
albatross	albatros (f)	['albaˌtʁʌs]
penguin	pingvin (f)	[peŋ'viˀn]

91. Fish. Marine animals

bream	brasen (f)	['bʁɑˀsən]
carp	karpe (f)	['kɑːpə]
perch	aborre (f)	['aˌbɒːɒ]
catfish	malle (f)	['malə]
pike	gedde (f)	['geðə]

| salmon | laks (f) | ['laks] |
| sturgeon | stør (f) | ['støˀɐ̯] |

herring	sild (f)	['silˀ]
Atlantic salmon	atlantisk laks (f)	[at'lanˀtisk 'laks]
mackerel	makrel (f)	[ma'kʁalˀ]
flatfish	rødspætte (f)	['ʁœðˌspɛtə]

zander, pike perch	sandart (f)	['sanˌaˀt]
cod	torsk (f)	['tɒːsk]
tuna	tunfisk (f)	['tuːnˌfesk]
trout	ørred (f)	['œɐ̯ʌð]

eel	ål (f)	['ɔˀl]
electric ray	elektrisk rokke (f)	[e'lɛktʁisk 'ʁʌkə]
moray eel	muræne (f)	[mu'ʁɛːnə]
piranha	piraya (f)	[pi'ʁaja]

shark	haj (f)	['hajˀ]
dolphin	delfin (f)	[dɛl'fiˀn]
whale	hval (f)	['væˀl]

crab	krabbe (f)	['kʁabə]
jellyfish	gople, meduse (f)	['gʌplə], [me'duːsə]
octopus	blæksprutte (f)	['blɛkˌspʁutə]

| starfish | søstjerne (f) | ['søˌstjæɐ̯nə] |
| sea urchin | søpindsvin (i) | ['sø 'penˌsviˀn] |

seahorse	søhest (f)	['sø‚hɛst]
oyster	østers (f)	['østʌs]
shrimp	reje (f)	['ʁajə]
lobster	hummer (f)	['hom'ʌ]
spiny lobster	languster (f)	[laŋ'gustʌ]

92. Amphibians. Reptiles

snake	slange (f)	['slaŋə]
venomous (snake)	giftig	['gifti]

viper	hugorm (f)	['hɔg‚oɡ'm]
cobra	kobra (f)	['koːbʁa]
python	pyton (f)	['pytʌn]
boa	boa (f)	['boːa]

grass snake	snog (f)	['snoʔ]
rattle snake	klapperslange (f)	['klapʌ‚slaŋə]
anaconda	anakonda (f)	[ana'kʌnda]

lizard	firben (i)	['fiɡ'be'n]
iguana	leguan (f)	[legu'æ'n]
monitor lizard	varan (f)	[vɑ'ʁɑ'n]
salamander	salamander (f)	[sala'man'dʌ]
chameleon	kamæleon (f)	[kamələ'o'n]
scorpion	skorpion (f)	[skɒpi'o'n]

turtle	skildpadde (f)	['skel‚paðə]
frog	frø (f)	['fʁœ']
toad	tudse (f)	['tusə]
crocodile	krokodille (f)	[kʁokə'dilə]

93. Insects

insect, bug	insekt (i)	[en'sɛkt]
butterfly	sommerfugl (f)	['sʌmʌ‚fu'l]
ant	myre (f)	['myːʌ]
fly	flue (f)	['fluːə]
mosquito	stikmyg (f)	['stek‚myg]
beetle	bille (f)	['bilə]

wasp	hveps (f)	['vɛps]
bee	bi (f)	['bi']
bumblebee	humlebi (f)	['hɔmlə‚bi']
gadfly (botfly)	bremse (f)	['bʁamsə]

spider	edderkop (f)	['ɛð'ʌ‚kʌp]
spiderweb	edderkoppespind (i)	['ɛð'ʌkʌpə‚sben']

dragonfly	**guldsmed** (f)	['gulˌsmeð]
grasshopper	**græshoppe** (f)	['gʁasˌhʌpə]
moth (night butterfly)	**natsværmer** (f)	['natˌsvæɡˀmʌ]
cockroach	**kakerlak** (f)	[kakʌ'lak]
tick	**flåt, mide** (f)	['flɔˀt], ['mi:ðə]
flea	**loppe** (f)	['lʌpə]
midge	**kvægmyg** (f)	['kvɛjˌmyg]
locust	**vandregræshoppe** (f)	['vandʁʌ 'gʁasˌhʌpə]
snail	**snegl** (f)	['snajˀl]
cricket	**fårekylling** (f)	['fɔ:ɒˌkyleŋ]
lightning bug	**ildflue** (f)	['ilflu:ə]
ladybug	**mariehøne** (f)	[ma'ʁiˀəˌhœ:nə]
cockchafer	**oldenborre** (f)	['ʌlənˌbɒ:ɒ]
leech	**igle** (f)	['i:lə]
caterpillar	**sommerfuglelarve** (f)	['sʌmʌˌfu:lə 'la:və]
earthworm	**regnorm** (f)	['ʁajnˌoɡˀm]
larva	**larve** (f)	['la:və]

T&P BOOKS

FLORA

T&P Books Publishing

tree	**træ** (i)	['tʁɛˀ]
deciduous (adj)	**løv-**	['løw-]
coniferous (adj)	**nåle-**	['nɔlə-]
evergreen (adj)	**stedsegrønt,** **eviggrønt**	['stɛðsəˌgʁœnˀt], ['eːviˌgʁœnˀt]
apple tree	**æbletræ** (i)	['ɛˀbləˌtʁɛˀ]
pear tree	**pæretræ** (i)	['pɛʌˌtʁɛˀ]
sweet cherry tree	**moreltræ** (i)	[moˈʁalˌtʁɛˀ]
sour cherry tree	**kirsebærtræ** (i)	['kiɐ̯səbæɐ̯ˌtʁɛˀ]
plum tree	**blommetræ** (i)	['blʌməˌtʁɛˀ]
birch	**birk** (f)	['biɐ̯k]
oak	**eg** (f)	['eˀj]
linden tree	**lind** (f)	['lenˀ]
aspen	**asp** (f)	['asp]
maple	**løn** (f), **ahorn** (f)	['lœnˀ], ['aˌhoɐ̯ˀn]
spruce	**gran** (f)	['gʁan]
pine	**fyr** (f)	['fyɐ̯ˀ]
larch	**lærk** (f)	['læɐ̯k]
fir tree	**ædelgran** (f)	['ɛˀðəlˌgʁan]
cedar	**ceder** (f)	['seːðʌ]
poplar	**poppel** (f)	['pʌpəl]
rowan	**røn** (f)	['ʁœnˀ]
willow	**pil** (f)	['piˀl]
alder	**el** (f)	['ɛl]
beech	**bøg** (f)	['bøˀj]
elm	**elm** (f)	['ɛlˀm]
ash (tree)	**ask** (f)	['ask]
chestnut	**kastanie** (i)	[kaˈstanjə]
magnolia	**magnolie** (f)	[mɑwˈnoˀljə]
palm tree	**palme** (f)	['palmə]
cypress	**cypres** (f)	[syˈpʁas]
mangrove	**mangrove** (f)	[maŋˈgʁoːvə]
baobab	**baobabtræ** (i)	[bɑoˈbabˌtʁɛˀ]
eucalyptus	**eukalyptus** (f)	[œwkaˈlyptus]
sequoia	**sequoia** (f), **rødtræ** (i)	[sekˈwojə], ['ʁœðˌtʁɛˀ]

95. Shrubs

| bush | busk (f) | ['busk] |
| shrub | buskads (i) | [bu'skæˀs] |

| grapevine | vinranke (f) | ['viːnˌʁɑŋkə] |
| vineyard | vingård (f) | ['viːnˌgɒˀ] |

raspberry bush	hindbærbusk (f)	['henbæɐ̯ˌbusk]
blackcurrant bush	solbærbusk (f)	['soːlbæɐ̯ˌbusk]
redcurrant bush	ribsbusk (f)	['ʁɛbsˌbusk]
gooseberry bush	stikkelsbær (i)	['stekəlsˌbæɐ̯]

acacia	akacie (f)	[a'kæˀɕə]
barberry	berberis (f)	['bæɐ̯ˀbʌʁis]
jasmine	jasmin (f)	[ɕas'miˀn]

juniper	ene (f)	['eːnə]
rosebush	rosenbusk (f)	['ʁoːsənˌbusk]
dog rose	Hunde-Rose (f)	['hunə-'ʁoːsə]

96. Fruits. Berries

fruit	frugt (f)	['fʁɔgt]
fruits	frugter (f pl)	['fʁɔgtʌ]
apple	æble (i)	['ɛˀblə]
pear	pære (f)	['pɛˀʌ]
plum	blomme (f)	['blʌmə]

strawberry (garden ~)	jordbær (i)	['joɐ̯ˌbæɐ̯]
sour cherry	kirsebær (i)	['kiɐ̯səˌbæɐ̯]
sweet cherry	morel (f)	[mo'ʁalˀ]
grape	drue (f)	['dʁuːə]

raspberry	hindbær (i)	['henˌbæɐ̯]
blackcurrant	solbær (i)	['soːlˌbæɐ̯]
redcurrant	ribs (i, f)	['ʁɛbs]
gooseberry	stikkelsbær (i)	['stekəlsˌbæɐ̯]
cranberry	tranebær (i)	['tʁɑːnəˌbæɐ̯]

orange	appelsin (f)	[ɑpəl'siˀn]
mandarin	mandarin (f)	[mandɑ'ʁiˀn]
pineapple	ananas (f)	['ananas]
banana	banan (f)	[ba'næˀn]
date	daddel (f)	['daðˀəl]

lemon	citron (f)	[si'tʁoˀn]
apricot	abrikos (f)	[ɑbʁi'koˀs]
peach	fersken (f)	['fæɐ̯skən]

| kiwi | **kiwi** (f) | ['ki:vi] |
| grapefruit | **grapefrugt** (f) | ['gʁɛjp‚fʁɔgt] |

berry	**bær** (i)	['bæɐ̯]
berries	**bær** (i pl)	['bæɐ̯]
cowberry	**tyttebær** (i)	['tytə‚bæɐ̯]
wild strawberry	**skovjordbær** (i)	['skɒw 'joɐ̯‚bæɐ̯]
bilberry	**blåbær** (i)	['blɔˀ‚bæɐ̯]

97. Flowers. Plants

| flower | **blomst** (f) | ['blʌmˀst] |
| bouquet (of flowers) | **buket** (f) | [bu'kɛt] |

rose (flower)	**rose** (f)	['ʁo:sə]
tulip	**tulipan** (f)	[tuli'pæˀn]
carnation	**nellike** (f)	['nelˀekə]
gladiolus	**gladiolus** (f)	[gladi'o:lus]

cornflower	**kornblomst** (f)	['koɐ̯n‚blʌmˀst]
harebell	**blåklokke** (f)	['blʌ‚klʌkə]
dandelion	**mælkebøtte, løvetand** (f)	['mɛlkə‚bøtə], ['lø:ve‚tanˀ]
camomile	**kamille** (f)	[ka'milə]

aloe	**aloe** (f)	['æˀlo‚eˀ]
cactus	**kaktus** (f)	['kɑktus]
rubber plant, ficus	**ficus, stuebirk** (f)	['fikus], ['stu:ə‚biɐ̯k]

lily	**lilje** (f)	['liljə]
geranium	**geranie** (f)	[ge'ʁɑˀnjə]
hyacinth	**hyacint** (f)	[hya'senˀt]

mimosa	**mimose** (f)	[mi'mo:sə]
narcissus	**narcis** (f)	[nɑ'si:s]
nasturtium	**blomsterkarse** (f)	['blʌmˀstʌ‚kɑ:sə]

orchid	**orkide, orkidé** (f)	[ɒki'deˀ]
peony	**pæon** (f)	[pɛ'oˀn]
violet	**viol** (f)	[vi'oˀl]

pansy	**stedmoderblomst** (f)	['stɛmoɐ̯ ‚blʌmˀst]
forget-me-not	**forglemmigej** (f)	[fʌ'glɛmˀmɑ‚ɑjˀ]
daisy	**tusindfryd** (f)	['tusən‚fʁyðˀ]

poppy	**valmue** (f)	['val‚mu:ə]
hemp	**hamp** (f)	['hɑmˀp]
mint	**mynte** (f)	['møntə]

| lily of the valley | **liljekonval** (f) | ['liljə kɔn'valˀ] |
| snowdrop | **vintergæk** (f) | ['ventʌ‚gɛk] |

nettle	nælde (f)	['nɛlə]
sorrel	syre (f)	['syːʌ]
water lily	åkande, nøkkerose (f)	['ɔˀkanə], ['nøkəˌʁoːsə]
fern	bregne (f)	['bʁɑjnə]
lichen	lav (f)	['lɑw]

greenhouse (tropical ~)	drivhus (i)	['dʁiwˌhuˀs]
lawn	græsplæne (f)	['gʁasˌplɛːnə]
flowerbed	blomsterbed (i)	['blʌmˀstʌˌbeð]

plant	plante (f)	['plantə]
grass	græs (i)	['gʁas]
blade of grass	græsstrå (i)	['gʁasˌstʁɔˀ]

leaf	blad (i)	['blað]
petal	kronblad (i)	['kɾɔnˌblað]
stem	stilk (f)	['stelˀk]
tuber	rodknold (f)	['ʁoðˌknʌlˀ]

| young plant (shoot) | spire (f) | ['spiːʌ] |
| thorn | torn (f) | ['toɐ̯ˀn] |

to blossom (vi)	at blomstre	[ʌ 'blʌmstʁʌ]
to fade, to wither	at visne	[ʌ 'vesnə]
smell (odor)	lugt (f)	['lɔgt]
to cut (flowers)	at skære af	[ʌ 'skɛːʌ 'æˀ]
to pick (a flower)	at plukke	[ʌ 'plɔkə]

98. Cereals, grains

grain	korn (i)	['koɐ̯ˀn]
cereal crops	kornsorter (f pl)	['koɐ̯nˌsɒːtʌ]
ear (of barley, etc.)	aks (i)	['ɑks]

wheat	hvede (f)	['veːðə]
rye	rug (f)	['ʁuˀ]
oats	havre (f)	['hɑwʁʌ]

| millet | hirse (f) | ['hiɐ̯sə] |
| barley | byg (f) | ['byg] |

corn	majs (f)	['majˀs]
rice	ris (f)	['ʁiˀs]
buckwheat	boghvede (f)	['bɔwˌveːðə]

pea plant	ært (f)	['æɐ̯ˀt]
kidney bean	bønne (f)	['bœnə]
soy	soja (f)	['sʌja]
lentil	linse (f)	['lensə]
beans (pulse crops)	bønner (f pl)	['bœnʌ]

T&P BOOKS

COUNTRIES OF
THE WORLD

T&P Books Publishing

Afghanistan	**Afghanistan**	[aw'gæ'niˌstan]
Albania	**Albanien**	[al'bæ'njən]
Argentina	**Argentina**	[agɛn'ti'na]
Armenia	**Armenien**	[a'me'njən]
Australia	**Australien**	[aw'stʁa'ljən]
Austria	**Østrig**	['østʁi]
Azerbaijan	**Aserbajdsjan**	[asæɐ̯baj'djæ'n]
The Bahamas	**Bahamas**	[ba'ha'mas]
Bangladesh	**Bangladesh**	[bangla'dɛɕ]
Belarus	**Hviderusland**	['vi:ðəˌʁuslan']
Belgium	**Belgien**	['bɛl'gjən]
Bolivia	**Bolivia**	[bo'livia]
Bosnia and Herzegovina	**Bosnien-Herzegovina**	['bosniən hæɐ̯səgo'vi:na]
Brazil	**Brasilien**	[bʁa'siljən]
Bulgaria	**Bulgarien**	[bul'ga:iən]
Cambodia	**Cambodja**	[kæ:m'boða]
Canada	**Canada**	['kanæ'da]
Chile	**Chile** (i)	['tji:lə]
China	**Kina**	['ki:na]
Colombia	**Colombia**	[ko'lɔmbja]
Croatia	**Kroatien**	[kʁo'æ'tiən]
Cuba	**Cuba**	['ku:ba]
Cyprus	**Cypern**	['kypɒn]
Czech Republic	**Tjekkiet**	['tjɛˌkiəð]
Denmark	**Danmark**	['dænmak]
Dominican Republic	**Dominikanske Republik**	[domini'kæ:nskə ʁɛpu'blik]
Ecuador	**Ecuador**	[ekwa'do'ɐ̯]
Egypt	**Egypten**	[ɛ'gyptən]
England	**England**	['ɛŋ'lan]
Estonia	**Estland**	['ɛstlan]
Finland	**Finland**	['fenlan]
France	**Frankrig**	['fʁaŋkʁi]
French Polynesia	**Fransk Polynesien**	['fʁan'sk poly'ne'ɕən]
Georgia	**Georgien**	[ge'ɒ'gjən]
Germany	**Tyskland**	['tysklan']
Ghana	**Ghana**	['ganə]
Great Britain	**Storbritannien**	['stoɐ̯ bʁiˌtaniən]
Greece	**Grækenland**	['gʁɛ:kənlan']
Haiti	**Haiti**	[haiti:]
Hungary	**Ungarn**	['ɔŋga'n]

100. Countries. Part 2

Iceland	**Island**	['islan']
India	**Indien**	['endjən]
Indonesia	**Indonesien**	[endo'ne:ɕən]
Iran	**Iran**	['iʁɑn]
Iraq	**Irak**	['iʁɑk]
Ireland	**Irland**	['iɛlan']
Israel	**Israel**	[isʁɑ:əl]
Italy	**Italien**	[i'tæljən]
Jamaica	**Jamaica**	[ɕa'mɑjka]
Japan	**Japan**	['ja:pæn]
Jordan	**Jordan**	['joɛdan]
Kazakhstan	**Kasakhstan**	[ka'sɑk‚stan]
Kenya	**Kenya**	['kɛnja]
Kirghizia	**Kirgisistan**	[kiɛ'gisi‚stan]
Kuwait	**Kuwait**	[ku'vɑjt]
Laos	**Laos**	['læ:ɒs]
Latvia	**Letland**	['lɛtlan']
Lebanon	**Libanon**	['li:banɒn]
Libya	**Libyen**	['li:bjən]
Liechtenstein	**Liechtenstein**	['li:ktənʃtajn]
Lithuania	**Litauen**	['li‚taw'ən]
Luxembourg	**Luxembourg**	['lygsəm‚bɒ:]
Macedonia (Republic of ~)	**Makedonien**	[mɑkə'do:njən]
Madagascar	**Madagaskar**	[mada'gæskɑ]
Malaysia	**Malaysia**	[ma'lɑjɕiʌ]
Malta	**Malta**	['malta]
Mexico	**Mexiko**	['mɛksiko]
Moldova, Moldavia	**Moldova**	[mʌl'do'va]
Monaco	**Monaco**	[mo'nɑko]
Mongolia	**Mongoliet**	[mʌŋgo'lieð]
Montenegro	**Montenegro**	['mɒntə‚nɛgʁə]
Morocco	**Marokko**	[mɑ'roko]
Myanmar	**Myanmar**	[mjanmɛ]
Namibia	**Namibia**	[na'mibia]
Nepal	**Nepal**	['nepal']
Netherlands	**Nederlandene**	['ne:ðʌ‚lɛnnə]
New Zealand	**New Zealand**	[nju:'si:lan']
North Korea	**Nordkorea**	['noɛ ko'ʁɛ:a]
Norway	**Norge**	['nɒ:w]

101. Countries. Part 3

Pakistan	**Pakistan**	['pɑki‚stan]
Palestine	**Palæstina**	[palə'stinɛnə]

Panama	**Panama**	['panamə]
Paraguay	**Paraguay**	[pɑːɑgˈwʌj]
Peru	**Peru**	[peˈʁuː]
Poland	**Polen**	['poːlæn]
Portugal	**Portugal**	['pɒːtugəl]
Romania	**Rumænien**	[ʁuˈmɛˀnjən]
Russia	**Rusland**	['ʁuslanˀ]
Saudi Arabia	**Saudi-Arabien**	['sawdi ɑˈʁɑːbjən]
Scotland	**Skotland**	['skɒtlanˀ]
Senegal	**Senegal**	[seːnəgæːl]
Serbia	**Serbien**	['sæʁˀbiən]
Slovakia	**Slovakiet**	[slovaˈkiːəð]
Slovenia	**Slovenien**	[sloˈveːnjən]
South Africa	**Sydafrika**	['syð ˌafʁika]
South Korea	**Sydkorea**	['syð koˈʁɛːa]
Spain	**Spanien**	['spæˀnjən]
Suriname	**Surinam**	['suʁiˌnam]
Sweden	**Sverige**	['svɛʁiˀ]
Switzerland	**Schweiz**	['svajts]
Syria	**Syrien**	['syʁiən]
Taiwan	**Taiwan**	['tɑjˌvæˀn]
Tajikistan	**Tadsjikistan**	[taˈdɕikiˌstan]
Tanzania	**Tanzania**	['tansaˌniæ]
Tasmania	**Tasmanien**	[tasˈmaniːən]
Thailand	**Thailand**	['tɑjlɛnˀ]
Tunisia	**Tunis**	['tuːnis]
Turkey	**Tyrkiet**	[tyʁkiːəð]
Turkmenistan	**Turkmenistan**	[tuʁkˈmeˀniˌstan]
Ukraine	**Ukraine**	[ukʁɑˈiˀnə]
United Arab Emirates	**Forenede Arabiske Emirater**	[fʌˈenəðə ɑˈʁɑˀbiskə emiˈʁɑˀtʌ]
United States of America	**De Forenede Stater**	[di fʌˈenəðə 'stæˀtʌ]
Uruguay	**Uruguay**	[uʁugˈwɑj]
Uzbekistan	**Usbekistan**	[usˈbekiˌstan]
Vatican	**Vatikanstaten**	['vateˌkæːn 'stæˀtən]
Venezuela	**Venezuela**	[venəsuˈeːla]
Vietnam	**Vietnam**	['vjɛtnam]
Zanzibar	**Zanzibar**	['saːnsibɑː]

T&P BOOKS

GASTRONOMIC GLOSSARY

This section contains a lot of words and terms associated with food. This dictionary will make it easier for you to understand the menu at a restaurant and choose the right dish

T&P Books Publishing

English-Danish gastronomic glossary

aftertaste	bismag (f)	['bismæ'j]
almond	mandel (f)	['man'əl]
anise	anis (f)	['anis]
aperitif	aperitif (f)	[apeɐ̯i'tif]
appetite	appetit (f)	[ɑpə'tit]
appetizer	forret (f)	['fɔːʁɑt]
apple	æble (i)	['ɛ'blə]
apricot	abrikos (f)	[ɑbʁi'ko's]
artichoke	artiskok (f)	[ˌɑːti'skʌk]
asparagus	asparges (f)	[a'spɑ's]
Atlantic salmon	atlantisk laks (f)	[at'lan'tisk 'lɑks]
avocado	avokado (f)	[avo'kæ:do]
bacon	bacon (i, f)	['bɛjkʌn]
banana	banan (f)	[ba'næ'n]
barley	byg (f)	['byg]
bartender	bartender (f)	['bɑːˌtɛndʌ]
basil	basilikum (f)	[ba'sil'ikɔm]
bay leaf	laurbærblad (i)	['lɑwʌbæɡ̊ˌblɑð]
beans	bønner (f pl)	['bœnʌ]
beef	oksekød (i)	['ʌksəˌkøð]
beer	øl (i)	['øl]
beetroot	rødbede (f)	[ʁœð'be:ðə]
bell pepper	peber (i, f)	['pewʌ]
berries	bær (i pl)	['bæɡ̊]
berry	bær (i)	['bæɡ̊]
bilberry	blåbær (i)	['blɔ'ˌbæɡ̊]
birch bolete	galde rørhat (f)	['galə ˌʁɶ'ɡ̊hat]
bitter	bitter	['betʌ]
black coffee	sort kaffe (f)	['soɡ̊t 'kɑfə]
black pepper	sort peber (i, f)	['soɡ̊t 'pewʌ]
black tea	sort te (f)	['soɡ̊t ˌte']
blackberry	brombær (i)	['bʁɔmˌbæɡ̊]
blackcurrant	solbær (i)	['so:lˌbæɡ̊]
boiled	kogt	['kʌgt]
bottle opener	oplukker (f)	['ʌpˌlɔkʌ]
bread	brød (i)	['bʁœð']
breakfast	morgenmad (f)	['mɔːɒnˌmɑð]
bream	brasen (f)	['bʁɑ'sən]
broccoli	broccoli (f)	['bʁʌkoli]
Brussels sprouts	rosenkål (f)	['ʁo:sənˌkɔ'l]
buckwheat	boghvede (f)	['bɔwˌve:ðə]
butter	smør (i)	['smœɡ̊]
buttercream	creme (f)	['kʁɛ'm]
cabbage	kål (f)	['kɔ'l]

cake	kage (f)	['kæ:jə]
cake	lagkage (f)	['law‚kæ:jə]
calorie	kalorie (f)	[ka'loɐ̯ʔjə]
can opener	dåseåbner (f)	['dɔ:sə‚ɔ:bnʌ]
candy	konfekt, karamel (f)	[kɔn'fɛkt], [kɑɑ'mɛlʔ]
canned food	konserves (f)	[kɔn'sæɐ̯vəs]
cappuccino	cappuccino (f)	[kɑpu'tji:no]
caraway	kommen (f)	['kʌmən]
carbohydrates	kulhydrater (i pl)	['kʌlhy‚dʁɑʔdʌ]
carbonated	med kulsyre	[mɛ 'bʁu̇ʔs]
carp	karpe (f)	['kɑ:pə]
carrot	gulerod (f)	['gulə‚ʁoʔð]
catfish	malle (f)	['malə]
cauliflower	blomkål (f)	['blʌm‚kɔʔl]
caviar	kaviar (f)	['kavi‚ɑʔ]
celery	selleri (f)	['selʌ‚ʁiʔ]
cep	karljohan-rørhat (f)	[‚kɑ:ljo'han 'ʁœʔɐ̯hat]
cereal crops	kornsorter (f pl)	['koɐ̯n‚sɒ:tʌ]
cereal grains	gryn (i)	['gʁy̆ʔn]
champagne	champagne (f)	[ɕɑm'panjə]
chanterelle	kantarel (f)	[kantɑ'ʁalʔ]
check	regning (f)	['ʁɑjnen]
cheese	ost (f)	['ɔst]
chewing gum	tyggegummi (i)	['tygə‚gomi]
chicken	høne (f)	['hœ:nə]
chocolate	chokolade (f)	[ɕoko'læ:ðə]
chocolate	chokolade-	[ɕoko'læ:ðə-]
cinnamon	kanel (i, f)	[ka'neʔl]
clear soup	bouillon (f)	[bul'jʌŋ]
cloves	nellike (f)	['nelʔekə]
cocktail	cocktail (f)	['kʌk‚tɛjl]
coconut	kokosnød (f)	['ko:kos‚nøðʔ]
cod	torsk (f)	['tɔ:sk]
coffee	kaffe (f)	['kɑfə]
coffee with milk	kaffe (f) med mælk	['kɑfə mɛ 'mɛlʔk]
cognac	cognac, konjak (f)	['kʌnʔjɑg]
cold	kold	['kʌlʔ]
condensed milk	kondenseret mælk (f)	[kʌndən'seʔʌð mɛlʔk]
condiment	krydderi (i)	[kʁyðʌ'ʁiʔ]
confectionery	konditorvarer (f pl)	[kʌn'ditʌ‚va:ɑ]
cookies	småkager (f pl)	['smʌ‚kæ:jʌ]
coriander	koriander (f)	[kɒi'anʔdʌ]
corkscrew	proptrækker (f)	['pʁʌp‚tʁakʌ]
corn	majs (f)	['mɑjʔs]
corn	majs (f)	['mɑjʔs]
cornflakes	cornflakes (pl)	['koɐ̯n‚flɛks]
course, dish	ret (f)	['ʁat]
cowberry	tyttebær (i)	['tytə‚bæɐ̯]
crab	krabbe (f)	['kʁɑbə]
cranberry	tranebær (i)	['tʁɑ:nə‚bæɐ̯]
cream	fløde (f)	['flø:ðə]
crumb	krumme (f)	['kʁɔmə]

crustaceans	**krebsdyr** (i pl)	['kʁabsˌdyɐ̯ˀ]
cucumber	**agurk** (f)	[a'guɐ̯k]
cuisine	**køkken** (i)	['køkən]
cup	**kop** (f)	['kʌp]
dark beer	**mørkt øl** (i)	['mæɐ̯kt ˌøl]
date	**daddel** (f)	['daðˀəl]
death cap	**grøn fluesvamp** (f)	['gʁœn 'flu:əˌsvɑmˀp]
dessert	**dessert** (f)	[de'sɛɐ̯ˀt]
diet	**diæt** (f)	[di'ɛˀt]
dill	**dild** (f)	['dilˀ]
dinner	**aftensmad** (f)	['ɑftənsˌmɑð]
dried	**tørret**	['tœɐ̯ʌð]
drinking water	**drikkevand** (i)	['dʁɛkəˌvanˀ]
duck	**and** (f)	['anˀ]
ear	**aks** (i)	['ɑks]
edible mushroom	**spiselig svamp** (f)	['spi:səli 'svɑmˀp]
eel	**ål** (f)	['ɔˀl]
egg	**æg** (i)	['ɛˀg]
egg white	**hvide** (f)	['vi:ðə]
egg yolk	**blomme** (f)	['blʌmə]
eggplant	**aubergine** (f)	[obæɐ̯'ɕi:n]
eggs	**æg** (i pl)	['ɛˀg]
Enjoy your meal!	**Velbekomme!**	['vɛlbə'kʌmˀə]
fats	**fedt** (i)	['fet]
fig	**figen** (f)	['fi:ən]
filling	**fyld** (i, f)	['fylˀ]
fish	**fisk** (f)	['fesk]
flatfish	**rødspætte** (f)	['ʁœðˌspɛtə]
flour	**mel** (i)	['meˀl]
fly agaric	**fluesvamp** (f)	['flu:əˌsvɑmˀp]
food	**mad** (f)	['mɑð]
fork	**gaffel** (f)	['gɑfəl]
freshly squeezed juice	**friskpresset juice** (f)	['fʁɛskˌpʁasəð 'dʒu:s]
fried	**stegt**	['stɛgt]
fried eggs	**spejlæg** (i)	['spɑjlˌɛˀg]
frozen	**frossen**	['fʁɔsən]
fruit	**frugt** (f)	['fʁʌgt]
fruits	**frugter** (f pl)	['fʁɔgtʌ]
game	**vildt** (i)	['vilˀt]
gammon	**skinke** (f)	['skeŋkə]
garlic	**hvidløg** (i)	['viðˌlʌjˀ]
gin	**gin** (f)	['djen]
ginger	**ingefær** (f)	['eŋəˌfæɐ̯]
glass	**glas** (i)	['glas]
glass	**vinglas** (i)	['vi:nˌglas]
goose	**gås** (f)	['gɔˀs]
gooseberry	**stikkelsbær** (i)	['stekəlsˌbæɐ̯]
grain	**korn** (i)	['koɐ̯ˀn]
grape	**drue** (f)	['dʁu:ə]
grapefruit	**grapefrugt** (f)	['gʁɛjpˌfʁɔgt]
green tea	**grøn te** (f)	['gʁœnˀ ˌteˀ]
greens	**grønt** (i)	['gʁœnˀt]

halibut	helleflynder (f)	['hɛlə̩flønʌ]
ham	skinke (f)	['skeŋkə]
hamburger	kødfars (f)	['køð̩fɑˀs]
hamburger	hamburger (f)	['hæːm̩bœːgʌ]
hazelnut	hasselnød (f)	['hasəl̩nøðˀ]
herring	sild (f)	['silˀ]
honey	honning (f)	['hʌneŋ]
horseradish	peberrod (f)	['pewʌ̩ʁoˀð]
hot	hed, varm	['heðˀ], ['vɑˀm]
ice	is (f)	['iˀs]
ice-cream	is (f)	['iˀs]
instant coffee	pulverkaffe (f)	['pɔlvʌ̩kafə]
jam	syltetøj (i)	['syltə̩tʌj]
jam	syltetøj (i)	['syltə̩tʌj]
juice	juice (f)	['dʒuːs]
kidney bean	bønne (f)	['bœnə]
kiwi	kiwi (f)	['kiːvi]
knife	kniv (f)	['kniwˀ]
lamb	lammekød (i)	['lamə̩køð]
lemon	citron (f)	[si'tʁoˀn]
lemonade	limonade (f)	[limo'næːðə]
lentil	linse (f)	['lensə]
lettuce	salat (f)	[sa'læˀt]
light beer	lyst øl (i)	['lyst ̩øl]
liqueur	likør (f)	[li'køˀɐ̯]
liquors	alkoholiske drikke (f pl)	[alko'hoˀliskə 'dʁɛkə]
liver	lever (f)	['lewˀʌ]
lunch	frokost (f)	['fʁɔkʌst]
mackerel	makrel (f)	[mɑ'kʁalˀ]
mandarin	mandarin (f)	[mandɑ'ʁiˀn]
mango	mango (f)	['maŋgo]
margarine	margarine (f)	[mɑgɑ'ʁiːnə]
marmalade	marmelade (f)	[mɑmə'læːðə]
mashed potatoes	kartoffelmos (f)	[kɑ'tʌfəl̩mɔs]
mayonnaise	mayonnaise (f)	[majo'nɛːs]
meat	kød (i)	['køð]
melon	melon (f)	[me'loˀn]
menu	menu (f)	[me'ny]
milk	mælk (f)	['mɛlˀk]
milkshake	milkshake (f)	['milk̩ɕɛjk]
millet	hirse (f)	['hiɐ̯sə]
mineral water	mineralvand (i)	[minə'ʁal̩vanˀ]
morel	morkel (f)	['mɔːkəl]
mushroom	svamp (f)	['svamˀp]
mustard	sennep (f)	['senʌp]
non-alcoholic	alkoholfri	['alkohʌl̩fʁiˀ]
noodles	nudler (f pl)	['nuðˀlʌ]
oats	havre (f)	['hawʁʌ]
olive oil	olivenolie (f)	[o'liˀvən̩oljə]
olives	oliven (f pl)	[o'liˀvən]
omelet	omelet (f)	[omə'lɛt]
onion	løg (i)	['lʌjˀ]

orange	appelsin (f)	[apəl'siˀn]
orange juice	appelsinjuice (f)	[apəl'siˀn 'dʒuːs]
orange-cap boletus	skælstokket rørhat (f)	['skɛlˌstʌkəð 'ʁœˀɡhat]
oyster	østers (f)	['østʌs]
pâté	pate, paté (f)	[pa'te]
papaya	papaja (f)	[pa'paja]
paprika	paprika (f)	['papʁika]
parsley	persille (f)	[pæɡ'selə]
pasta	pasta (f)	['pasta]
pea	ærter (f pl)	['æɡˀtʌ]
peach	fersken (f)	['fæɡskən]
peanut	jordnød (f)	['joɡˌnøðˀ]
pear	pære (f)	['pɛˀʌ]
peel	skal, skræl (f)	['skalˀ], ['skʁalˀ]
perch	aborre (f)	['aˌbɒːɒ]
pickled	syltet	['syltəð]
pie	pie (f)	['pɑːj]
piece	stykke (i)	['støkə]
pike	gedde (f)	['ɡeðə]
pike perch	sandart (f)	['sanˌɑˀt]
pineapple	ananas (f)	['ananas]
pistachios	pistacier (f pl)	[pi'stæːɕʌ]
pizza	pizza (f)	['pidsa]
plate	tallerken (f)	[ta'læɡkən]
plum	blomme (f)	['blʌmə]
poisonous mushroom	giftig svamp (f)	['gifti svamˀp]
pomegranate	granatæble (i)	[gʁa'næˀtˌɛːblə]
pork	flæsk (i)	['flɛsk]
porridge	grød (f)	['gʁœðˀ]
portion	portion (f)	[pɒ'ɕoˀn]
potato	kartoffel (f)	[kɑ'tʌfəl]
proteins	proteiner (i pl)	[pʁotə'iˀnʌ]
pub, bar	bar (f)	['bɑˀ]
pudding	budding (f)	['buðeŋ]
pumpkin	græskar (i)	['gʁaska]
rabbit	kanin (f)	[ka'niˀn]
radish	radiser (f pl)	[ʁa'disə]
raisin	rosin (f)	[ʁo'siˀn]
raspberry	hindbær (i)	['henˌbæɡ]
recipe	opskrift (f)	['ʌpˌskʁɛft]
red pepper	rød peber (i, f)	['ʁœð 'pewʌ]
red wine	rødvin (f)	['ʁœðˌviˀn]
redcurrant	ribs (i, f)	['ʁɛbs]
refreshing drink	læskedrik (f)	['lɛskəˌdʁɛk]
rice	ris (f)	['ʁiˀs]
rum	rom (f)	['ʁʌmˀ]
russula	skørhat (f)	['skøɡˌhat]
rye	rug (f)	['ʁuˀ]
saffron	safran (i, f)	[sa'fʁɑˀn]
salad	salat (f)	[sa'læˀt]
salmon	laks (f)	['laks]
salt	salt (i)	['salˀt]

salty	**saltet**	['saltəð]
sandwich	**smørrebrød** (i)	['smœɐ̯ʌ̩bʁœð']
sardine	**sardin** (f)	[sɑ'di'n]
sauce	**sovs, sauce** (f)	['sɒw's]
saucer	**underkop** (f)	['ɔnʌˌkʌp]
sausage	**pølse** (f)	['pølsə]
seafood	**fisk og skaldyr**	[fesk 'ɒw 'skaldyɐ̯']
sesame	**sesam** (f)	['se:sɑm]
shark	**haj** (f)	['hɑj']
shrimp	**reje** (f)	['ʁɑjə]
side dish	**tilbehør** (i)	['telbeˌhø'ɐ̯]
slice	**skive** (f)	['ski:və]
smoked	**røget**	['ʁʌjəð]
soft drink	**alkoholfri drik** (f)	['alkohʌlˌfʁi' 'dʁɛk]
soup	**suppe** (f)	['sɔpə]
soup spoon	**spiseske** (f)	['spi:səˌske']
sour cherry	**kirsebær** (i)	['kiɐ̯səˌbæɐ̯]
sour cream	**cremefraiche,**	[kʁɛːm'fɛːˌɕ],
	syrnet fløde (f)	['syɐ̯nəð 'flø:ðə]
soy	**soja** (f)	['sʌja]
spaghetti	**spaghetti** (f)	[spa'gɛti]
sparkling	**med brus**	[mɛ 'bʁu's]
spice	**krydderi** (i)	[kʁyðʌ'ʁi']
spinach	**spinat** (f)	[spi'næ't]
spiny lobster	**languster** (f)	[laŋ'gustʌ]
spoon	**ske** (f)	['ske']
squid	**blæksprutte** (f)	['blɛkˌspʁutə]
steak	**bøf** (f)	['bøf]
still	**uden brus**	['uðən 'bʁu's]
strawberry	**jordbær** (i)	['joɐ̯ˌbæɐ̯]
sturgeon	**stør** (f)	['stø'ɐ̯]
sugar	**sukker** (i)	['sɔkʌ]
sunflower oil	**solsikkeolie** (f)	['so:lˌsekə ˌoljə]
sweet	**sød** (f)	['søð']
sweet cherry	**morel** (f)	[mo'ʁal']
taste, flavor	**smag** (f)	['smæ'j]
tasty	**lækker**	['lɛkʌ]
tea	**te** (f)	['te']
teaspoon	**teske** (f)	['te'ˌske']
tip	**drikkepenge** (pl)	['dʁɛkəˌpɛŋə]
tomato	**tomat** (f)	[to'mæ't]
tomato juice	**tomatjuice** (f)	[to'mæ:tˌdʒu:s]
tongue	**tunge** (f)	['tɔŋə]
toothpick	**tandstikker** (f)	['tanˌstekʌ]
trout	**ørred** (f)	['œɐ̯ʌð]
tuna	**tunfisk** (f)	['tu:nˌfesk]
turkey	**kalkun** (f)	[kal'ku'n]
turnip	**majroe** (f)	['mɑjˌʁo:ə]
veal	**kalvekød** (i)	['kalvəˌkøð]
vegetable oil	**vegetabilsk olie** (f)	[vegəta'bi'lsk 'oljə]
vegetables	**grøntsager** (pl)	['gʁœntˌsæ'jʌ]
vegetarian	**vegetar, vegetarianer** (f)	[vegə'tɑ'], [vegətɑi'æ'nʌ]

vegetarian	**vegetarisk**	[vegə'tɑˀisk]
vermouth	**vermouth** (f)	['væɠmut]
vienna sausage	**wienerpølse** (f)	['viˀnʌˌpølsə]
vinegar	**eddike** (f)	['ɛðikə]
vitamin	**vitamin** (i)	[vita'miˀn]
vodka	**vodka** (f)	['vʌdka]
waffles	**vaffel** (f)	['vɑfəl]
waiter	**tjener** (f)	['tjɛːnʌ]
waitress	**servitrice** (f)	[sæɠvi'tʁiːsə]
walnut	**valnød** (f)	['valˌnøðˀ]
water	**vand** (i)	['vanˀ]
watermelon	**vandmelon** (f)	['van meˈloˀn]
wheat	**hvede** (f)	['veːðə]
whiskey	**whisky** (f)	['wiski]
white wine	**hvidvin** (f)	['við,viˀn]
wild strawberry	**skovjordbær** (i)	['skɒw 'joɠˌbæɠ]
wine	**vin** (f)	['viˀn]
wine list	**vinkort** (i)	['viːnˌkɒːt]
with ice	**med is**	[mɛ 'iˀs]
yogurt	**yoghurt** (f)	['joˌguɐˀt]
zucchini	**squash, zucchini** (f)	['sgwʌɕ], [su'kiːni]

Danish-English gastronomic glossary

ål (f)	['ɔˀl]	eel
æble (i)	['ɛˀblə]	apple
æg (i pl)	['ɛˀg]	eggs
æg (i)	['ɛˀg]	egg
ærter (f pl)	['æɐ̯ˀtʌ]	pea
øl (i)	['øl]	beer
ørred (f)	['œɐ̯ʌð]	trout
østers (f)	['østʌs]	oyster
aborre (f)	['ɑˌbɔːɒ]	perch
abrikos (f)	[abʁi'koˀs]	apricot
aftensmad (f)	['ɑftənsˌmað]	dinner
agurk (f)	[a'guɐ̯k]	cucumber
aks (i)	['ɑks]	ear
alkoholfri	['alkohʌlˌfʁiˀ]	non-alcoholic
alkoholfri drik (f)	['alkohʌlˌfʁiˀ 'dʁɛk]	soft drink
alkoholiske drikke (f pl)	[alko'hoˀliskə 'dʁɛkə]	liquors
ananas (f)	['ananas]	pineapple
and (f)	['anˀ]	duck
anis (f)	['anis]	anise
aperitif (f)	[apeɐ̯i'tif]	aperitif
appelsin (f)	[apəl'siˀn]	orange
appelsinjuice (f)	[apəl'siˀn 'dʒuːs]	orange juice
appetit (f)	[apə'tit]	appetite
artiskok (f)	[ˌɑːti'skʌk]	artichoke
asparges (f)	[a'spɑˀs]	asparagus
atlantisk laks (f)	[at'lanˀtisk 'lɑks]	Atlantic salmon
aubergine (f)	[obæɐ̯'ɕiːn]	eggplant
avokado (f)	[avo'kæːdo]	avocado
bær (i pl)	['bæɐ̯]	berries
bær (i)	['bæɐ̯]	berry
bøf (f)	['bøf]	steak
bønne (f)	['bœnə]	kidney bean
bønner (f pl)	['bœnʌ]	beans
bacon (i, f)	['bɛjkʌn]	bacon
banan (f)	[ba'næˀn]	banana
bar (f)	['bɑˀ]	pub, bar
bartender (f)	['bɑːˌtɛndʌ]	bartender
basilikum (f)	[ba'silˀikɔm]	basil
bismag (f)	['bismæˀj]	aftertaste
bitter	['betʌ]	bitter
blåbær (i)	['blɔˀˌbæɐ̯]	bilberry
blæksprutte (f)	['blɛkˌspʁutə]	squid
blomkål (f)	['blʌmˌkɔˀl]	cauliflower
blomme (f)	['blʌmə]	egg yolk

blomme (f)	['blʌmə]	plum
boghvede (f)	['bɔwˌve:ðə]	buckwheat
bouillon (f)	[bul'jʌn]	clear soup
brød (i)	['bʁœð']	bread
brasen (f)	['bʁɑ'sən]	bream
broccoli (f)	['bʁʌkoli]	broccoli
brombær (i)	['bʁɔmˌbæɡ]	blackberry
budding (f)	['buðeŋ]	pudding
byg (f)	['byg]	barley
cappuccino (f)	[kɑpu'tji:no]	cappuccino
champagne (f)	[ɕɑm'panjə]	champagne
chokolade (f)	[ɕoko'læ:ðə]	chocolate
chokolade-	[ɕoko'læ:ðə-]	chocolate
citron (f)	[si'tʁo'n]	lemon
cocktail (f)	['kʌkˌtɛjl]	cocktail
cognac, konjak (f)	['kʌn'jɑg]	cognac
cornflakes (pl)	['koɐ̯nˌflɛks]	cornflakes
creme (f)	['kʁɛ'm]	buttercream
cremefraiche,	[kʁɛ:m'fʁɛ:ɕ],	sour cream
syrnet fløde (f)	['syɡnəð 'flø:ðə]	
dåseåbner (f)	['dɔ:səˌɔ:bnʌ]	can opener
daddel (f)	['dɑð'əl]	date
dessert (f)	[de'sɛɡ't]	dessert
diæt (f)	[di'ɛ't]	diet
dild (f)	['dil']	dill
drikkepenge (pl)	['dʁɛkəˌpɛŋə]	tip
drikkevand (i)	['dʁɛkəˌvan']	drinking water
drue (f)	['dʁu:ə]	grape
eddike (f)	['ɛðikə]	vinegar
fedt (i)	['fet]	fats
fersken (f)	['fæɡskən]	peach
figen (f)	['fi:ən]	fig
fisk (f)	['fesk]	fish
fisk og skaldyr	[fesk 'ɒw 'skaldyɡ']	seafood
flæsk (i)	['flɛsk]	pork
fløde (f)	['flø:ðə]	cream
fluesvamp (f)	['flu:əˌsvɑm'p]	fly agaric
forret (f)	['fɔ:ʁat]	appetizer
friskpresset juice (f)	['fʁɛskˌpʁasəð 'dʒu:s]	freshly squeezed juice
frokost (f)	['fʁɔkʌst]	lunch
frossen	['fʁɔsən]	frozen
frugt (f)	['fʁɔgt]	fruit
frugter (f pl)	['fʁɔgtʌ]	fruits
fyld (i, f)	['fyl']	filling
gås (f)	['gɔ's]	goose
gaffel (f)	['gɑfəl]	fork
galde rørhat (f)	['galə ˌʁœ'ɡhat]	birch bolete
gedde (f)	['geðə]	pike
giftig svamp (f)	['gifti svɑm'p]	poisonous mushroom
gin (f)	['djen]	gin
glas (i)	['glas]	glass
græskar (i)	['gʁaskɑ]	pumpkin

grød (f)	['gʁœð⁷]	porridge
grøn fluesvamp (f)	['gʁœn 'flu:ə‚svɑm⁷p]	death cap
grøn te (f)	['gʁœn⁷ ‚te⁷]	green tea
grønt (i)	['gʁœn⁷t]	greens
grøntsager (pl)	['gʁœnt‚sæ⁷jʌ]	vegetables
granatæble (i)	[gʁɑ'næ⁷t‚ɛ:blə]	pomegranate
grapefrugt (f)	['gʁɛjp‚fʁɔgt]	grapefruit
gryn (i)	['gʁy⁷n]	cereal grains
gulerod (f)	['gulə‚ʁo⁷ð]	carrot
høne (f)	['hœ:nə]	chicken
haj (f)	['hɑj⁷]	shark
hamburger (f)	['hæ:m‚bœ:gʌ]	hamburger
hasselnød (f)	['hasəl‚nøð⁷]	hazelnut
havre (f)	['hɑwʁʌ]	oats
hed, varm	['heð⁷], ['vɑ⁷m]	hot
helleflynder (f)	['hɛlə‚flønʌ]	halibut
hindbær (i)	['hen‚bæɡ]	raspberry
hirse (f)	['hiɡsə]	millet
honning (f)	['hʌneŋ]	honey
hvede (f)	['ve:ðə]	wheat
hvide (f)	['vi:ðə]	egg white
hvidløg (i)	['við‚lʌj⁷]	garlic
hvidvin (f)	['við‚vi⁷n]	white wine
ingefær (f)	['eŋə‚fæɡ]	ginger
is (f)	['i⁷s]	ice
is (f)	['i⁷s]	ice-cream
jordbær (i)	['joɡ‚bæɡ]	strawberry
jordnød (f)	['joɡ‚nøð⁷]	peanut
juice (f)	['dʒu:s]	juice
kål (f)	['kɔ⁷l]	cabbage
kød (i)	['køð]	meat
kødfars (f)	['køð‚fɑ⁷s]	hamburger
køkken (i)	['køkən]	cuisine
kaffe (f)	['kɑfə]	coffee
kaffe (f) med mælk	['kɑfə mɛ 'mɛl⁷k]	coffee with milk
kage (f)	['kæ:jə]	cake
kalkun (f)	[kal'ku⁷n]	turkey
kalorie (f)	[ka'loɡ⁷jə]	calorie
kalvekød (i)	['kalvə‚køð]	veal
kanel (i, f)	[ka'ne⁷l]	cinnamon
kanin (f)	[ka'ni⁷n]	rabbit
kantarel (f)	[kantɑ'ʁal⁷]	chanterelle
karljohan-rørhat (f)	[‚kɑ:ljo'han 'ʁœ⁷ɡhat]	cep
karpe (f)	['kɑ:pə]	carp
kartoffel (f)	[kɑ'tʌfəl]	potato
kartoffelmos (f)	[kɑ'tʌfəl‚mɔs]	mashed potatoes
kaviar (f)	['kavi‚ɑ⁷]	caviar
kirsebær (i)	['kiɡsə‚bæɡ]	sour cherry
kiwi (f)	['ki:vi]	kiwi
kniv (f)	['kniv⁷]	knife
kogt	['kʌgt]	boiled
kokosnød (f)	['ko:kos‚nøð⁷]	coconut

kold	['kʌlˀ]	cold
kommen (f)	['kʌmən]	caraway
kondenseret mælk (f)	[kʌndən'seˀʌð mɛlˀk]	condensed milk
konditorvarer (f pl)	[kʌn'ditʌˌvɑːɑ]	confectionery
konfekt, karamel (f)	[kɔn'fɛkt], [kɑɑ'mɛlˀ]	candy
konserves (f)	[kɔn'sæɡvəs]	canned food
kop (f)	['kʌp]	cup
koriander (f)	[kɒi'anˀdʌ]	coriander
korn (i)	['koɡˀn]	grain
kornsorter (f pl)	['koɡnˌsɒːtʌ]	cereal crops
krabbe (f)	['kʁɑbə]	crab
krebsdyr (i pl)	['kʁabsˌdyɡˀ]	crustaceans
krumme (f)	['kʁʊmə]	crumb
krydderi (i)	[kʁyðʌ'ʁiˀ]	condiment
krydderi (i)	[kʁyðʌ'ʁiˀ]	spice
kulhydrater (i pl)	['kʌlhyˌdʁɑˀdʌ]	carbohydrates
lækker	['lɛkʌ]	tasty
læskedrik (f)	['lɛskəˌdʁɛk]	refreshing drink
løg (i)	['lʌjˀ]	onion
lagkage (f)	['lawˌkæːjə]	cake
laks (f)	['laks]	salmon
lammekød (i)	['lam9ˌkøð]	lamb
languster (f)	[laŋ'gustʌ]	spiny lobster
laurbærblad (i)	['lawʌbæɡˌblɑð]	bay leaf
lever (f)	['lewˀʌ]	liver
likør (f)	[li'køˀɡ]	liqueur
limonade (f)	[limo'næːðə]	lemonade
linse (f)	['lensə]	lentil
lyst øl (i)	['lyst ˌøl]	light beer
mælk (f)	['mɛlˀk]	milk
mørkt øl (i)	['mœɡkt ˌøl]	dark beer
mad (f)	['mað]	food
majroe (f)	['majˌʁoːə]	turnip
majs (f)	['majˀs]	corn
majs (f)	['majˀs]	corn
makrel (f)	[mɑ'kʁalˀ]	mackerel
malle (f)	['malə]	catfish
mandarin (f)	[mandɑ'ʁiˀn]	mandarin
mandel (f)	['manˀəl]	almond
mango (f)	['maŋgo]	mango
margarine (f)	[mɑgɑ'ʁiːnə]	margarine
marmelade (f)	[mɑmə'læːðə]	marmalade
mayonnaise (f)	[majo'nɛːs]	mayonnaise
med brus	[mɛ 'bʁuˀs]	sparkling
med is	[mɛ 'iˀs]	with ice
med kulsyre	[mɛ 'bʁuˀs]	carbonated
mel (i)	['meˀl]	flour
melon (f)	[me'loˀn]	melon
menu (f)	[me'ny]	menu
milkshake (f)	['milkˌɕɛjk]	milkshake
mineralvand (i)	[minə'ʁalˌvanˀ]	mineral water
morel (f)	[mo'ʁalˀ]	sweet cherry

morgenmad (f)	['mɒːɒnˌmað]	breakfast
morkel (f)	['mɒːkəl]	morel
nellike (f)	['nelˀekə]	cloves
nudler (f pl)	['nuðˀlʌ]	noodles
oksekød (i)	['ʌksəˌkøð]	beef
oliven (f pl)	[o'liˀvən]	olives
olivenolie (f)	[o'liˀvənˌoljə]	olive oil
omelet (f)	[oməˈlɛt]	omelet
oplukker (f)	['ʌpˌlɔkʌ]	bottle opener
opskrift (f)	['ʌpˌskʁɛft]	recipe
ost (f)	['ɔst]	cheese
pære (f)	['pɛˀʌ]	pear
pølse (f)	['pølsə]	sausage
papaja (f)	[pa'paja]	papaya
paprika (f)	['papʁika]	paprika
pasta (f)	['pasta]	pasta
pate, paté (f)	[pa'te]	pâté
peber (i, f)	['pewʌ]	bell pepper
peberrod (f)	['pewʌˌʁoˀð]	horseradish
persille (f)	[pæɡ'selə]	parsley
pie (f)	['pɑːj]	pie
pistacier (f pl)	[pi'stæːɕʌ]	pistachios
pizza (f)	['pidsa]	pizza
portion (f)	[pɒ'ɕoˀn]	portion
proptrækker (f)	['pʁʌpˌtʁakʌ]	corkscrew
proteiner (i pl)	[pʁote'iˀnʌ]	proteins
pulverkaffe (f)	['pɔlvʌˌkafə]	instant coffee
rød peber (i, f)	['ʁœð 'pewʌ]	red pepper
rødbede (f)	[ʁœð'beːðə]	beetroot
rødspætte (f)	['ʁœðˌspɛtə]	flatfish
rødvin (f)	['ʁœðˌviˀn]	red wine
røget	['ʁʌjəð]	smoked
radiser (f pl)	[ʁɑ'disə]	radish
regning (f)	['ʁajnɛŋ]	check
reje (f)	['ʁajə]	shrimp
ret (f)	['ʁat]	course, dish
ribs (i, f)	['ʁɛbs]	redcurrant
ris (f)	['ʁiˀs]	rice
rom (f)	['ʁʌmˀ]	rum
rosenkål (f)	['ʁoːsənˌkɔˀl]	Brussels sprouts
rosin (f)	[ʁo'siˀn]	raisin
rug (f)	['ʁuˀ]	rye
sød	['søðˀ]	sweet
safran (i, f)	[sa'fʁɑˀn]	saffron
salat (f)	[sa'læˀt]	lettuce
salat (f)	[sa'læˀt]	salad
salt (i)	['salˀt]	salt
saltet	['saltəð]	salty
sandart (f)	['sanˌɑˀt]	pike perch
sardin (f)	[sɑ'diˀn]	sardine
selleri (f)	['selʌˌʁiˀ]	celery
sennep (f)	['senʌp]	mustard

servitrice (f)	[sæɐvi'tɕi:sə]	waitress
sesam (f)	['se:sɑm]	sesame
sild (f)	['silˀ]	herring
skælstokket rørhat (f)	['skɛlˌstʌkəð 'ʁœˀɐ̯hat]	orange-cap boletus
skørhat (f)	['skøɐ̯ˌhat]	russula
skal, skræl (f)	['skalˀ], ['skʁalˀ]	peel
ske (f)	['skeˀ]	spoon
skinke (f)	['skeŋkə]	ham
skinke (f)	['skeŋkə]	gammon
skive (f)	['ski:və]	slice
skovjordbær (i)	['skɒw 'joɐ̯ˌbæɐ̯]	wild strawberry
småkager (f pl)	['smʌˌkæ:jʌ]	cookies
smør (i)	['smœɐ̯]	butter
smørrebrød (i)	['smœɐ̯ʌˌbʁœðˀ]	sandwich
smag (f)	['smæˀj]	taste, flavor
soja (f)	['sʌja]	soy
solbær (i)	['so:lˌbæɐ̯]	blackcurrant
solsikkeolie (f)	['so:lˌsekə ˌoljə]	sunflower oil
sort kaffe (f)	['soɐ̯t 'kɑfə]	black coffee
sort peber (i, f)	['soɐ̯t 'pewʌ]	black pepper
sort te (f)	['soɐ̯t ˌteˀ]	black tea
sovs, sauce (f)	['sɒwˀs]	sauce
spaghetti (f)	[spa'gɛti]	spaghetti
spejlæg (i)	['spɑjlˌɛˀg]	fried eggs
spinat (f)	[spi'næˀt]	spinach
spiselig svamp (f)	['spi:səli 'svɑmˀp]	edible mushroom
spiseske (f)	['spi:səˌskeˀ]	soup spoon
squash, zucchini (f)	['sgwʌʃ], [su'ki:ni]	zucchini
stør (f)	['støˀɐ̯]	sturgeon
stegt	['stɛgt]	fried
stikkelsbær (i)	['stekəlsˌbæɐ̯]	gooseberry
stykke (i)	['støkə]	piece
sukker (i)	['sɔkʌ]	sugar
suppe (f)	['sɔpə]	soup
svamp (f)	['svɑmˀp]	mushroom
syltet	['syltəð]	pickled
syltetøj (i)	['syltəˌtʌj]	jam
syltetøj (i)	['syltəˌtʌj]	jam
tørret	['tœɐ̯ʌð]	dried
tallerken (f)	[ta'læɐ̯kən]	plate
tandstikker (f)	['tanˌstekʌ]	toothpick
te (f)	['teˀ]	tea
teske (f)	['teˀˌskeˀ]	teaspoon
tilbehør (i)	['telbeˌhøˀɐ̯]	side dish
tjener (f)	['tjɛ:nʌ]	waiter
tomat (f)	[to'mæˀt]	tomato
tomatjuice (f)	[to'mæːtˌdʒu:s]	tomato juice
torsk (f)	['tɒ:sk]	cod
tranebær (i)	['tʁɑ:nəˌbæɐ̯]	cranberry
tunfisk (f)	['tu:nˌfesk]	tuna
tunge (f)	['tɔŋə]	tongue
tyggegummi (i)	['tygəˌgomi]	chewing gum

tyttebær (i)	['tytə,bæɐ̯]	cowberry
uden brus	['uðən 'bʁu's]	still
underkop (f)	['ɔnʌ,kʌp]	saucer
vaffel (f)	['vɑfəl]	waffles
valnød (f)	['val,nøð']	walnut
vand (i)	['van']	water
vandmelon (f)	['van me'lo'n]	watermelon
vegetabilsk olie (f)	[vegeta'bi'lsk 'oljə]	vegetable oil
vegetar, vegetarianer (f)	[vegə'tɑ'], [vegətɑi'æ'nʌ]	vegetarian
vegetarisk	[vegə'tɑ'isk]	vegetarian
Velbekomme!	['vɛlbə'kʌm'ə]	Enjoy your meal!
vermouth (f)	['væɡmut]	vermouth
vildt (i)	['vil't]	game
vin (f)	['vi'n]	wine
vinglas (i)	['vi:n,glas]	glass
vinkort (i)	['vi:n,kɔ:t]	wine list
vitamin (i)	[vita'mi'n]	vitamin
vodka (f)	['vʌdka]	vodka
whisky (f)	['wiski]	whiskey
wienerpølse (f)	['vi'nʌ,pølsə]	vienna sausage
yoghurt (f)	['jo,guɐ't]	yogurt